Se><ualities

Sexualities: Contemporary Psychoanalytic Perspectives presents a broad selection of contemporary psychoanalytic thinking on sexuality from a wide range of psychoanalytic traditions. Sexuality remains at the heart of much psychoanalytic theory and practice but it is a complex and controversial subject. Edited by **Alessandra Lemma and Paul E. Lynch**, this volume includes a range of international contributions that examine contemporary issues and trace common themes needed to understand any sexuality, including the basics of sexuality and the myriad ways in which sexuality is lived.

The clinical examples provided here demonstrate contemporary psychoanalytic techniques to uncover meanings that are both fresh and enlightening, and address heterosexuality, homosexuality, gender and perversion from a psychoanalytic perspective. Divided into four parts, the book includes the following:

- Historical context
- Foundational concepts: Contemporary elaborations
- Homosexuality
- Perversion revisited

Throughout *Sexualities: Contemporary Psychoanalytic Perspectives* the reader will find psychoanalytic wisdom that is transferrable to work with patients of all sexualities, and will see that the essentials of sexuality may be more similar than they are different for homo- and heterosexuality. Psychoanalysts and psychoanalytic psychotherapists, as well as academics interested in the subjects of psychoanalysis, gender, sexuality or homosexuality, will find this book an invaluable resource.

Alessandra Lemma, PhD is Director of the Psychological Therapies Development Unit at the Tavistock and Portman NHS Foundation Trust. She is a Fellow of the British Psychoanalytic Society and Visiting Professor in the Psychoanalysis Unit, University College London. She is a Consultant Adult Psychotherapist at the Portman Clinic where she specializes in working with transsexuals. She has published extensively on psychoanalysis, the body and trauma.

Paul E. Lynch, MD is on the faculty of the Boston Psychoanalytic Society and Institute, the Massachusetts Institute for Psychoanalysis, and the China American Psychoanalytic Alliance. He teaches about psychoanalysis, gender and sexuality, and has been a popular speaker on issues of homosexuality and psychoanalysis. He is also a Clinical Instructor of Psychiatry at the Tufts University School of Medicine.

Sexualities

Contemporary psychoanalytic perspectives

Edited by Alessandra Lemma and Paul E. Lynch

Routledge
Taylor & Francis Group

LONDON AND NEW YORK

First published 2015
by Routledge
27 Church Road, Hove, East Sussex, BN3 2FA

and by Routledge
711 Third Avenue, New York, NY 10017

Routledge is an imprint of the Taylor & Francis Group, an informa business

British Library Cataloguing in Publication Data
A catalogue record for this book is available from the British Library

Library of Congress Cataloging in Publication Data
Sexualities : contemporary psychoanalytic perspectives / edited by
Alessandra Lemma and Paul E. Lynch.
pages cm
1. Sex (psychology) 2. psychoanalysis. I. Lemma, Alessandra. II. Lynch,
Paul E., 1959-
BF175.5.S48S487 2015
155.3–dc23
2014048378

ISBN: 978-0-415-71865-3 (hbk)
ISBN: 978-0-415-71866-0 (pbk)
ISBN: 978-1-315-71460-8 (ebk)

Typeset in Times New Roman
by Swales & Willis Ltd, Exeter, Devon, UK

Printed and bound by CPI Group (UK) Ltd, Croydon, CR0 4YY

For Andy and John

Contents

Contributors

Marilia Aisenstein is a Training Analyst of the Hellenic Psychoanalytical Society and the Paris Psychoanalytical Society. She has been president of the Paris Society and of the Paris Psychosomatic Institute, member of the editorial board of the *Revue Française de Psychanalyse*, co-founder and editor of the *Revue Française de Psychosomatique*. She presently works in private practice and gives seminars in both the Hellenic and the Paris Societies and is the Chair of the Executive committee of the Paris Society's Psychoanalytical Clinic. She has written three books on psychosomatics and hypochondria and numerous papers in French and international journals.

Elizabeth Allison PhD is a psychoanalyst and Deputy Director of the Psychoanalysis Unit at University College London. She received her doctorate from Oxford University and her current research interests include the application of psychoanalytic ideas to the study of literature.

Nicola Barden is the Director of Student Services at the University of Winchester. She has counselled students in higher education for over twenty years, which has brought with it plenty of scope for thinking about the formation of gendered and sexual identities. She is registered with the United Kingdom Council for Psychotherapy and the British Association for Counselling and Psychotherapy, and was Chair of the BACP from 2005 to 2008.

Peter Fonagy PhD, FMedSci, FBA, OBE is Freud Memorial Professor of Psychoanalysis and Head of the Research Department of Clinical, Educational and Health Psychology at University College London; Chief Executive of the Anna Freud Centre, London; and Consultant to the Child and Family Programme at the Menninger Department of Psychiatry and Behavioral Sciences at Baylor College of Medicine. He is a Senior Investigator for the National Institute of Health Research and holds professorships at both Harvard and Yale. He is a clinical psychologist and a training and supervising analyst in the British Psychoanalytical Society in child and adult analysis. He is also National Clinical Lead of the NHS Children and Young People's Improving Access to Psychological Therapies and Director of the UCL Partners Integrated

Mental Health and Wellbeing Programme. His clinical interests centre around issues of borderline psychopathology, violence and early attachment relationships. His work attempts to integrate empirical research with psychoanalytic theory.

Leezah Hertzmann is Senior Psychoanalytic Couple Psychotherapist at the Tavistock Centre for Couple Relationships (TCCR), and an individual psychoanalytic psychotherapist and supervisor in private practice. She has a particular interest in psychoanalytic theory and technique in clinical work with lesbian and gay couples, and is a member of the British Psychoanalytic Council special task group on homosexuality. Amongst her other work, Leezah has developed a Mentalization-based intervention for parents in entrenched conflict, which is currently being evaluated in a randomized controlled trial, undertaken with colleagues at University College London. Leezah convenes a clinical workshop with colleagues in TCCR, developing a psychoanalytically informed Mentalization model of intervention for high conflict couples for whom more traditional psychoanalytic approaches are less suited. She has published in this area and on psychoanalytic work with lesbian and gay couples.

Dagmar Herzog PhD is Professor of History and Daniel Rose Faculty Scholar, Graduate Center, City University of New York. She has won a Guggenheim Fellowship to study the history of psychoanalysis in the postwar era. She has studied, written, and taught extensively on the history of sexuality, and has published several books, including: *Sexuality in Europe: A Twentieth-Century History* (Cambridge UP, 2011); *Sex in Crisis: The New Sexual Revolution and the Future of American Politics* (Basic, 2008); *Sex after Fascism: Memory and Morality in Twentieth-Century Germany* (Princeton, 2005); *Intimacy and Exclusion: Religious Politics in Pre-Revolutionary Baden* (Princeton, 1996; Transaction, 2007).

Alessandra Lemma PhD is Director of the Psychological Therapies Development Unit at the Tavistock and Portman NHS Foundation Trust. She is a Consultant Adult Psychotherapist at the Portman Clinic where she specializes in working with transsexuals. She is a Fellow of the British Psychoanalytical Society and Visiting Professor, Psychoanalysis Unit, University College London and Honorary Professor of Psychological Therapies in the School of Health and Human Sciences at Essex University. She is the Clinical Director of the Psychological Interventions Research Centre at UCL. She is Visiting Professor, Istituto Winnicott, Sapienza University of Rome and Centro Winnicott, Rome. She is the Editor of the *New Library of Psychoanalysis* book series (Routledge) and one of the regional Editors for the *International Journal of Psychoanalysis*. She has published extensively on psychoanalysis, the body and trauma.

Vittorio Lingiardi MD is a Professor and Director of the Clinical Psychology Specialization Program at the Faculty of Medicine and Psychology, Sapienza

University of Rome. He is a member of the International Association for Relational Psychoanalysis and Psychotherapy and the International Association for Analytical Psychology. He has written many books on psychiatric and psychoanalytic topics, including *Men in Love* (Milan, 1997, translated into English: Open Court, Chicago, 2002) and *The Mental Health Professions and Homosexuality: International Perspectives* (with J. Drescher, New York, 2003).

Paul E. Lynch MD is a psychoanalyst in private practice in Boston, MA. He is on the faculty of the Boston Psychoanalytic Society and Institute, and the Massachusetts Institute for Psychoanalysis, and has taught about Gender and Sexuality in Psychoanalysis for many years. He received the American Psychoanalytic Association's Karl A. Menninger Award in 2002. He is also on the faculty of the Tufts University School of Medicine, where he supervises psychotherapy.

Donald Moss MD is a psychoanalyst in private practice in New York City. He is on the faculty of the Institute for Psychoanalytic Education, NYU Medical Center, and is author of *Thirteen Ways of Looking at a Man* (Routledge, 2012), *Hating in the First Person Plural* (Other Press, 2003), and *Stories* (2000). He serves on the editorial boards of *Journal of the American Psychoanalytic Association, Psychoanalytic Quarterly, American Imago,* and *Studies in Gender and Sexuality.*

Avgi Saketopoulou PhD is a psychoanalyst in private practice in New York City. She is a graduate of the NYU Postdoctoral Program in Psychotherapy and Psychoanalysis, where she received the Ruth Stein Prize in 2011. In 2014 she received the Ralph Roughton award from the American Psychoanalytic Association, and the Symonds Prize from *Studies in Gender and Sexuality.* She serves on the editorial boards of *Psychoanalytic Dialogues* and of *Studies in Gender and Sexuality.*

Mary Target PhD is a Fellow of the Institute of Psychoanalysis, Professional Director of the Anna Freud Centre, London, and Professor of Psychoanalysis at University College London. She is Course Director of UCL's Masters in Theoretical Psychoanalytic Studies and Doctorate in Child and Adolescent Psychoanalytic Psychotherapy. She carries out research on child and adult attachment, personality functioning and mentalization, and has a half-time adult psychoanalytic practice. She serves on several committees of the Institute of Psycho-Analysis and the International Psychoanalytical Association, and on the editorial boards of a number of psychoanalytic journals. She has published widely, including her influential paper 'Is our sexuality our own? A developmental model of sexuality based on early affect mirroring' (Target, 2007, *British Journal of Psychotherapy, 23,* 517–530), which builds on a co-authored book, *Affect Regulation, Mentalization and the Development of the Self* (Fonagy, Gergely, Jurist and Target, Other Press, 2002).

Heather Wood PhD is a psychoanalytic psychotherapist and Consultant Adult Psychotherapist and Clinical Psychologist at the Portman Clinic, Tavistock and Portman NHS Foundation Trust in London, which offers outpatient psychoanalytic psychotherapy to children and adults with problems of violence, criminality and compulsive sexual behaviours. With a special interest in psychoanalytic perspectives on the compulsive use of internet pornography and the related subject of paedophilia, she has taught widely on these subjects as well as publishing recent papers in *Psychoanalytic Psychotherapy* and book chapters in Lemma and Caparotta (Routledge, 2014) and Bower, Hale and Wood (Karnac, 2013).

Acknowledgements

Wood, H. (2014) Working with problems of perversion. *British Journal of Psychotherapy*, 30 (4) 16 pages. Reprinted with permission.

Michael Cunningham, A Home at the End of the World. Reprinted with permission.

Excerpt from 'Two Loves' by Bosie, Lord Alfred Douglas – © the Executors of the Literary Estate of Lord Alfred Douglas Decd – all rights reserved. Reprinted with permission.

Introduction

Let's talk about sex or . . . maybe not . . .

Alessandra Lemma and Paul E. Lynch

Many people are abnormal in their sexual life who in every other respect approximate to the average and have, along with the rest, passed through a process of human cultural development in which sexuality remains the weak spot.

(Freud, 1905: 149)

No healthy person, it appears, can fail to make some addition that might be called perverse to the normal sexual aim.

(Freud, 1905: 160)

(Being in love) . . . has the power to remove repressions and re-instate perversions.

(Freud, 1914: 100)

'So what's all this sex stuff about then?' provocatively asked a patient, after devoting much of his session to persuading one of us (AL) that his sexual fantasies were of no import, that they had no connection *whatsoever* with the chronic panic attacks that had brought him to analysis. This was something *I* wanted to talk about, he said, and that he considered redundant.

Getting our minds around sex, around the notion of ourselves as sexual beings, is indeed a tall order. This patient may well have been in a rigid state of anxious denial about the possible connection between the contents of his sexual fantasies and his presenting symptoms, but his position only differs in degree from the natural resistance present in all of us to thinking and talking about sex. It is a challenge to come clean about our sexual desire even in the confessional booth of our mind or on the couch for that matter. Because we are so afraid to be seen as the erotic outlier, sex remains shrouded in a degree of secrecy that seems at odds with contemporary confessional popular culture.

Despite our resistances, for contemporary Western society, sexuality has come to define, as Foucault (1976, 1984a, 1984b) argued, the 'truth about ourselves.' However we must recall that 'sexuality' is a term that was only introduced at the end of the nineteenth century, which suggests that what we mean by it is not an unchanging concept but a historically bound phenomenon. Into the twenty-first century this 'truth about ourselves' is never a static internal narrative; rather it is always in a dynamic interaction with social processes. Indeed writing about sexuality in the age of techno-culture challenges us to rethink sexuality. As the internet revolution is changing so much about us – how we work, how we relate – why would it not change our sexuality too? Because of the ready availability of internet pornography, even the very young are now exposed to imagery they would once have had to work hard to seek out. We cannot but be interested in how this kind of hyper-sexuality will impact on the embodied experience of sex with an actual person: the real thing may feel like a disappointment unable to match the dopamine hit available from the screen and the more arduous reality of living out and sustaining desire in the context of a real attachment relationship. Although virtual space may provide helpful opportunities for what Lynch (Chapter 7) refers to as 'restorative experimentation,' we cannot ignore the potentially more destructive uses of virtual reality when it comes to the development of sexuality (Lemma, 2013). The immediate availability of sexual stimuli outpaces the developmental challenges we all face as we negotiate our own individual sexual trajectories.

Explanations of sexuality, as they relate to both sexual behaviour and identity, have long been controversial issues within psychology, psychiatry and psychoanalysis evidencing that even so-called scientific disciplines betray the difficulty of defining without moralizing. The attempt by many to force sex and morality together often leads to absurd and dangerous positions. Homosexuality, for example, was classified as a mental illness in the Diagnostic and Statistical Manual of Mental Disorders until 1973. Even though homosexuality is no longer regarded with the degree of opprobrium that was evident in the past we cannot deny the continued existence of prejudice and the consequent struggles faced by many gay, lesbian and bisexual people, not least within institutional psychoanalysis where 'malignant prejudices' (Fonagy and Higgit, 2007) about what is normal sexuality set the foundations, as Fonagy and Allison (Chapter 6) suggest, for defining 'homosexual pleasure as an illness' (p. 129).

Despite the fact that societal norms have become more enlightened most of us still feel that there is something about our sexual selves that cannot be easily revealed. This is because our sexual desires always pose questions we cannot readily account for to others or to ourselves. Perhaps, as Kohon suggests, the challenge is to accept that there 'exist[s] a radical antagonism between human sexuality and the task of making any sense of it. . . . What if we cannot ever fully account for our sexual phantasies, which are outrageous, enjoyable, perverse, wonderful, horrific, and sometimes totally politically incorrect?' (Kohon, 1999: 21–22).

Perhaps because of sexuality's shadows, its power to disrupt has resulted in the need to control it, not just through the operation of intrapsychic and interpersonal defences, but also at the level of societal/institutional structures. Gustave Flaubert was put on trial for his allegedly pornographic *Madame Bovary* and Charles Baudelaire ended up in court for his collection of poems *Les Fleurs du Mal,* which included poems depicting lesbian relations – a fact that did not escape the censor's knife.

A legal history, however, reveals that there are no 'eternal' sex laws. What is contrary to the norm of one group could be a blessing for another (Berkowitz, 2013). For the Greeks of the classical period, with the exception of incest, there was virtually no prohibition on specific sexual practices. Their morality was not concerned with the nature of what gave pleasure, but rather the quantity and intensity of the use of pleasure. If Greece advocated the moderation of the drive, Catholic Rome went much further and forbade even desire, imposing prohibitions through the external authority of God and defining the content of what was now to be forbidden. Indeed throughout ancient civilizations sex has always been micromanaged by the law and religion with the surprising exception of same sex relations, which were ignored almost entirely by law until the Hebrews labelled homosexuality a crime on a par with murder.

If we feel stuck in heteronormative ways a brief detour into the sexual behaviour of living organisms reveals it to be far more diverse than our theories. Virtually all plant and many animal species are intersex, that is living organisms are often both sexes simultaneously, which means that there are not really 'two sexes' at all (Laidman, 2000). Many animal species routinely practice transsex, by changing from one sex to another, either once or several times. In some families of fish, transsex is so much the norm that biologists have created a term for those 'unusual' fish that do not change sex – gonochoristic. Other animals practice transvestism by visually, chemically or behaviourally resembling the 'opposite' sex. And over 4000 known species are parthenogenic: all the organisms are female and they reproduce without sex.

This diversity confronts cultural ideas about family, monogamy, fidelity, parental care, heterosexuality, and 'sexual difference.' It is incumbent upon all mental health clinicians to consider the extent to which their current practice is indebted to heteronormative assumptions. We need to be aware that considerable debate exists even within evolutionary theory about homosexual behaviour specifically, for example, and sex and sexual practices more generally. The 'abnormality' of homosexual behaviour is axiomatic to traditional accounts, whereas competing critical research favours the acknowledgement of sex and sexual diversity among living organisms. From the perspective of this latter approach, the continued emphasis on attempts to 'explain' homosexual behaviour betrays a cultural impetus rather than one based on evidence from a range of disciplines.

The focus of this book is psychoanalytic and hence we are not addressing such interdisciplinary dialogues in this volume, but we nevertheless consider that such dialogues are essential to reasoned debate.

(Re)Sexualizing psychoanalysis

Sex has been micromanaged through law and religion because of its subversive, socially destabilizing potential. It was Freud who first bravely placed sex at the heart of psychic development and highlighted its destabilizing power in our psyche and hence the defences brought into play to manage this. His corpus of work might even be described as an attempt to understand the self-imposed prohibitions that are not only the cause but also the result of an internal need for regulation of the sexual drive.

Freud's original boldness with respect to sexuality has not been upheld with equal vigour by some of the important contemporary psychoanalytic schools that have followed in his wake where we observe instead the displacement of sex from centre-stage position to make way for relational considerations. Here the sexual drive is replaced by new conceptualizations of primary love and attachment. This has resulted, as Corbett (2009) provocatively put it, in a trend discernible in much contemporary analytic thinking, whereby 'the burlap of desire too quickly becomes the pashmina of mutual recognition' (p. 216).

Psychoanalytic gender theories have undergone profound changes in recent decades, often spurred by feminist theory and new openness to homosexuality as a normal variant of sexuality. The focus of this new openness has of necessity been first on shedding bias and automatic assumptions of pathology, and less on the sexuality in homosexuality or heterosexuality. Even at this time in psychoanalytic history, it remains difficult to explore sexuality without coming across cultural binds and blind spots that prejudice our theory and practice, given the depth with which sexuality is ensconced in culture. Gender, like attachment and relational concerns, may be more comfortably conceived of – more easily detached or abstracted – as compared with the visceral reality that sex entails.

Perhaps conceptual pashminas are needed because, as Herzog (Chapter 1) outlines, at the heart of the psychoanalytic community itself there has always been, ironically, an ingrained ambivalence about talking about sex. She suggests that the question of sex brought forward by Freud opened up psychoanalysis to the reproach that it was not only a Jewish affair but also a 'dirty' one to boot. Increasingly, however, analysts are trying to reverse this trend, arguing that psychoanalytic theory needs to be re-sexualized (e.g. Fonagy, 2012; Kohon, 2012). Kohon suggests that the de-sexualization of psychoanalytic theory is no more than 'an extension of a very specific form of resistance regarding sexuality in all of us. Freud's original discovery is at the heart of this resistance' (2012: 47).

Freud's contributions on this subject are numerous, but here we want to draw attention to five strands of his thinking that are especially germane to the themes approached by the contributors to this book.

First, Freud squarely placed the focus on *psychosexual development*, not only on the development of the psyche, highlighting that sexuality, along with other processes governing life, is the product of development: our sexuality in all its guises (e.g. as behaviour, as fantasy) always bears traces of our earliest experiences and attachments.

Second, he singled out the *infantile aspect of sexuality*. Contemporary theory has rightly stressed the importance of early interpersonal experience and the internalized objects that derive from it undergoing various transformations due to the operation of defences. However such a relational focus is not psychoanalytic unless we also consider the role of unconscious fantasy and conflict in the development of the mind. Nowhere is this more important than in relation to an understanding of sexuality. Sexuality is not simply an instinct and behaviour as Bowlby (1969) acknowledged; it also organizes intrapsychic experience and fantasy. In other words, early attachment relations provide the interpersonal context within which the experience of embodiment, and hence of our sexuality, unfolds (Schilder, 1950; Diamond and Blatt, 2007; Weinstein, 2007) and infantile sexuality is in turn shaped by these interactions (i.e. external experience with others is relived as autoerotic activity). In our work we need to understand the patient's experience of *sexuality in infancy* but this is not the same as *infantile sexuality*, the residues of which are to be found in the unconscious (Scarfone, 2002).

Third, Freud (1905) captured the *normative abnormality of sexuality* – an insight that flowed naturally from his shrewd observation that object choice and the drive are independent of each other. Freud (1905) makes clear that our so-called normal sexuality encompasses perverse aspects whether through the means chosen to find pleasure, in fore-pleasure, or in the sexual fantasies that are played out during sexual experience. This paved the way for the enlightened contributions of Stoller (1979) who helped us to see that we are all perverts to an extent, underlining the human capacity to manage intense affects and trauma through the sexualization of anxiety. This was then also further elaborated in the work of Glasser (1979, 1992) who suggested that perversions have very little to do with sex (in the sense of a bodily intimacy), but are about the use of sexualization as a defence to deal with primitive terrors in relationships. Four of the chapters in this book are concerned specifically with the question of sexual perversions (Lemma, Moss, Saketopoulou, Wood), but embedded in the thinking of all the authors is a recognition that sexual experience can be variously motivated by intimate connection or defensive sexualization – sexuality as love and sexuality as perversion.

Fourth in Freud's theory we find the notion of an inherent *bisexuality;* hence diversity and complexity are at the core of human sexual experience. He argued that we are all bisexual: whether this is manifest or latent, libido is nevertheless distributed over objects of both sexes. Arguably he uses the term to mean different things at different points in his theorizing: an innate biological predisposition *and* a type of mental functioning characterized by the ability to integrate or balance identifications with each parent (Birksted-Breen, 1993). McDougall (2000) concurred that our 'megalomanic childhood desires' include both the wish to be (to identify with) both parents – to possess the genitals and magical powers of both parents, and also the wish to have both parents sexually (p. 157). Many psychoanalysts have emphasized that 'normative' development requires our universal bisexuality to undergo a mourning process as we work toward acceptance of monosexuality, forced by the reality-based recognition of the difference between the sexes. McDougall (1993, 1995, 2000, 2001) maintained the importance of sustained homosexual and heterosexual psychic representations of identification and object choice for the enrichment and stabilization of love and social relationships, and for the stimulation of creativity (e.g. 2000: 160). Rejecting the notion of biological bisexuality, she insisted that our gender identity and our sexual identity stem from important transmissions first 'from the biparental unconscious, to which, later, is added the input of sociocultural discourse of which the parents are themselves an emanation' (p. 158). Butler (1995) described the melancholic consequence of the failure to mourn early desires to be and have both parents, as when such identifications and desires are foreclosed by societal taboo – a never loved, never lost identity that affirms sexual orientation by disavowing that an attachment or desire ever existed. For Benjamin (1995), the child's 'overinclusive' identifications with both parents are not removed from the unconscious by the recognition of difference, but rather remain available after the Oedipal phase 'to transcend reality by means of fantasy, which can be reconfigured in the sexual symbolic' (p. 140).

Finally, despite Freud's famous paraphrasing of Napoleon with the statement 'anatomy is destiny' (1912: 189), he also underlined how sex is not just a biological function but also an *emotionally charged experience.* He stated that infantile sexuality reaches its peak in the Oedipus complex – 'an emotional attachment.' (1925: 220). That is, the sexual is not reducible to biology alone, but also involves powerful emotional forces. Moreover, as subsequent theorists have more fully articulated, and as will be further elaborated in the chapters of this book, under- standing sexuality requires a two-person psychology to do justice to the emotional significance of sex and the defences it mobilizes. In other words, sex is about much more than reproductive necessity.[1]

Whilst the integration of drive theory and object relations theory results in a richer account of psychosexuality than either theory alone can achieve, maybe even this integration has been used too narrowly to capture the complexity of human sexual experience (Stein, 2008) – an experience that defies a simple, 'neat' formulation, an experience whose very essence is that it can never be fully rep- resented. This is partly because the drive lies between its embodied home and its representation: it can hardly be expressed. The anchoring towards a representation through images or words amounts to the leap between drive and desire, which is what our patients typically bring to analysis.

Development and the 'work of desire'

In her chapter, Target explores the capacities for sexual pleasure and for love rooted in psychosexual development that is based in early affect mirroring – an integration of drive and relational models that takes into account biology, real events and real relationships, and the elaboration of emotional development and self-understanding within attachment relationships. She incorporates important aspects of Laplanche's thinking (1995) about the development of the unconscious and of psychosexuality via the unconscious communications of the mother, and extends this thinking to show how the development of mystery, enigma and alien- ness in sexuality may develop out of the normal difficulty of mirroring sexual drive pressures. Target uses this model to explain why excitement has to be expe- rienced in and with the other, and goes on to show in her clinical examples how this model may also explain a decrease in the intensity of excitement with a given partner over the course of a relationship.

Freud, as we have seen, understood that psychic development is rooted in the body, and consequently he emphasized the measure of the demand for work imposed on the psyche due to its link with the body. The drive is a borderline concept situated between the body and the mind. There is something – a pressure, a source, an energy – that arises from the body and is looking for a way out and a discharge through an object and an aim. To this end, Aisenstein (Chapter 3) returns to Freudian theory to show the masochistic structure of desire – the development of a pleasure in waiting. Moss (Chapter 3) further develops this notion of the 'work of desire.' Desire is measured in terms of time: it is about anticipation and the delay of gratification – it is in the gap thus created that we are pushed to represent our experience. Not surprisingly this creates conflict and many clinical presentations could be construed as manifestations of a failure to manage the implications of desire and of being desired.

Moss draws a clinically helpful distinction between two categories of patient: those for whom desire is a catastrophe and those who are conflicted by the work of desire. Aisenstein develops the dynamic peculiar to the former group and focuses on patients who, as she puts it, are 'anti desire,' that is individuals for whom desire is experienced as a narcissistic failure. Moss's and Aisenstein's contributions speak to a core aspect of sexuality, namely that at the heart of our sexuality lies otherness. This otherness needs to be integrated into the subjective experience of sexuality. In other words, every desire concentrates on an other, and more specifically the existence of the other confronts us with both our dependence and passivity – positions that mobilize anxiety. The 'elusive, ineffable quality' of the sexual other (Stein, 2008) poses a challenge complicating our very experience of desire and of our wish to be desired.

Desire does not exist in a vacuum: it is developmentally shaped by the social system within which it is vested. For the infant this system comprises the earliest relationships with caregivers. Additionally, it is also important to incorporate into our analytic formulations the systemic cultural forces that frame the experience and expression of sexuality and gender (Benjamin, 1988; Dimen, 1991; Goldner, 1991, 2011; Harris, 1991, 2011; Suchet, 2011) so as to challenge more simplistic equations of biological sex, gender and sexual desire (Butler, 1998, 2003; Foucault, 1976). Approaching sexuality thus requires a wide-angled lens so as to formulate the interpersonal and intrapsychic processes that give rise to a highly idiosyncratic experience of the child's embodiment and its emergent sexuality.

Desire, as French psychoanalysts like Laplanche (1995) have pointed out, is shaped and socially constructed by the parents' unconscious 'enigmatic' sexual messages. Laplanche specifically proposes that the other constitutes the subject and moreover that it is an asymmetrical intersubjectivity that enables the creation of human sexuality. For Laplanche the enigmatic message is constitutive of the child's unconscious. Staying true to a drive model, Laplanche nevertheless acknowledges the importance of the relational context within which the drive develops:

There must be a preexistent somatic reactivity, a general organic excitability, but [that] something else is needed to make this into a drive.

(Laplanche, 2002: 52)

After being awakened in the child by the mother, the aspects of sexuality that have not been understood or assimilated become repressed and add to the feeling of strangeness and mystery we have about sexuality. Sexuality is inherently mysterious and 'excessive' (Stein, 1998) because the child cannot translate the adult's message into a conscious representation.

Fonagy (2008) elaborates the role of the parent's sexuality set out by Laplanche within an attachment and mentalizing framework. He suggests that the parent shapes the infant's experience of sexuality through its non-responsiveness to the infant's desire. He argues that *partial failures* of mirroring occur because the manifestations of this desire (which comprises sexuality and aggression) generate too much unpleasure in the caregiver, making him or her reluctant to respond fully contingently and giving no meaning to the infant's desire. As a consequence of this failure Fonagy proposes that adult sexual desire is characterized by a sense of incongruence and striving to be fully experienced that leads us to seek another body through which an internal experience can find voice. Indeed this failure of mentalizing may, along with other developmental experiences, lead to considerable conflict and shame linked with the experience of sexuality which could manifest later as perversion or a more marked failure to organize one's own pleasure and desire in an optimal secondary level way. Lemma (Chapter 10) puts forward the possibility that one function of sex with prostitutes may be understood as an attempt by some men to integrate psychosexuality where the prostitute acts as a validating mirror for the man's sexual desire.

Laplanche and Fonagy, though different in their emphases, nevertheless both introduce the possibility that at its best sexuality comes to life through a vitalizing maternal seduction. The excess that is sexuality always begins with an unconscious communication from the other: the parents' sexuality as not yet comprehended by the child, the transmission of affect and excitement by the parent without actual seduction. Of course the excitement associated with desire can become overwhelming to the immature psyche if it is not processed by the parent.

They raise interesting questions about whether the caregiver overlooks or entices the infant's excitement (Target, 2007; Fonagy, 2008). Does the mother sexualize the now sexual child or does she add to this? This inevitably also raises the possibility that the seduction can be of a more perverse nature, of a distorting and alienating mirroring or 'intromission' (Laplanche) into the baby's sexuality. Notwithstanding these considerations, what most analysts converge on is the belief that adult sexuality expresses residues of early exchanges between mother and baby. These exchanges form the matrix of later sexual development (Lichtenberg, 2008).

All the chapters in this book, with the exception of Lingiardi's and to an extent Barden's, are concerned with the nature of desire, with the nature of the object of desire, and not with the question of gender per se. Sex and gender are closely linked, of course, but they are not the same thing. Typically the distinction between the two defines sex as relating to the object of our desire whereas gender concerns more specifically gender identification: the feminine and the mascline and the myriad, unique blends of these poles that define us.[2] As such gender does not emanate from biology but is seen to reflect cultural and psychological meanings – a position that uncomfortably steers towards a mind-body dualism where on the one hand we have a sexual body and on the other we have a culturally and linguistucally determined gender. Maintaining a dialectical tension between essentialist and constructivist positions is not easy, but it is essential to the development of analytic thought (see Diamond, 2006). Lingiardi (Chapter 5) elaborates many dialectical tensions between gender expressions and identifications and the experience of sexual orientation.

Moreover it is not at all clear that notions of femininity and masculinity exhaust all possible gender identities. In this book we have not included a chapter about transsexuality. This is because transsexuality, in our view, is often unhelpfully conflated with problems of sexual orientation or desire, whereas it concerns primarily the nature of gender identifications, and hence the nature of one's core identity, as opposed to manifesting problems with the object of desire, though these may also co-exist. We might say, along with Laplanche, that gender organizes sexuality rather than being organized by it.

Homosexuality

Before the Hebrews labelled male homosexuality an abomination there was almost no restriction on it. But the Jewish God hated it so much that he wrecked the cities of Sodom and Gomorrah to prove it. This is, of course, an untrue story: there is no evidence that either city was a hotbed of homosexual activity. Nevertheless the tale of the accused cities became the single most influential myth to transmit anti-homosexual practice. Though the Hebrew kingdoms were short-lived, Judaism spawned Christianity and then Islam and hence Hebrew law influenced Western sexual attitudes more than any other collection of ideas, equating the body, the state and the collective moral good as enshrined in the Torah. The tale of Sodom and Gomorrah was adopted wholesale by the Christian church and became the basis for some of the most influential anti-homosexual laws, setting in stone the foundations for generations of intolerance that seeped into psychoanalytic thinking and practice.

Unlike Jesus, Freud did make statements about homosexuality, but they were very conflicting comments about 'abnormality,' 'inversion' and 'developmental arrest,' along with praise for some great homosexuals like Plato, Leonardo and Michelangelo. Let us indeed return to Freud, not because we must resurrect him at every opportunity, failing then to acknowledge the very many important contributions since his time, but because in so many ways he was a perfectly modern and humane thinker about sex and sexuality. In Freud's 'Letter to an American Mother' in 1935, he told her, 'Homosexuality is assuredly no advantage, but it is nothing to be ashamed of, no vice, no degradation, it cannot be classified as an illness.' After telling her that he cannot promise to abolish homosexuality with an analysis, he added,

> What analysis can do for your son runs in a different line. If he is unhappy, neurotic, torn by conflicts, inhibited in his social life, analysis may bring him harmony, peace of mind, full efficiency, whether he remains a homosexual or gets changed . . .

And yet despite Freud's non-pathologizing stance towards homosexuality, heterosexuality has been the dominant psychoanalytic narrative, anchored in Oedipal theory (see Barden, Chapter 4) where the only healthy pathway recognized is to renounce inherent bisexuality, identify with the parent of the same sex, and shift our desire to the opposite sex.

The importance of object constancy as the hallmark of a healthy relationship can and does exist independently of sexual aim or reproductive necessity. Yet amongst psychoanalysts the category of homosexuality has long been equated with pathology (as a subset of perversion) and accorded the status of what Tannenbaum (2003), in another context, calls a 'public idea': an idea that names a problem and prescribes a solution simultaneously. Coterminous with this development, some contemporary philosophers had begun to question the validity of categories for gender and sexual identity that psychoanalysts had now reified into essentialist, defining features of mental health (Butler, 1990). More radical critics began to follow this lead by deconstructing the certainty of interpretations whose starting point was an analyst's knowledge claims about pre-defined psycho-erotic patterns.

In a helpful contribution to the debate Elizabeth Auchincloss and Susan Vaughan (2001) pointed out conceptual muddles in previous efforts to assert a psychoanalytic theory of homosexuality. The province of what is 'normal,' for example, belongs to disciplines such as sociology and epidemiology that are equipped with the intellectual tools and the data to offer answers. The sample of patients seen by psychoanalysts, even if it could be aggregated across analysts and different groups of patients (and heterosexuals and homosexuals compared), is still not going to answer the question whether any or all of these were normal. However much analysts might claim privileged knowledge of the symbolic significance of the clinical material they report, in practice they are reliant on keeping an open ear to what patients are willing and unwilling to say to them in confidence about their innermost, and hitherto unconscious feelings. In all probability there is a correlation between keeping an open mind, keeping an open ear, and eliciting further disclosures that shed genuine new light on the problem (Lemma and Clarke, 2011). At any rate, what emerges, at least in the United States, where the official position started to change some two decades ago (Roughton and Margolis, 1996), is a more sophisticated clinical and scientific discourse around homosexuality, based on a more collaborative and productive relationship between psychoanalysts and their homosexual patients (see Fonagy and Allison, Chapter 6).

Lynch (Chapter 7) draws attention to how a child's homosexual longings may create horror in the parent. The lack of empathic recognition (or mentalization) for homoerotic hedonic desires can present an *extra* hurdle in psychic development, especially for the integration of sex and intimacy in gay men. Moreover, as Hertzman (Chapter 8) explores in her chapter, for some lesbian and gay couples, and particularly those who have grown up with a heterosexual parental couple, the representation of an intimate heterosexual couple union does not belong to their conscious experience. Both partners desire to be in a couple relationship, but the heterosexual one they grew up with and have internalized in development as a dynamic object is for some homosexual partners burdened by the addition of gender role and identity conflicts. Psychoanalysis and specifically psychoanalytic couple theory has viewed our encounter with the internal parental couple relationship as both a fundamental psychic event in the course of our development (Ruszczynski, 1993) and, until recently, as a heteronormatively constructed concept.

The challenge for psychoanalytic theory, as Barden (Chapter 4) eloquently discusses, is how to approach homosexuality without the lens of classical Oedipal theory that insists that desire and identification are separate:

> ... to confuse them resulted in the disaster that was unresolved oedipus, bound to an infantile state, unable to turn outwards from the maternal coupling towards the world and its adult opportunities. Homosexuality in this scenario must be a developmental inhibition, a variation or diversion from the norm ...
>
> (p. 83)

We see in the chapters of this book that even classical concepts such as drive theory and Oedipal theory, when unbound from heteronormative bias, can be integral to contemporary theories, integrated with relational theories, and help us to understand the experience of sexuality and its crucial component, desire.

Sexual aberrations or perversions

The concept of sexual perversion is one that elicits a great deal of agreement among psychoanalysts – agreement that the term 'perversion' had come to take on such pejorative connotations that it ceased to be useful for psychoanalytic discourse. For some decades, perversion was used to define anything outside of 'normal' sexuality, and the definition of 'normal' was rather narrow. In recent decades, as psychoanalysts recognized the limitations of normative classification, the utility of a category for the perverse faded, as it included too many and too diverse a number of subcategories to remain coherent.

As with many psychiatric and psychoanalytic diagnoses, the problem of classification is least difficult with the more severely symptomatic. Therefore, the strict fetishist is comfortably seen as having diverted sexual energy from an original sexual object, and the paedophile as having made not only a diversion but a diversion toward a prohibited object and sociopathy. Categorization is delineated with far less consensus when symptoms are less desperate, sexual behaviours are more mutually engaged between adults, and when they are just one part of a sexual repertoire rather than a sole interest. To know whether a woman who loves her husband and enjoys being anally penetrated by him is perversely diverting from genital sexuality, or is a creatively enjoying a sexual adventure with her husband, we would have to know more about the psychic underpinnings of the behaviour. Disagreements persist today about where the line can be drawn between the normal and the perverse, and about whether lines can be drawn at all.

For psychoanalysts, the focus shifts from generalizations about categories of behaviour to explorations of the psychodynamics of the individual, particularly that which is not conscious. Kaplan's (1991) 'perverse strategy,' is a mental strategy intent on deceiving the self and the observer about unconscious meanings, and diverts attention from latent motives, fantasies, wishes, and desires. The pervasiveness of Kaplan's underlying perverse strategy runs the gamut from the desperation and fixity of classically perverse sexual behaviours to the fetishistic icons of everyday life, 'banalities that are always fetched up into something other than what they actually are – [*Madam Bovary's*] napkins in the shape of bishops' hats . . .' (p. 203), and underlie the performance of gender role behaviours that impersonate and caricature gender stereotypes and ideals (e.g. male aggression, or female innocence and submission).

In keeping with Kaplan's recognition of the pervasiveness of perverse strategies, McDougall (1995) raised the spectre of a 'perverse psychoanalytic relationship,' and the elements of countertransference that may be perverse. She noted that psychoanalysts were perhaps too ready to speak of patients as perverts, thereby distancing themselves, and not often enough examining the analyst's contributions to the psychoanalytic endeavour for its perverse elements (p. 217). Dimen (2001) broadens this psychoanalytic consideration in 'Perversion is Us,' showing how power structures intertwine in psychoanalytic concepts of perversion. Reconsidering some of the major psychoanalytic contributions to theories of perversion by Chasseguet-Smirgel, Kernberg, Khan and others, we see how little developed is the analyst's understanding of their countertransference, often used blithely only to amplify the analyst's point of view. Re-assessing classical theories in historical context, Dimen makes a dramatic yet simple conclusion:

> If perversion can coexist with health, if its status as illness varies with cultural time and place, then, conversely, any sexuality may be symptomatic – or healthy. . . . Put another way, sexuality has nothing inherently to do with mental health or mental illness.
>
> (2001: 857)

Moss (Chapter 9) considers the concept of sexual aberrations in psychoanalytic practice and theory, in the bidirectional interaction of theory and experience, and particularly in the ways that analysts may reject or embrace the concept in our never ending struggles to liberate and to contain (control, interpret, etc.) sexuality. Wood (Chapter 12) notes the heterogeneity of perversity among patients, both in the variety of symptoms and in terms of depth of pathology. Drawing on the dynamics and clinical issues of more severely symptomatic patients, she illustrates many transference and countertransference implications that will be of interest to all clinicians.

Lemma (Chapter 10) looks at one behaviour, the use of prostitutes, without the standard assumption that it must always and only be perverse – failing to relate to the other as separate from the self, as anything but a narcissistic appendage. She shows that, rather than only evacuating unwanted feelings into the prostitute, some men may use the prostitute to mirror a sexual self, thereby possibly fostering development in the service of integrating a sexual self. Saketopoulou (Chapter 11) broadens our purview in the realm of the interpersonal field to include unrepresented or unformulated experience that may present itself in unexpected ways. With a provocative case example, she shows us that by remaining receptively curious about the forward reach of perverse acts, rather than listening only for repetitive genetic material or evidence of what the patient is moving away from, we may find generative psychic possibilities in some perverse sexual practices. A keen observer will find some differences in the way that even our authors use the concept of perversion, yet the authors in this book share a commitment to remain psychoanalytically open and curious to unconscious meaning and to what is being enacted in any analysis. The idea that a label of 'perversion' conveys an answer or a full explanation is absent here, and in most of contemporary psychoanalysis, where the observation of a behaviour is only the beginning of a search for unconscious meaning.

About this book

As will be apparent from a quick perusal of the contents page, this book reflects a somewhat idiosyncratic collection. Yes, all the chapters concern sexuality with a particular focus on the question of the vicissitudes of desire and of the object of desire, but the selection is most certainly not representative of the diversity that defines sexuality in contemporary culture. Our restricted focus inevitably reflects one of our primary concerns, namely how psychoanalysis has positioned itself in relation to the question of homosexuality. Consequently several of the chapters in this book are concerned with exploring homosexuality (Barden, Fonagy and Allison, Hertzmann, Lynch) from a number of vantage points. We have knowingly overrepresented this focus because we consider that psychoanalytic thinking in this domain has not developed as much as it needs to.

In keeping with Freud we also wanted to include chapters about heterosexuality and its vicissitudes alongside the ones on homosexuality to underscore the fact that there is much to be questioned and understood about human sexuality irrespective of the sex of the object of desire. Sexuality, freed from the limitations of narrowly prescribed gender roles, is a far more varied enterprise than the original formula of Freud's Oedipal complex. Yet, we see in the chapters that follow that essential aspects of sexuality can be identified – e.g. sexuality develops in the context of parental care, may be experienced as a source of inner conflict, and can be employed creatively or defensively – and that essentials of sexuality may be more similar than different for homo- and hetero-sexuality.

We may experience the given body in highly idyosyncratic ways and its physical contours need not define us in any essentialiast manner, but the body is the site where difference is visible and has to be managed, somehow, no matter how we manipulate the surface of our body. Notwithstanding this embodied reality, we need to keep in mind that psychoanalytic thinking originated with a man whose primary contribution to understanding human nature was to disrupt the comforting notion of so-called normality. It is our collective responsibility as we approach the variation in human sexual experience to keep the 'disruption alive' (Barden, Chapter 4).

Notes

1   Even if we cast the net wider to animals we discover that many species don't have sex solely or primarily in order to reproduce. Although generally ignored, pleasure is an organizing force in relations between non-human animals. Many female animals engage in sex when they are already pregnant, and many animals masturbate (Bagemihl, 1999). Birth control is not restricted to human animals: many non-human animals practice forms of birth control through vaginal plugs, defecation, abortion through the ingestion of certain plants, ejection of sperm and, in the case of chimpanzees, nipple stimulation (Bagemihl, 1999).
2   For an excellent discussion of gender please refer to Birksted-Breen (1993).

References

Auchinloss, E. & Vaughan, S. (2001). Psychoanalysis and homosexuality: do we need a new theory? *Journal of the American Psychoanalytic Association*, 49, 1157–1186.
Bagemihl, B. (1999). *Biological Exuberance: Animal Homosexuality and Natural Diversity*. New York: St Martin's Press.
Benjamin, J. (1995). Sameness and difference: toward an 'overinclusive' model of gender development. *Psychoanalytic Inquiry,* 15, 125–142.
Benjamin, J. (1998). *Shadow of the Other: Intersubjectivity and Gender in Psychoanalysis*. New York: Routledge.
Berkowitz, E. (2013). *Sex and Punishment: 4000 Years of Judging Desire*. London: Westbourne Press.
Birksted-Breen, D. (1993). *The Gender Conundrum*. London: Routledge.
Bowlby, J. (1969). *Attachment and Loss*. New York: Basic Books.
Butler, J. (1990). *Gender Trouble: Feminism and the Subversion of Identity*. New York: Routledge.
Butler, J. (1995). Melancholy gender: refused identification. *Psychoanalytic Dialogues*, 5, 165–180.
Butler, J. (1998). Analysis to the core: commentary on papers by James H. Hansell and Dianne Elise. *Psychoanalytic Dialogues*, 8, 373–377.
Butler, J. (2003). Violence, mourning, politics. *Studies in Gender and Sexuality*, 4, 9–37.
Butler, J. (2004). *Undoing Gender*. New York: Routledge.

Corbett, K. (2009). *Boyhoods: Rethinking Masculinities*. New Haven, CT: Yale University Press.

Diamond, M. (2006). Masculinity unraveled: the roots of male gender identity and the shifting of male ego ideals throughout life. *Journal of the American Psychoanalytic Association*, 54 (4), 1099–1130.

Diamond, M. & Blatt, S. (2007). *Attachment and Sexuality*. London: Routledge

Dimen, M. (1991). Deconstructing difference: gender, splitting and transitional space. *Psychoanalytic Dialogues*, 1, 335–352.

Dimen, M. (2001). Perversion is us? Eight notes. *Psychoanalytic Dialogues*, 11, 825–860.

Fonagy, P. (2008). A genuinely developmental theory of sexual enjoyment and its implications for psychoanalytic technique. *Journal of the American Psychoanalytic Association*, 56, 11–36.

Fonagy, P. (2012). *A scientific theory of homosexuality for psychoanalysis*. Plenary Lecture, Psychoanalytic Psychotherapy NOW conference January, 2012, London, UK.

Fonagy, P., & Higgitt, A. (2007). The development of prejudice: an attachment theory hypothesis explaining its ubiquity. In H. Parens, A. Mahfouz, S.W. Twemlow and D.E. Scharff (Eds.) *The Future of Prejudice*. Plymouth: Jason Aronson.

Foucault, M. (1976). *The History of Sexuality I*. Paris: Editions Gallimard.

Foucault, M. (1984a). *The History of Sexuality II*. Paris: Editions Gallimard.

Foucault, M. (1984b). *The History of Sexuality III*. Paris: Editions Gallimard.

Freud, S. (1905). Three essays on the theory of sexuality. *The Standard Edition of the Complete Psychological Works of Sigmund Freud*, Vol. VII (125–244).

Freud, S. (1912). On the universal tendency to debasement in the sphere of love (contributions to the psychology of love II). *The Standard Edition of the Complete Psychological Works of Sigmund Freud*, Vol. XI (1910): Five Lectures on Psycho-Analysis, Leonardo da Vinci and Other Works, 177–190.

Freud, S. (1914). On narcissism. *The Standard Edition of the Complete Psychological Works of Sigmund Freud*, Vol. XIV (1914–1916): On the History of the Psycho-Analytic Movement, Papers on Metapsychology and Other Works.

Freud, S. (1925). The resistances to psycho-analysis. *The Standard Edition of the Complete Psychological Works of Sigmund Freud*, Vol. XIX (1923–1925): The Ego and the Id and Other Works, 211–224.

Freud, S. ([1935]1960). Letter to an American mother, in E. Freud (Ed.) *The Letters of Sigmund Freud*. New York: Basic Books.

Glasser, M. (1979). Some aspects of the role of aggression in the perversions. In I. Rosen (Ed.) *Sexual Deviations*. Oxford: OUP.

Glasser, M. (1992). Problems in the psychoanalysis of certain narcissistic disorders. *International Journal of Psychoanalysis*, 73, 493–503.

Goldner, V. (1991). Toward a critical relational theory of gender. *Psychoanalytic Dialogues*, 1 (3), 249–272.

Goldner, V. (2011). Trans: gender in free fall. *Psychoanalytic Dialogues*, 21 (2), 153–158.

Harris, A. (1991). Gender as contradiction. *Psychoanalytic Dialogues*, 1 (3), 197–224.

Hird, M. (2004). *Sex, Gender and Science*. Basingstoke: Palgrave Press.

Kaplan, L. (1991). *Female Perversions: The Temptations of Emma Bovary*, New York: Doubleday.

Kohon, G. (2012). On Peter Fonagy and Elizabeth Allison's scientific theory of homosexuality. Paper given at the Scientific Meeting of the British Psychoanalytical Society on October 17, 2012. *Bulletin of the British Psychoanalytical Society*, 48 (7), September 2012.

Laidman, J. (2000). Reproduction a touch-and-go thing for fungus. *Nature*, July 24, 1–3.

Laplanche, J. (1995). Seduction, persecution, revelation. *International Journal of Psychoanalysis*, 76, 663–682.

Laplanche, J. (2002). Sexuality and attachment in metapsychology. In D. Widlöcher, *Infantile Sexuality and Attachment*. London: Karnac.

Lemma, A. (2013). An order of pure decision. In A. Lemma. *Minding the Body*, London: Routledge.

Lemma, A. & Clarke, J. (2011). Editorial. *Psychoanalytic Psychotherapy*, 25 (4), 303–307.

Lichtenberg, J.D. (2008). *Sensuality and Sexuality across the Divide of Shame*. New York: The Analytic Press.

McDougall, J. (1993). Sexual identity, trauma, and creativity. *International Forum of Psychoanalysis*, 2, 204–218.

McDougall, J. (1995). *The Many Faces of Eros: A Psychoanalytic Exploration of Human Sexuality*. New York: W. & W. Norton.

McDougall, J. (2000). Sexuality and the neosexual. *Modern Psychoanalysis*, 25 (1), 155–166.

McDougall, J. (2001). Gender identity and creativity. *Journal of Gay and Lesbian Psychotherapy*, 5 (1), 5–28.

Mackay, J. (2001). Why have sex? *British Medical Journal*, 322, 623.

Roughton, R. & Margolis, M. (1996). Homosexuality and analysis. Letter to the editor. *New York Times*, October 10.

Ruszczynski, S. (1993). Narcissistic object relating. In S. Ruszczynski and J. Fisher (Eds.) *Intrusiveness and Intimacy in the Couple*. London: Karnac.

Scarfone, D. (2002). Sexuel et actuel. In D. Widlöcher (Ed.) *Sexualité infantile et attachement*. Paris: PUF.

Schilder, P. (1950). *The Image and Appearance of the Human Body: Studies in the Constructive Energies of the Psyche*. New York: IUP.

Stein, R. (1998). The poignant, the excessive and the enigmatic in sexuality. *International Journal of Psychoanalysis*, 79, 253–268.

Stein, R.A. (2008). The otherness of sexuality: excess. *Journal of the American Psychoanalytic Association*, 56, 43–71.

Stoller, R.J. (1976). Sexual excitement. *Archives of General Psychiatry*, 33 (August), 899–909.

Stoller, R. (1979). *Sexual Excitement: Dynamics of Erotic Life*. New York: Pantheon.

Suchet, M. (2011). Crossing over. *Psychoanalytic Dialogues*, 21 (2), 172–191.

Tannenbaum, S.J. (2003). Evidence-based practice in mental health: practical weaknesses meet political strengths. *Journal of Evaluation in Clinical Practice*, 9, 287–301.

Target, M. (2007). Is our sexuality our own? A developmental model of sexuality based on early affect mirroring. *British Journal of Psychotherapy*, 23, 517–530.

Weinstein, L. (2007). When sexuality reaches beyond the pleasure principle. In M. Diamond, & S. Blatt (Eds.) *Attachment and Sexuality*, London: Routledge.

Part I

Historical context

Chapter 1

What happened to psychoanalysis in the wake of the sexual revolution?

A story about the durability of homophobia and the dream of love, 1950s–2010s

Dagmar Herzog

> For me, the offense that we who engage in public talk regarding sexuality commit is to hold up images of the self and of the 'normal' that alienate people from their experience of themselves. For example, there is the prevalent view that mature and healthy, in addition to heterosexual, sex must be deeply imbued with sentiments of love. That may sound very attractive, but I don't think that describes very many people's experience.
>
> (Sociologist and *Sexual Conduct* co-author William Simon in a 1999 interview)

This is a story about the intertwined histories of psychoanalysis, psychiatry, sexology, and cultural change. It is a story about the perplexingly stubborn hold of homophobia on the profession of psychoanalysis in the post-World War II era. It is also a story about the more subtly egregious and harder to see mis-uses of the dream of love. For the relationships between sex and love – their connections and disconnections – are not obvious, and never have been. People on both sides of the couch know this in their hearts. But as it happens, psychoanalytic literature was rather more frank about the complexities of desire in the first decades of the movement than it would be in the conditions of diaspora after Freud's death. And the disavowal of desire's complexities was even more powerful in the postwar U.S. than it would be in postwar Europe – precisely in the two decades when the prestige of psychoanalysis in American medicine and culture made its dramatic ascent.

Inventing the love doctrine, 1948–1968

The first major paradigm shift in postwar U.S. psychoanalytic thinking about sex would emerge in direct reaction to – indeed *against* – Alfred Kinsey. Kinsey's *Sexual Behavior in the Human Male* and *Sexual Behavior in the Human Female*, published in 1948 and 1953, were widely read and discussed in the U.S. media. Instantly, they were understood full well, by the public and journalists alike, as an endorsement, in the guise of scientific empiricism, of a greater 'democratic pluralism of sexuality' – as the psychoanalytically inclined literary critic Lionel

Trilling put it at the time, evincing considerable distaste and discomfort at the idea (Trilling, 1948: 475). Through their statistics alone, the Reports constituted a frontal attack on the idea of constricting sex to monogamous heterosexual marriage. But they did more than that. They took ordinary people's experiences seriously. As the reviewer in *The Nation* noted, until the first Report, 'only two organized groups have been entitled to talk about sex – the churches and the psychoanalysts.' Alfred Kinsey made it possible for everyone to talk. No wonder, then, that 'clergymen and psychoanalysts are among the most militant enemies of the report' (Gumpert, 1948: 471). Among other things, Kinsey asserted that there was no difference between men and women in their capacity for orgasm, or for marital infidelity, or for sexual interest in general. And he actively advanced the view that homosexuality was a natural variant of human sexuality – and indeed a remarkably prevalent one.

What had changed in the half-century since Sigmund Freud had first weighed in on the topics of sexual desire, aims, and objects? Freud's work was full of contradictory impulses and recurrent self-revisions, but he was unquestionably more open and curious about the intricacies of desire than many of the psychoanalysts who followed in his wake. On the one hand, there were in Freud's published work the normative assumptions that what he called 'a normal sexual life' required: making an object choice external to the self; connecting the drive for pleasure to reproductive aims; fusing component instincts and putting any remaining partial (polymorphous, oral, anal) drives into the service of genital primacy (S. Freud, 1962: 73). On the other hand, there were also repeated declarations that: homosexuals were not necessarily any more mentally unstable than heterosexuals; homosexuals could in fact serve as analysts themselves; and there was as little prospect of converting homosexuals to heterosexuality as the reverse. Moreover, and emphatically, Freud declared (in a 1915 footnote added to his *Three Essays on the Theory of Sexuality*): 'Psycho-analytic research is most decidedly opposed to any attempt at separating off homosexuals from the rest of mankind as a group of a special character' (S. Freud, 1962: 11).[1]

In the decades between Freud and Kinsey, however, the psychoanalytic community tended increasingly towards more negative assessments of homosexuality – even as, in the early movement, there was still a lively mix of opinions and theories (in the midst, significantly, of an ongoing effort to profile psychoanalysis in relationship to other then-emerging sexological propositions). The Hungarian analyst Sándor Ferenczi, for instance, a close collaborator of Freud's, veered between: earnest confession of 'the homosexual impulses' in himself (Ferenczi, 1914: 39) as well as 'the homosexual component that is hidden in everyone' (Ferenczi, 1952: 43); amused, cheeky descriptions of how well a particular man he knew was managing his own homosexuality – despite being married to a woman (Ferenczi, 1926: 250); and a smorgasbord of side remarks in case studies of patients, ranging from one homosexual patient's 'indissoluble fixation on his mother' (Ferenczi, 1934: 5) to another patient's 'far-going homosexual bondages' (Ferenczi, 1949: 233). Most consequential for the future, however, was Ferenczi's attempt to distinguish conceptually between different types of male homosexual interest. Reacting, in a talk given in 1911 and published in 1914, to the well-known German homosexual rights activist Magnus Hirschfeld's theories of a 'third' or 'intermediate sex,' Ferenczi advanced the notion that one should distinguish between what he called 'subject-homo-erotism' (evinced by a more feminine man, i.e. by someone inverted in his own gender role and thus an exemplar of Hirschfeld's 'intermediate sex' – these types Ferenczi thought were not convertible to heterosexuality) and 'object-homo-erotism' (as exemplified by more masculine-appearing men who nonetheless desired other men – these types Ferenczi deemed to be suffering from 'obsessional neurosis,' and he asserted that they could in fact be converted and could learn to desire women (Ferenczi, 1952: 300, 303)).

Along related lines, in the early work of Helene Deutsch, there was a stark vacillation between, on the one hand, a genuine, at times intrusive-voyeuristic and at other times almost envious, concern with investigating the sexual practices of lesbians and, on the other, the eager attempt to develop further Freud's reflections on lesbian object-choice – above all by shifting theoretical interest to the pre-Oedipal stage of the mother–child relationship (Deutsch, 1932). In Karen Horney's often impressive feminist critiques of Freud's theories of sexuality, as well as in her eventual skepticism of the validity of libido theory in general, there was at least ambivalence about the status of same-sex desire (Horney, 1924: 60–61; Horney, 1939: 80–81). Strikingly, Horney's occasional negative comments about homosexual men were accompanied by negative assertions about most heterosexual men as well (Horney, 1932: 352). But already in Melanie Klein's drive-centered, pre- (or early) Oedipally- focused work with children, and in Marie Bonaparte's studies of incest and of children's sexual play with each other, there were inserted strongly negative assertions about the pathology of homosexuality (Klein, 1932: 46, 78; Bonaparte, 1953: 130–131). So too, in Ronald Fairbairn's writings, and in the midst of his innovative larger project of deeroticizing the concept of libido and promoting the importance of object relations, there was explicit annoyance at so many male homosexuals' refusal to see themselves as disturbed and disinterest in changing their orientation; in a 1946 essay Fairbairn described homosexuality with clear distaste as 'the natural sexual expression of a personality which has become perverse in its essential structure' (Fairbairn, 1952: 291–293; Royston, 2001: 43). In the more ego- and defense-oriented work of Sigmund Freud's daughter Anna, there was the proud pronouncement, as of 1949, that while her father had not believed in the possibility of conversion of orientation, she, Anna, could report excellent success in this area with a number of male homosexuals. Basing herself expressly on Ferenczi's distinctions between 'subject-' and 'object-homo-erotism,' Anna Freud insisted that the most important things to look at in the attempt to arrive at accurate diagnoses and treatment approaches were not men's behaviors but rather their fantasies (especially with regard to their identifications as either passive or active – or, in alternation, both – in the midst of the sexual act). Therapeutic success in 'divert[ing] their libido from one sex to the other' would emerge from the analyst's interpretations of these oscillating identifications (A. Freud, 1949: 195; Waldhorn, 1951: 337).

By the post-World War II era, the dramatically rapid spread of psychoanalytic ideas into the American mainstream via the mass media and popular advice books was marked by an ever more firmly consolidated consensus among analysts that homosexuality was by definition abnormal. From Chicago to New York and from Boston to Topeka and back to Baltimore, and despite ongoing vigorous conflicts in views with regard to psychoanalytic theory and technique more generally, there was remarkable agreement that homosexuals were disturbed and needed to be cured – i.e. that they were, in fact, the separate category of person that Sigmund Freud had insisted they were not. Whether in the 'neo-Freudian' trend first inspired by the writings of Franz Alexander and then developed further by both Karen Horney and Harry Stack Sullivan (the latter of whom, although homosexual himself, publicly made homophobic pronouncements) or among the 'ego psychologists' around Heinz Hartmann, Ernst Kris, and Grete and Edward Bibring (all of whom worked closely together with Anna Freud), whether in the group around Sándor Radó (whose antihomosexual ideas were built on his vehement objections to Sigmund Freud's foundational concept of bisexuality) or in the work of the eminent non-émigré psychoanalyst and explicitly Christian 'dean' of American psychiatry Karl Menninger – not to mention in the subsequent psychoanalytic projects of Robert Bak and Phyllis Greenacre on perversions and fetishes – the psychoanalytic community in the U.S. generated a welter of uninterrogated assumptions and declarative assertions that would shape the conversation about same-sex desire for decades to come.[2]

The incoherence of the claims about the patheticness and/or pathology of homosexuality was as palpable as was the imposing confidence with which those assertions were delivered. Male homosexuality was seen as a way of attempting to avoid castration by the father – or as a way to unite with the father. It signaled an overidentification with a seductive or domineering mother – or it was a sign of a profound fear of the female genitals. It functioned as a hapless way to repair one's sense of inadequacy as a male – or it was a powerful sexual compulsion that required better control. The prolific, popular New York-based analyst Edmund Bergler wrote with authority: 'Homosexuals are essentially disagreeable people . . . [displaying] a mixture of superciliousness, fake aggression, and whimpering . . . subservient when confronted with a stronger person, merciless when in power . . . You seldom find an intact ego . . . among them' (Bergler, 1956: 28–29). Psychoanalysts were not quite as obsessed with lesbianism, but comparably confused things would be said about it as well. Was the same-sex-desiring woman identifying *with* an emotionally withholding Oedipal father or defending herself *against* her (frustrated) desire for that father? Were lesbians stuck in a still all-too-masculine 'clitoridal' phase – or did they have castrating impulses toward their own sons? Or were they above all striving for a return to the undifferentiated mother–child fusion of infancy?

It is difficult in hindsight to assess how much the hostility to homosexuality was driven by the lasting sense, inherited from Freud, that homosexual impulses, however well hidden, existed in every individual, including within the analysts themselves, and how much the animus was driven by the effort to make psychoanalysis acceptable to mainstream, Main Street America. This was, it bears remembering, a culture which was by no means free of anti-Semitism. And although there were certainly also gentile, native-born analysts, it was not irrelevant that this was a culture still strongly skeptical of the European-accented, often left-leaning and oddball-seeming, 'queer birds' that had emigrated to the U.S. in the 1930s (Danto, 2012: 217).

Yet I want to propose that the animus against homosexuality could also be seen as part of a much deeper-seated ambivalence within the psychoanalytic community about the centrality of sex of *any* kind to the psychoanalytic project. For sex was both the topic analysts thought they were the experts on *and* they were deeply anxious about being too strongly associated with. This uncertainty and discomfort had much to do not least with the aggressive Nazi, as well as conservative Christian, attacks of the 1930s on psychoanalysis as not only an overly 'Jewish' enterprise, but also an overly sex-obsessed and therefore 'dirty' one (Herzog, 2005: 22, 277fn56). And such ambivalence was, of course, both perceptive *and* problematic.

Certainly, as Freud himself as well as his defectors, loyalists, and subsequent adapters recurrently noted, human beings were also motivated by ego-strivings and aggression and nonsexual relational impulses and not just libido. Furthermore, it is noteworthy that already in the early years of the psychoanalytic movement, really from the beginning of the twentieth century on, sexual mores, especially in Central Europe, had been loosening (the very invention of psychoanalysis, after all, was also a symptom of that more general loosening and by no means its cause); from the start, then, sexual repression alone could never have explained the emotional troubles with which Freud and his early followers were initially confronted. It is thus not surprising that the first defectors balked specifically at the centering of sexual concerns ('The Old Wise Man,' 1955). And it is thus logical also that many of the early faithful shifted their attention away from drives to objects. But the issue of libido was always palpably present, hovering over the enterprise, at once necessary to the entire conceptual framework and yet continually threatening to make the enterprise seem dirty and tawdry and trivial. (It is indicative, for instance, that in his ongoing campaign to make psychoanalysis socially acceptable in the U.S., Menninger in an interview with *Time* expressed annoyance that 'many ministers and laymen apparently assume that the Freudians are in favor of general sexual promiscuity.' For Menninger,

> this assumption is false, and its reiteration is a lie, a slander. . . . Psychoanalysts do not favor promiscuity, do not encourage it, do not attempt to relieve any patient's guilt about it. . . . Quite the reverse, most of them spend hours and hours attempting to relieve patients from the compulsive feeling of need for these very 'immoralities.'

Or, as *Time* summarized with a flourish, the aim was 'simply to get people's sex lives back to normal' ('Psychiatry,' 1951: 65–66).)

This, then, was the context into which the Kinsey Reports had burst. No longer skittish about being associated with sex, analysts thrown on the defensive by the Reports' wild popularity rushed both to announce their longstanding expertise on the topic of sex (*we* are the ones who know the most about masturbation, infidelity, etc., they averred) and to denigrate Kinsey's work, directly challenging his views on the normalcy of homosexuality and the reality and strength of female sexual interest. But their largest move was to insist that Kinsey treated humans 'zoologically.' Kinsey was an ignoramus about *love*.

Thus the Columbia University social psychiatrist Sol Ginsburg complained about Kinsey's apparent 'need to separate sex from love, tenderness, concern with the feelings and needs of one's partner . . . such a separation of the genital from other aspects of one's sexual attitudes and satisfactions itself represents an abnormality in individuals' (Ginsburg, 1954: 39). Menninger for his part declared: 'As for an orgasm being the chief criterion of sexuality, everyone knows that one orgasm can differ from another as widely as do kisses.' The examples he gave were telling:

> The orgasm of a terrified soldier in battle, that of a loving husband in the arms of his wife, that of a desperate homosexual trying to prove his masculinity and that of a violent and sadistic brute raping a child are not the same phenomena.

And Menninger approvingly cited yet another author who had argued that 'Unless the movement toward sexual integration is an expression of love for the other person there can be no normal sexual ecstasy. . . Sexual promiscuity or experimentation or athleticizing . . . without feelings of tenderness and affection is . . . destructive' (Menninger, 1953: 70). Others made nearly the same point. Iago Galdston at New York University attacked Kinsey for praising primitive peoples like the Nepalese Lepcha 'among whom "sexual activity is practically divorced from emotion . . . like food and drink it does not matter from whom you receive it, as long as you get it.". . . In Kinsey's scheme of things there seems to be little room for love' (Galdston, 1954: 46–47). And psychoanalyst Edward S. Tauber of the (interpersonal relations-focused) William Alanson White Institute, meanwhile, found it awful that ordinary Americans rushed to read the Kinsey Reports in order to discover 'that their difficulties are statistically "normal," despite the fact that their sexual behavior fails to be an expression of real warmth and tenderness.' 'A healthy psychosexual adjustment,' Tauber intoned,

> would mean that the individual has the ability to have a durable intimate relationship with a person of the opposite sex . . . This would be an adjustment which expressed love and tenderness, and was not an expression of non-sexual aims or sado-masochistic trends.
>
> (Tauber, 1954: 184, 188)

Not a single analyst reacted positively to Kinsey.

A number of things are worth noting about this phenomenon. One is that it really was new. While homophobic views had been solidifying for quite some time, then, what was novel was the development of what might well be called 'the love doctrine.' Freud himself, moreover, and significantly, had remarked on the frequent *disconnect* – also specifically among heterosexuals – between love and sexual desire (Freud, 1910, 1912). This claim that loveless sex was pathological was a postwar innovation. It emerged in direct response to Kinsey.[3] Second is that it was not innocent. There was nothing banal or benign about this disavowal of the extraordinary prevalence of loveless sex also *within* heterosexual marriages and the tone-deafness this displayed especially towards *women's* all-too-frequent sense of alienation within marital sex. Third, the paradigm would be enormously influential. Psychoanalysis ascended in the decades of the Cold War precisely by offering a secular 'moral sensibility' that reinforced conservative family values under the sign of 'health,' one that was expressly contemptuous of homosexuality and of any expression of female sexuality outside of marriage. Some people fit the norms effortlessly. But the wastage of lives – the traumas of homosexuals subjected to relentless disrespect and conversion attempts, the miseries within numberless heterosexual marriages – was immense (Heinze, 2004; Lewes, 2005; Staub, 2011).

From Oedipus to Narcissus, 1966–1979

All of this would be undone by the sexual revolution: first the Pill, then the deluge of porn, the explosion of public chatter about free love and the ubiquitous incitement to loosen mores even more. What had previously been covert became demonstratively overt. On the one hand, there were intimidating new standards of sexual performance. On the other hand, the women's and gay rights movements would turn what had been the casual power of the misogynist double standard and the privilege of heterosexual masculinity into scandals requiring massive redress.

And not least: the sexual revolution also arrived in the heartland of America with William Masters and Virginia Johnson and their blockbuster book, *Human Sexual Response* (1966). Here once again, in other words, were sex experts who challenged the sovereignty of psychoanalysis directly. Masters and Johnson explicitly sold their behaviorist sex therapeutic techniques for curing premature ejaculation and anorgasmia as *the* antidote to psychoanalysis. Two weeks in a hotel in St. Louis making daily love with your spouse was certainly marketable as an improvement over seven years on the couch.

Among other things, moreover, the women's movement, building expressly on the findings of Masters and Johnson, engaged in a frontal assault on the core psychoanalytic notion that there was a distinction to be made between clitoral and vaginal orgasms and that only the latter were properly mature (Sherfey, 1966). Feminists also criticized the assumptions prevalent in the analytic community that women were intellectually inferior to men and that their purpose was to serve men. And they challenged analysts' disdain for women's professional and sexual agency (Buhle, 1998).

For their part, gay rights activists were especially incensed by the psychiatric pathologization of homosexuality (within the DSM, the *Diagnostic and Statistical Manual of Mental Disorders*), not least because it was understood to lend the authority of medicine to the legal discrimination against homosexuals prevailing across the U.S. From 1970 on, provocative disruptions became common at meetings of the American Psychiatric Association and related organizations. At the APA in 1970, at a panel on homosexuality and transsexualism, the presentation of Irving Bieber, one of the most influential homophobic analysts, was greeted with comments to the effect that 'you're a motherfucker,' and that if his book 'talked about black people the way it talks about homosexuals you'd be drawn and quartered and you'd deserve it.' A presentation on aversion therapy to convert homosexuals by the Australian psychiatrist Nathaniel McConaghy was met with catcalls like 'where did you take your residency, Auschwitz?' Similarly, there was a 'zap' at the New York Hilton when the Association for the Advancement of Behavior Therapy met in 1972 – under the banner slogan 'Torture Anyone?' (Bayer, 1987: 103–105). A movement was underway to get the diagnostic category of homosexuality removed (Drescher and Merlino, 2007).

At the same moment, psychoanalysis was experiencing a steep decline in status and influence. There were at least four reasons for this decline. First was the sexual revolution itself. One of the central Freudian presumptions had after all been that psychological problems were caused by sexual repression. Inevitably, that particular aspect of the Freudian framework would crumble completely in the face of a society filled with frank sexual stimuli and incitements. Moreover, and however paradoxically, since the 1940s at the latest, both the 'neos' around Horney and the 'egos' around Hartmann had become even more hesitant about the classic Freudian centering of sexual matters than the early defectors had been. Horney challenged the significance of the Oedipus complex most vigorously and directly (Horney, 1939). But Hartmann too, although he stayed loyal to Oedipus, had mostly left sex to the side (Hartmann et al., 1949; Kris et al., 1954). By the 1960s and 1970s, as sex filled the public sphere, psychoanalysts seemed completely out of step with the public's concerns; neither Freud's original ideas nor the subsequently developed theories fit the situation.

Second, there was the rise of self-help and pop psychology (with millions of book titles sold) and a more general disrespect for the whole notion of 'expertise' in a culture that increasingly embraced antiauthoritarianism. Third, also within psychiatry, analysis was increasingly felt to be unscientific – at best an art, but certainly not a science – an approach that could not keep pace with pharmaceutical and other biomedical research and discoveries. And the final reason was economic: analysis was simply too expensive, and there was a proliferating welter of other opportunities (from recreational drug use to 'New Age' and other alternative therapies) for dealing with personal and interpersonal ills and the desire for self-improvement and greater life enjoyment.

As it happens, and for a complicated and overdetermined set of reasons, psychiatry in the U.S. would rescue its own reputation and cultural esteem by dumping psychoanalysis overboard, and binding its professional future to a biomedical research agenda – and this had tremendous consequences for gay rights. The key figure in this transformation would be the psychiatrist Robert L. Spitzer, who was no particular fan of either feminism or gay liberation. But he was adamantly intent on making psychiatry more scientific and he was open to hearing gay rights advocates make a scientific case for the removal of homosexuality from the DSM.[4] At the same time, however, Spitzer was attuned to the concern that the profession should not be seen as capitulating to 'outside agitators' and he was committed to continuing to give antihomosexual experts a hearing. He thus organized a panel at the May 1973 APA convention in Honolulu which pitted psychiatrists who favored removal of the category (these were Robert Stoller and Judd Marmor, both, as it happens, also analysts, and Richard Green) and the gay rights activist Ronald Gold against two of the most prominent proponents of ongoing pathologization of homosexuality, analysts Irving Bieber and Charles Socarides.

While the Honolulu panel was to be an important tipping point, no less important were the several years of quiet strategic planning that had put more liberal and sympathetic psychiatrists into key positions within the APA ('81 Words,' 2002). In November of 1973 the Board of Trustees of the APA voted to remove the category of homosexuality from the DSM. This was a major victory for gay and lesbian liberation, even as it also caused many in the psychoanalytic subcommunity of American psychiatry to withdraw from further discussion of the issue in disgruntlement at what was obviously a rebuff to their perspectives, and even as the official shift did not necessarily signal a change of heart in the rank and file of American psychiatry either.[5]

Meanwhile, however, in these same years, analysts in the U.S. and internationally were reviving with renewed intensity and in new terms a long-recurring dispute over whether the analytic patient base was moving towards more borderline and narcissistically disturbed patients (Lunbeck, 2006). British object relations theorists had been shifting analytic attention from Oedipal to pre-Oedipal pathology already since the 1940s, but the 1970s saw an especially heated round of this dispute – coinciding quite specifically with the crisis in psychoanalytic pestige more generally. Significantly, the dispute coincided as well with the sense that leading American practitioners' longstanding emphasis on the Oedipus complex had been linked to pre-sexual revolution assumptions about sexual repression as a source of difficulty; as the American analyst Edward M. Weinshel noted at the International Congress on Psycho-Analysis held in London in 1975, there was a growing consensus among analysts that primitive and 'archaic' aggressions were a far larger element in patients' problems than sex *per se* (even as Weinshel himself – and invoking on this point also Anna Freud – surmised that sexual problems persisted in new forms in the midst of the sexual revolution (Weinshel, 1976: 456–457). In this context, an increasing number of American analysts thought the time had come to shift from Oedipus to Narcissus (Quinn, 1981). Importantly, the narcissism problem under discussion was not understood in the quotidian sense as meaning self-involvement, vanity, and the advancement of self-interest, but rather, on the contrary, the sign of a profound *deficiency* in self-love. While some of the impetus for rethinking character disorders had come from diverse British object relations approaches and particularly the American Otto Kernberg's innovative adaptation of Kleinian ideas for work with borderline patients, the major lightning-rod figure in the conflicts of the 1970s was the Chicago analyst and developer of 'self psychology' Heinz Kohut. Patients might be filled with inchoate rage and anxiety even when they presented as manipulatively seductive, but whatever sexually seductive or aggressively hostile impulses were being directed at the therapist were, in the Kohutian framework, not strong drives being dealt with in transference with the analyst but rather the breakdown products of a weak and poorly formed self (Auchincloss and Glick, 1996/97: 25).

This paradigm shift, despite all its various internal contradictions and ongoing areas of controversy, would, however ironically, give both homophobia and sexism new leases on life. The turn to a preoccupation with narcissism was, after all, not just a realistic assessment of a changing client base, nor just a sign of the profession's maturing insight that perhaps all along, for decades, patients had been misunderstood as Oedipally challenged neurotics when really the source of their troubles had lain in severe damage produced in the dyadic dynamics of the pre-Oedipal phase – although those two options were hotly debated in the mid-1970s. The shift to pre-Oedipal issues needs also to be understood in the context of a reaction both to the declining significance of analysis within American psychiatry and to the feminist and gay challenges. Psychoanalysis *had* to reinvent itself.

Just as in the 1950s analysts had not responded directly to the Kinsey challenge, but instead rerouted the discussion to the purported pathology of loveless sex, here too there was a sideways response. Rather than letting go of homophobia, its contents morphed.[6] Analytic discussion turned on new theories that homosexuality had its pathogenic source not in a failure to 'navigat[e] the straits of Oedipus' (Green, 1988), but instead – as Harry Gershman and Charles Socarides among others argued – in the failure to establish 'a sound and solid gender identity' due to 'an incomplete resolution from the mother-child symbiosis that precedes the Oedipal period.' Gershman described homosexuals in a way that resonated powerfully with the kinds of symptoms typically associated with narcissistic character disorders. In Gershman's view, homosexuals were driven by a 'compulsive sexuality [that] serves to allay anxiety and inferiority feelings. . . . It is linked to [the patient's] need for control, to his masochistic self-contempt, and to his need . . . to stimulate himself in order to overcome his profound emptiness, resignation, and hopelessness' (Gershman, 1975: 303, 310). Given these developments, it is perhaps no surprise that the American Psychoanalytic Association did not manage formally to adopt a nondiscrimination policy with regard to homosexuality until 1991 – and the International Psychoanalytic Association did not do so until 2002 (Roughton, 2002, 2003).

In one last twist, despite their growing marginalization within psychiatry and their seemingly dwindling impact within American society, analysts' notion that narcissism was the new condition ailing humanity took astonishingly strong root in cultural commentary. Christopher Lasch's hugely successful *The Culture of Narcissism*, published in 1979, is perhaps the best example. Americans in general, he thought, evinced a 'dependence on the vicarious warmth provided by others . . . a sense of inner emptiness, boundless repressed rage, and unsatisfied oral cravings.' Lasch was especially contemptuous of both feminism and sexual liberation, scoffing at feminists' complaints about 'the myth of the vaginal orgasm' while also noting, not without insight but nonetheless without sympathy, that men were often terrified of women's new 'sexual demands,' because these called up 'early fantasies of a possessive, suffocating, devouring, and castrating mother.' And he was resolute in his condemnation of everything associated with the sexual revolution, from oral sex to homosexuality to promiscuity to the celebration of polymorphous perversity (Lasch, 1979: 15, 33, 40, 50, 193, 203). Whether any of this had ever been based on sound evidence about individual analytic patients or about the culture as a whole remains an open question (Reiche, 2004: 41–49). The diagnosis of what purportedly went wrong in the 1970s, and the damning association of both feminism and loosened sexual mores with 'narcissism' – a word thrown around freely even when the term was misunderstood – has stuck.

Stoller's dissent, 1973–1991

One voice stood out with particular eloquence in its dissent from the crescendo chorus insisting on maintaining a sense of high-minded superiority to the perversions and pathology purportedly evinced by unapologetically sexually active women and homosexuals. Robert J. Stoller was the Los Angeles-based psychiatrist and psychoanalyst who, at the APA meeting in Honolulu in May 1973, had offered the most creative indictment of the homophobia endemic to his profession. His antihomophobic colleagues Judd Marmor and Richard Green had also made excellent points, among them that 'from an objective biological viewpoint there is nothing "unnatural" about homosexual object choice' (indeed it could be thought of as akin to vegetarianism – a similarly unusual choice in the midst of a world in which 'most human beings are "naturally" meat-eaters') or that labeling homosexuals according to the degree of intensity of their same-sex desires was 'unpleasantly reminiscent of the Hitlerian process of trying to determine what fraction of black or Jewish ancestry a person might be permitted to have' (those were both Marmor), or that (as Green pointed out) there were plenty of heterosexuals who used sex neurotically 'to control others, as a substitute for feelings of self-worth, or as a defense against anxiety and depression' – and yet there was no DSM category for them ('A Symposium,' 1973: 1209, 1213–1214). But no one turned the mirror around onto the heterosexual male norm as forcefully – at once mockingly and earnestly – as Stoller did.

Importantly, Stoller did not dispense with psychoanalysis (of which he was a passionate practitioner) but rather wed it to a pro-sex feminist and pro-gay agenda. Stoller noted that 'there is no such *thing* as homosexuality' and thus there were in any event no grounds for having a diagnosis for it in the DSM. However, if diagnoses there must be, he said – reminding his listeners that there were after all *many* 'variants of overt heterosexuality, e.g. compulsive promiscuity, use of pornography, preference for prostitutes, adult masturbation,' then indeed 'we can all be given a diagnosis.' For – even among those who seemed conformist to norms on the surface – 'everyone has his own style and distinctive fantasy content that he daydreams or stages with objects.' In fact, Stoller was dubious that anyone achieved the purported ideal of 'a male preferring a female and vice versa, in which both wholeheartedly enjoy the sexual and loving aspects of their relationship.' Although, he conceded, that ideal 'may well be buried there in most of us,' he observed that it was manifestly evident at best 'in only a few.' And Stoller went on to propose that if a finer diagnostic schema for sexual preferences were to be developed, then some more realistic examples of such preferences should be chosen. What might some of those preferences be? One has to imagine here the audience, predominantly straight, and at least outwardly propriety-preoccupied. And there was Stoller blithely extemporizing some possibilities: 'e.g., heterosexual, monogamous, with accompanying fantasies of being raped by a stallion; homosexual, with foreskin fetishism; heterosexual, with preference for cadavers; homosexual, with disembodied penises (tearoom promiscuity); heterosexual, voyeurism; homosexual [male], expressed only in fantasies during intercourse with wife' ('A Symposium,' 1973: 1208). The barbed joke was aimed directly at the audience.

In the years that followed, Stoller emphasized the key point that what was erotic for one person was utterly nonerotic for another. While Masters and Johnson had researched arousal anatomically, Stoller was interested in how excitement worked *emotionally*. He was interested in fantasies – both conscious and unconscious – and how in every individual (but *always differently* from how it worked in everyone else) there was an intricate calibration of safety and riskiness, scripted storylines and fetishistic image scraps (with their convoluted combination of dehumanizing abstraction and rehumanizing concreteness) that maximized sexual excitement for that person. Drawing on examples from his own practice but also from pro-sex feminist writing on fantasy (for example Nancy Friday's *My Secret Garden*), using as his data patients' daydreams as well as masturbatory and during-sex fantasies (whether taken from pornography or self-invented), Stoller began to develop a theory that the point of the fantasies was 'to undo frustration, trauma, and intrapsychic conflict' – and that there was often a theme (however well hidden) of desire for revenge for past humiliations (Stoller, 1976: 899, 905).

The intellectual and political implications were immense. For one thing, Stoller eroded the boundary between normal and abnormal, instead seeing human beings on a spectrum in which, when it came to sexual excitement, almost no one fit the normative ideal of loving, unhostile relationships – hostility over past hurts was a theme in countless individuals' fantasies (whether they seemed on the surface to be about sadism or about masochism, one's own loss of control or one's power to frustrate and then thrill the other characters in the script), even as each individual's script (continually reworked over the course of a lifetime) was unique. In Stoller's view, painful experiences were at the root of all perversions – but almost everyone was a pervert in some way. Second, Stoller was adamantly antimisogynist and antihomophobic. The women in his essay were as inventive in their perverse imaginations as the men – and he was utterly accepting of their sexual agency, both within and outside of marriage. And Stoller was scathing about the denigration of homosexuals as somehow different from run-of-the-mill heterosexuals, convinced that if more details on heterosexuals' fantasies were to be collected,

> we shall become more lenient or more aware of our hypocrisy when we allege, as in law codes, that all sorts of behaviors that do not damage others must be massively punished. We try to make the outlandish folks function as scapegoats for the rest of us, but anyone – analyst or other – who collects erotic thoughts knows that many citizens, avowedly heterosexual, conspicuously normal . . . are also filled with hatred and wishes.
>
> (Stoller, 1976: 908)

Over and over, in subsequent publications, Stoller mocked the idea that homosexuals were narcissists and perverts with 'vulnerable' egos and 'archaically cathected objects' who were unable to renounce 'primitive gratification' and could not master their 'libidinal and aggressive impulses' (these were quotes from the homophobic analyst Charles Socarides) by giving examples of *heterosexual* males who had quite the same problems. In fact, he concluded with a flourish, 'How many happy heterosexuals do you know? How many of them are untainted by archaic and primitive narcissistic cathexes?' (Stoller, 1985: 175–177).[7]

In sum, Stoller was positioning himself in resistance to three prior movements. For one thing, he diverged from the rise of the biomedical model of psychiatry promoted by Robert Spitzer's DSM-III by maintaining a commitment to analysis as a practice and emotions as a focus. Second, he resisted the ongoing misogyny and homophobia still prevalent among analysts. And third, he repudiated the love doctrine developed by analysts in reaction against Kinsey.

Stoller died in 1991. He remains mostly remembered for his writings on gender identity and his sympathetic work with transsexuals. Stoller's subversive, deeply nonmisogynist and nonhomophobic impulse was ignored almost entirely by his psychiatric and psychoanalytic peers.[8] He was a prominent and respected figure who published in the most important journals, but when his ideas about how hostilities and traumas may be found at the root of perversions were adopted by fellow analysts and other psychiatrists in the U.S., it was almost never with the same fiercely compassionate anti-normativity that Stoller evinced, but rather with far more conservative agendas. Worse, and however ironically, prominent analysts assimilated Stoller's ideas about trauma and hostility to *reinforce* a normative – and indeed also overtly homophobic – version of the love doctrine (Kernberg, 1995; Auchincloss and Vaughan, 2001: 1168).

Nonetheless, Stoller's ideas about sexual excitement would be put to use for a quite different but also extremely important purpose. From the late 1970s on, they would prove absolutely essential to the international revitalization of the Kinsey tradition of sex research. To put it succinctly: Although ignored or misappropriated by his peers, Stoller's ideas would be taken up by some of the most prominent and influential sex researchers in the world – sociologists and psychologists and medical doctors in both West Germany and the United States (with influence eddying out also to other European nations).

Already before Stoller, sex researchers at the Kinsey Institute had begun to rethink a strictly biologistic perspective and to call attention to the *social* dimensions of sexual experience. The breakthrough text was John Gagnon and William Simon's *Sexual Conduct*, published in 1973. But it was young West Germans, struggling to rescue sex research both from the lingering after-effects of Nazi racism and from the moralistically conservative backlash against Nazism's licentious reputation that had defined the post-World War II moment – and building on Kinseyan empiricism while simultaneously holding to a Marcusean skepticism about whether the capitalism-driven sexual revolution was really the liberation activists had been hoping for – who found Stoller's (at once analytic and nonnormative) perspective most useful. Stoller's notion that the fantasies involved in sexual excitement and pleasure were inevitably ones of revenge and victory over past hurts and humiliations was thought to be too harsh. Sexual pleasure, as the Hamburg-based sexologist Eberhard Schorsch noted in an influential 1978 essay, also involved moments of intense longing for imagined or remembered infantile states of paradisical happiness and perfection, and the orgasm could be understood not just as a triumph wrested from past traumas but an incomparably fantastic momentary combination of dissolution of boundaries *and* heightened self-experience (Schorsch, 1978).

Nonetheless, Stoller helped Schorsch not just to rethink the project of sex research, but *to rethink the nature of sex itself.* The point was to challenge the very notion of sex as a primarily physiological drive and instead emphasize sex as an emotionally loaded phenomenon, an activity that human beings sought over and over – and *over again* – *not* in order to release some kind of built-up tension (in any event a masculinist notion, as the feminism-sympathetic Schorsch was all too aware) but rather in order continually to re-play, and each time re-solve, a convoluted but pressing inner psychological drama. The theoretical framework of sex research, in short, needed to proceed from the mind – its recesses and contradictions – and not from physiological function alone. The implications for sex therapy for individual dysfunctions and for couples' incompatibilities – as well as for cultural criticism on the politics of sex – would be profound as well, as Stoller helped German sexologists turn around the old Freudian assumption that many problems in life that seemed nonsexual had their (hidden) roots in sexual desire or conflictedness, and instead emphasize how much that was originally *non*sexual (whether emerging from an individual's lifestory or from the wider social context) was being brought into every sexual encounter (Arentewicz and Schmidt, 1983; Schmidt, 1986; Gschwind, 2001).

'Gay-friendly' analysis and its discontents, 1991–2014

It was only in 1991, when the American Psychoanalytic Association passed its nondiscrimination declaration, that openly gay or lesbian individuals in the U.S. could begin to move toward being certified as analysts. In other parts of the world it would take yet longer – and despite the International Psychoanalytic Association's official move towards nondiscrimination in 2002, in many countries – including Britain, France, and Germany – the matter remained unsettled (Lingiardi and Drescher, 2003; Robcis, 2013). The process in the U.S. had taken years of careful behind-the-scenes negotiations.

Several factors made the formal shift to nondiscrimination possible. One factor was what can only be called 'the feminism-ization of psychoanalysis,' growing out of the broader feminist revolution in psychotherapy in the course of the 1980s. Feminist critiques of the authoritarianism and misogyny structuring analytic encounters and theoretical publications alike, as well as the rise of pop psych and competing therapies (often shorter-term and more client-centered) had created a climate in which the ideals of empathy and a more democratic alliance between doctor and patient had begun to take hold also in more traditional analytic circles (Ballou et al., 2008: xv–xvi). In fact, even the shift to the narcissism paradigm, and despite that paradigm's homophobic uses, had contributed to the growth of a strand within analysis – spearheaded by Kohut but embraced by many others – which emphasized using the analytic space as a (Donald Winnicott-style) 'holding environment' more than a place of withholding (the stereotypical analyst's silence interrupted only by the occasional stern interpretation). Another huge factor was the rise, over the course of the 1980s, of ardent enthusiasm for, and sophisticated contributions to, psychoanalytic theorizing among non-M.D. psychologists, many of them drawn to relational and intersubjective approaches (only some of which were expressly antihomophobic but all of which tended towards the erosion of the analyst's sense of secure superiority vis-à-vis the patient) (Mitchell, 1978, 1981; Chodorow, 1992; Lesser, 1993). The 1985 lawsuit, settled in 1989, which at long last permitted the entry of analytically interested psychologists into the American Psychoanalytic Association benefited the Association most of all, as it brought an enormous infusion of energy into what had become a constricted and declining enterprise (Lane and Meisels, 1994; History Panel, 2013).

A further significant factor was the broad positive reception among therapeutic professionals and in the mainstream media of the analytically inclined psychologist Kenneth Lewes' landmark study, *The Psychoanalytic Theory of Male Homosexuality*, published in 1988. Lewes documented in detail the preposterousness and absurdism of the antihomosexual theories put forward over the decades since Freud and the cruelty and cowardice that had marked the profession's handling of the topic. And yet another major additional step forward in synthesizing the extant critical thinking would come in 1992, when the sociologist and analyst Nancy Chodorow published her influential essay 'Heterosexuality as a Compromise Formation.' Building on her prior feminist work while also drawing extensively on both Stoller and Lewes, Chodorow brilliantly called for treating heterosexuality as just as problematic as homosexuality had been thought to be, and insisted on the importance of pluralizing homosexualities and heterosexualities alike (Chodorow, 1992). In subsequent years, Chodorow would also be a key figure in promoting for a wider readership the splendidly perceptive early antihomophobic essays of relational psychologist Stephen Mitchell, and in making the case for *individualizing* all theorization of gender and sexuality (Mitchell, 1978; Mitchell, 1981; Chodorow, 2002; Chodorow 2012).

The turnaround in professional trends was dramatic. Five hundred psychoanalytic essays and books had been written on the topic of homosexuality before the early 1980s. Of those, as Lewes noted years later when he retrospectively surveyed this landscape, 'less than half a dozen claimed homosexuality might be part of a satisfactory psychic organization.' (Lewes, 2005: 17). As of the early twenty-first century, however, the excitement over the transformation of analysis as it sought to undo its nine-plus decades of post-Freudian contempt for homosexuality would be seen as one of the most vital growth areas within the field. The 1990s saw countless workshops, committees, initiatives, conference papers and publications – even journal launchings – that showed how eager the analytic community was to renew itself by *learning from* gays and lesbians (Auchincloss and Vaughan, 2001: 1158). In addition, more and more openly gay and lesbian individuals became analysts.

This turnaround, however, has also come with its own set of unintended side-effects. It is painfully ironic that with all the fresh new homo-friendly analytic approaches, we have nonetheless in the U.S. also witnessed a return, albeit in a variant form, of the love doctrine that had initially been invented in reaction against Kinsey – and that was nothing if not an insecure effort to assimilate psychoanalysis into a profoundly repressive and conformist Cold War culture. This is the final turn to the story. Gay-friendly psychoanalysts have now invented a love doctrine of their own. Kenneth Lewes has been most articulate in his alarm at the recent gay-friendly analysis' emphasis on 'attachment as a primary motivation,' and its concomitant underestimation of the importance of 'phallic drives,' which he sees as evincing a profound disrespect for those who 'did not come out as gay because they wanted a relationship or a family, but only the bare, forked activity of sex again and again, in all its variety, anarchy, repetition, and insatiability.' Lewes' concern – as elaborated in an important 2005 essay in the journal *Fort Da* – has been to defend the sexual outlaws and dissidents, the ones who did and do not fit into the new domestic paradigm – not least because he is convinced that talking those patients into believing that what they are most searching for is a singular relationship can only cause profound dependence and above all depression; it shames patients into disowning their own desires. Sex, also specifically anonymous sex, he argues, can after all serve as a life-affirming strategy for warding off despair – and in Lewes' view, it is by no means incompatible with social responsibility or healthy psychological functioning. The new supposedly gay-friendly love doctrine, in short, deprives gays and straights alike of a deeper and more honest understanding of the ways sexual desire and pleasure – or as Lewes has put it, 'the intensity of our sexual lives and imaginations' – need not only be sutured to the couple form, but can also be significant strategies of life-affirming resistance to – again in Lewes' words – 'social conformity. . . homogenization, and mediocrity' (Lewes, 2005: 17–19, 32). By no means is Lewes hostile to the dream of love, having concluded a prior essay with a vision of 'the promised land all people strive for: the experience of love, which, not checked by fear, shame and humiliation, expresses itself in affection, respect, and gratitude' (Lewes, 1998: 359). But in his 2005 essay Lewes is adamant in his concern that the ascent of the relational schools' insistence on 'yearnings for attachment and affiliation' as humans' primary motivation can be damaging to patients who do not fit the normative mold and is part of a longer analytic tradition of flight from and discomfort with sex (Lewes, 2005: 16–19).

Lewes' emphatic dissent has already been thoughtfully challenged by the psychoanalyst Paul Lynch. Lynch criticizes what he sees as the one-sidedness of Lewes' manifesto and notes that among his own gay male patients 'rare is the patient who doesn't to some degree want it all' – i.e. intensity and freedom *and* intimacy and durability (Lynch, Chapter 7). The future, in short, remains open. But there is no question that sexuality researchers of all disciplines – too often misled these days by the current wave of enthusiastically touted but all too often appallingly poorly conceptualized neuroscientific research projects – would do well to learn from controversies over the complexities of desire in the history of psychoanalysis.[9] Sexuality researchers would above all benefit enormously from a renewed consideration of foundational, quintessentially *psychoanalytic*, insights into: the profound significance of contradictory and conflicting impulses; the utter inextricability of social context and psychic interiority; the place of ambivalence in intimate relationships; the complicatedness of the relationships between excitement and satisfaction; the vast individual diversity of human experiences and longings; and the extraordinary power of the unconscious in fantasies and behaviors alike.

Notes

1 Useful overviews of Freud's pro-homosexual attitudes can be found in Green, 1988; Fuss, 1995; Domenici and Lesser, 1995; Dean and Lane, 2001. From Freud's subsequently published correspondence, we also know just how often Freud struggled with what he – in his own words – called an 'unruly homosexual feeling' in himself, even as the yearning for the men for whom this feeling in him stirred (Fliess, Ferenczi, Jung, and Jones) was not so much a frankly physical one but rather an intensive longing for emotional intimacy and, not least, for obedience to him as the revered patriarch (Lunbeck, 2014).
2 For uncritical and affirmative summaries of prominent analysts' starkly antihomosexual views, see Waldhorn, 1951; Bieber, 1962; and Gershman, 1975. For further – but critically

assessed – examples of hostile views on male homosexuality, see Lewes 1988; and Roughton, 2002. On lesbianism, see Glassgold and Iasenza, 2000; and O'Connor and Ryan, 2004. On Sullivan, see Wake, 2011: 4, 132. For a sampling of the work on perversions, see Bak, 1968.

3 Revealingly, the reaction to the Kinsey Reports was quite different in Continental Europe. There the diagnosis was not that Kinsey lacked a commitment to marital love, but rather that Americans lacked sexual skill, sensuality, and eroticism (Herzog, 2009).

4 The studies of psychologist Evelyn Hooker, which demonstrated experts' inability to detect any difference between homosexual and heterosexual men with respect to their 'mental adjustment,' became the most crucial evidence in this context (Hooker, 1957).

5 Four years after the vote, 69 percent of 2500 psychiatrists responding to a survey conducted by the journal *Medical Aspects of Human Sexuality* still affirmed that 'homosexuality is usually a pathological adaptation, as opposed to a normal variation,' and only 18 percent disagreed, with the rest being uncertain. 70 percent said that 'homosexuals' problems have more to do with their own inner conflicts than with stigmatization by society at large'; and 60 percent said homosexuals were less capable of 'mature, loving relationships' than heterosexuals ('Sick again?,' 1978). The love doctrine, as it were – and this despite the sexual revolution – remained a reference point.

6 Kohut himself, as late as 1980, told an interviewer with pride that he was able to cure a homosexual patient. Audiofile of Susan Quinn interview with Kohut, 3/29–3/30, 1980, Oral History Interviews, Boston Psychoanalytic Society and Institute.

7 Another favorite Stoller tactic was the list that proved the narcissist and pervert in everyone, one in which he deliberately mixed the unusual with the all-too-common in such a way that no one could avoid feeling called out and put on the spot. A typical example in his 1985 book was the list, of 'in males, some of the heterosexual realities with which clinicians are familiar: . . . voyeurism, exhibitionism, satyriasis, preference for prostitutes, . . . masturbation with pornography as more exciting than using live females, . . . klismaphilia [pleasure from receiving enemas] (the stimulus delivered by a female), telephone scatologia, . . . excitement with other men's wives but not with one's own, and preference for fat women, thin women, tall women, short women, blonde women, red-headed women, steatopygous women, big-busted women, small-busted women, black women, white women, Italian women, Jewish women, Gabonese women, Thai women, women with a cute little penis (a.k.a. clitoris), ladies, actresses, policewomen, poetesses, and women who are jet copilots.' 'Where,' Stoller asked rhetorically, 'is our paragon?' (Stoller, 1985: 176–177).

8 Only a historian, John Forrester, in his marvelous – at once appreciative and perceptively critical – essay on voyeurism and ethics in Stoller's clinical work, is the exception to the more general rule of inattention or misreading (Forrester, 2007).

9 Influential but ill-thought-out examples of the new neuroscientific work on sex and love include: Holstege et al., 2003; Aron et al., 2005; Acevedo et al., 2012; Pfaus et al., 2012; Young and Alexander, 2012.

References

81 Words (2002, 18 January). This American Life, National Public Radio. Retrieved June 5, 2013 from http://www.thisamericanlife.org/radio-archives/episode/204/transcript.

Acevedo, B. P., Aron, A., Fisher, H. E., & Brown, L. L. (2012). Neural Correlates of Long-Term Intense Romantic Love. *Social Cognitive and Affective Neuroscience, 7,* 2, 145–159.

Arentewicz, G., & Schmidt, G. (1983). *The Treatment of Sexual Disorders: Concepts and Techniques of Couple Therapy.* New York: Basic.

Aron, A., et al. (2005). Reward, Motivation, and Emotion Systems Associated with Early-Stage Intense Romantic Love. *Journal of Neurophysiology*, *94*, 1, 327–377.

Auchincloss, E. L., & Glick, R. (1996/1997). The Psychoanalytic Model of the Mind. In Michels, R., et al. (Eds.) *Psychiatry* (pp. 1–29). Philadelphia and New York: Lippincott-Raven.

Auchincloss, E. L., & Vaughan, S. C. (2001). Psychoanalysis and Homosexuality: Do We Need a New Theory? *Journal of the American Psychoanalytic Association*, *49*, 1157–1186.

Bak, R. C. (1968). The Phallic Woman – The Ubiquitous Fantasy in Perversions. *Psychoanalytic Study of the Child*, *23*, 15–36.

Ballou, M., Hill, M., & West, C. (Eds.) (2008). *Feminist Theory and Practice: A Contemporary Perspective*. New York: Springer.

Bayer, Ronald. (1987) *Homosexuality and American Psychiatry: The Politics of Diagnosis*. Princeton, NJ: Princeton UP.

Bergler, E. (1956). *Homosexuality: Disease or Way of Life?* New York: Hill and Wang.

Bieber, I., et al. (1962). *Homosexuality: A Psychoanalytic Study*. New York: Basic.

Bonaparte, M. (1953). The Male's Constructive Role in Female Sexuality. In *Female Sexuality* (pp. 116–138). London: Imago.

Buhle, M. J. (1998). *Feminism and its Discontents: A Century of Struggle with Psychoanalysis*. Cambridge, MA: Harvard UP.

Chodorow, N. J. (1992). Heterosexuality as a Compromise Formation: Reflections on the Psychoanalytic Theory of Sexual Development. *Psychoanalysis and Contemporary Thought*, *15*, 3, 267–304.

Chodorow, N. J. (2002). Prejudice Exposed on Stephen Mitchell's Pioneering Investigations of the Psychoanalytic Treatment and Mistreatment of Homosexuality. *Studies in Gender and Sexuality*, *3*, 61–72.

Chodorow, N. (2012). *Individualizing Gender and Sexuality: Theory and Practice*. New York: Routledge.

Danto, E. A. (2012) 'Have You No Shame?' – American Redbaiting of Europe's Psycho-analysts. In Damousi, J., & Plotkin, M. B. (Eds.) *Psychoanalysis and Politics: Histories of Psychoanalysis under Conditions of Restricted Political Freedom* (pp. 213–231). New York: Oxford UP.

Dean, T., & Lane, C. (2001). *Homosexuality and Psychoanalysis*. Chicago, IL: Chicago UP.

Deutsch, H. (1932). On Female Homosexuality. *Psychoanalytic Quarterly*, *1*, 484–510.

Domenici, T., & Lesser, R. (Eds.) (1995). *Disorienting Sexuality: Psychoanalytic Reappraisals of Sexual Identities*. New York: Routledge.

Drescher, J., & Merlino, J. P. (Eds.) (2007). *American Psychiatry and Homosexuality: An Oral History*. Binghamton, NY: Haworth.

Fairbairn, W. R. D. (1952). The Treatment and Rehabilitation of Sexual Offenders (1946). In *Psychoanalytic Studies of the Personality* (pp. 289–296). London: Tavistock Publications.

Ferenczi, S. (1914). Letter from Sándor Ferenczi to Sigmund Freud, December 18, 1914. *The Correspondence of Sigmund Freud and Sándor Ferenczi Volume 2, 1914–1919*, 38–39.

Ferenczi, S. (1926). Letter from Sándor Ferenczi to Sigmund Freud, February 21, 1926. *The Correspondence of Sigmund Freud and Sándor Ferenczi Volume 3, 1920–1933*, 249–251.

Ferenczi, S. (1934). Thalassa: A Theory of Genitality. *Psychoanalytic Quarterly*, *3*, 1–29.

Ferenczi, S. (1949). Notes and Fragments [1930–32]. *International Journal of Psycho-Analysis, 30*, 231–242.

Ferenczi, S. (1952). *First Contributions to Psycho-Analysis.* Vol. 45, International Psychoanalytical Library. (331 pp.). London: The Hogarth Press and the Institute of Psycho-Analysis. (Original work published 1914).

Forrester, J. (2007). The Psychoanalytic Case: Voyeurism, Ethics, and Epistemology in Robert Stoller's *Sexual Excitement.* In Creager, A. N. H., Lunbeck, E., & Norton Wise, M. (Eds.) *Science without Laws: Model Systems, Cases, Exemplary Narratives* (pp. 189–211). Durham, NC: Duke UP.

Freud, A. (1949). Report on the Sixteenth International Psychoanalytic Congress. *Bulletin of the International Psychoanalytic Association, 30*, 178–208.

Freud, S. (1910). A Special Type of Choice of Object Made by Men (Contributions to the Psychology of Love I). *The Standard Edition of the Complete Psychological Works of Sigmund Freud, Volume XI (1910): Five Lectures on Psycho-Analysis, Leonardo da Vinci and Other Works* (pp. 163–176).

Freud, S. (1912). On the Universal Tendency to Debasement in the Sphere of Love (Contributions to the Psychology of Love II). *The Standard Edition of the Complete Psychological Works of Sigmund Freud, Volume XI (1910): Five Lectures on Psycho-Analysis, Leonardo da Vinci and Other Works* (pp. 177–190).

Freud, S. (1962). *Three Essays on the Theory of Sexuality* (J. Strachey, Trans.). New York: Basic Books. (Original work published 1905)

Fuss, D. (1995). *Pink Freud.* Special issue of *GLQ, 2.*

Gagnon, J., & Simon, W. (1973). *Sexual Conduct: The Social Sources of Human Sexuality.* Chicago, IL: Aldine.

Galdston, I. (1954) So Noble an Effort Corrupted. In Geddes, D. P. (Ed.) *An Analysis of the Kinsey Reports on Sexual Behavior in the Human Male and Female* (pp. 41–48). New York: Mentor Books.

Gershman, H. (1975). The Effect of Group Therapy on Compulsive Homosexuality in Men and Women. *American Journal of Psychoanalysis, 35*, 303–312.

Ginsburg, S. W. (1954). Atomism of Behavior. In Geddes, D. P. (Ed.) *An Analysis of the Kinsey Reports on Sexual Behavior in the Human Male and Female* (pp. 32–40). New York: Mentor Books.

Glassgold, J., & Iasenza, S. (2000). *Lesbians and Psychoanalysis: Revolutions in Theory and Practice.* New York: Free Press.

Green, R. (1988, 11 December). Navigating the Straits of Oedipus. *New York Times.*

Gschwind, H. (2001). Das Sexuelle Symptom in der Sprechstunde. In Sigusch, V. (Ed.) *Sexuelle Störungen und ihre Behandlung* 3rd ed. (pp. 124–137). Stuttgart: Thieme.

Gumpert, M. (1948, 1 May). The Kinsey Report. *The Nation, 166*, 471.

Hartmann, H., Kris, E., & Loewenstein, R. M. (1949). Notes on the Theory of Aggression. *Psychoanalytic Study of the Child, 3*, 9–36.

Heinze, A. R. (2004). *Jews and the American Soul: Human Nature in the Twentieth Century.* Princeton, NJ: Princeton UP.

Herzog, D. (2005). *Sex after Fascism: Memory and Morality in Twentieth-Century Germany.* Princeton, NJ: Princeton UP.

Herzog, D. (2009, Winter). Fear and Loathing. *Lapham's Quarterly, 2*, 187–191.

History Panel. (2013, September 30). *Division 39 Insight.* Retrieved May 8, 2015 from http://division39blog.org/2013/09/history-panel/.

Holstege, G., et al. (2003, October 8). Brain Activation during Human Male Ejaculation. *Journal of Neuroscience, 23*, 27, 0185–0193.

Hooker, E. (1957). The Adjustment of the Male Overt Homosexual. *Journal of Projective Techniques*, *21*, 18–31.

Horney, K. (1924). On the Genesis of the Castration Complex in Women. *International Journal of Psycho-Analysis*, *5*, 50–65.

Horney, K. (1932). Observations on a Specific Difference in the Dread Felt by Men and by Women Respectively for the Opposite Sex. *International Journal of Psycho-Analysis*, *13*, 348–360.

Horney, K. (1939). *New Ways in Psychoanalysis*. New York: W. W. Norton.

Kernberg, O. F. (1995). *Love Relations: Normality and Pathology*. New Haven, CT: Yale UP.

Klein, M. (1932). *The Psycho-Analysis of Children*. Vol. 22, International Psychoanalytical Library (379 pp.). London: The Hogarth Press.

Kris, E., et al. (1954). Problems of Infantile Neurosis: A Discussion. *Psychoanalytic Study of the Child*, *9*, 16–71.

Lane, R. C., & Meisels, M. (Eds.) (1994). *A History of the Division of Psychoanalysis of the American Psychological Association*. Hillsdale, NJ: Lawrence Erlbaum Associates.

Lasch, C. (1979) *The Culture of Narcissism: American Life in an Age of Diminishing Expectations*. New York: Norton.

Lesser, R. (1993). A Reconsideration of Homosexual Themes: Commentary on Trop and Stolorow's 'Defense Analysis in Self Psychology'. *Psychoanalytic Dialogues*, *3*, 639–641.

Lewes, K. (1988). *The Psychoanalytic Theory of Male Homosexuality*. New York: Simon and Schuster.

Lewes, K. (1998). A Special Oedipal Mechanism in the Development of Male Homosexuality. *Psychoanalytic Psychology*, *15*, 3, 341–359.

Lewes, K. (2005). Homosexuality, Homophobia, and Gay-Friendly Psychoanalysis. *Fort Da*, *11A*, 13–34.

Lingiardi, V. & Drescher, J. (Eds.) (2003). *The Mental Health Professions and Homosexuality: International Perspectives*. Binghamton, NY: The Haworth Medical Press.

Lunbeck, E. (2006). Borderline Histories: Psychoanalysis Inside and Out. *Science in Context*, *19*, 151–173.

Lunbeck, E. (2014). *The Americanization of Narcissism*. Cambridge, MA: Harvard UP.

Menninger, K. (1953, December). One View of the Kinsey Report. *GP*, *8*, 67–72.

Mitchell, S. (1978). Psychodynamics, Homosexuality, and the Question of Pathology. *Psychiatry*, *41*, 254–263.

Mitchell, S. (1981). The Psychoanalytic Treatment of Homosexuality: Some Technical Considerations. *International Review of Psycho-Analysis*, *8*, 63–80.

O'Connor, N., & Ryan, J. (2004). *Wild Desires and Mistaken Identities: Lesbianism and Psychoanalysis*. London: Karnac.

The Old Wise Man. (1955, 14 February). *Time*, *65*, 64–72.

Pfaus, J. G., et al. (2012). Who, What, Where, When (and Maybe Even Why)? How the Experience of Sexual Reward Connects Sexual Desire, Preference, and Performance. *Archives of Sexual Behavior*, *41*, 1, 31–62.

Psychiatry and Religion. (1951, 16 April). *Time*, *57*, 65–66.

Quinn, S. (1981, 30 June). Oedipus vs. Narcissus. *New York Times*.

Reiche, R. (2004). Haben frühe Störungen zugenommen? In *Triebschicksal der Gesellschaft: Über den Strukturwandel der Psyche* (pp. 41–62). Frankfurt/Main: Campus.

Robcis, C. (2013). *The Law of Kinship: Anthropology, Psychoanalysis, and the Family in France*. Ithaca, NY: Cornell University Press.

Roughton, R. E. (2002, Summer). Rethinking Homosexuality: What It Teaches Us about Psychoanalysis. *Journal of the American Psychoanalytic Association, 50*, 733–763.

Roughton, R. E. (2003). The International Psychoanalytic Association and Homosexuality. *Journal of Gay and Lesbian Psychotherapy, 7*, 189–196.

Royston, R. (2001). Sexuality and Object Relations. In Harding, C. (Ed.) *Sexuality: Psychoanalytic Perspectives* (pp. 35–51). Philadelphia, PA: Taylor & Francis

Schmidt, G. (1986). *Das Grosse Der Die Das: Über das Sexuelle*. Herbstein: März.

Schorsch, E. (1978). Die Stellung der Sexualität in der psychischen Organisation des Menschen. *Der Nervenarzt, 49*, 456–460.

Sherfey, M. J. (1966). The Evolution and Nature of Female Sexuality in Relation to Psychoanalytic Theory. *Journal of the American Psychoanalytic Association, 14*, 28–125.

Sick Again? (1978, 20 February). *Time, 111*, 102.

Staub, M. (2011). Person Envy. In *Madness Is Civilization: When the Diagnosis Was Social, 1948–1980* (pp. 139–165). Chicago, IL: Chicago UP.

Stoller, R. J. (1976, August). Sexual Excitement. *Archives of General Psychiatry, 33*, 899–909.

Stoller, R. J. (1985). *Observing the Erotic Imagination*. New Haven, CT: Yale UP.

Stoller, R. J., et al. (1973, November). A Symposium: Should Homosexuality be in the APA Nomenclature? *American Journal of Psychiatry, 130*, 1207–1216.

Tauber, E. S. (1954). The Reading of Kinsey as a Meaningful Experience. In Geddes, D. P. (Ed.) *An Analysis of the Kinsey Reports on Sexual Behavior in the Human Male and Female* (pp. 183–192). New York: Mentor Books.

Trilling, L. (1948, April). Sex and Science: The Kinsey Report. *Partisan Review, 15*, 460–476.

Wake, N. (2011). *Private Practices: Harry Stack Sullivan, the Science of Homosexuality, and American Liberalism*. New Brunswick, NJ: Rutgers UP.

Waldhorn, H. F. (1951). Meetings of the New York Psychoanalytic Society. *Psychoanalytic Quarterly, 20*, 337–338.

Weinshel, E. M. (1976). Concluding Comments on the Congress Topic. *International Journal of Psycho-Analysis, 57*, 451–460.

Young, L., & Alexander, B. (2012). *The Chemistry Between Us: Love, Sex, and the Science of Attraction*. New York: Current/Penguin.

Part II

Foundational concepts

Contemporary elaborations

Chapter 2

A developmental model of sexual excitement, desire and alienation

Mary Target

Introduction

This chapter will build on earlier thinking by Peter Fonagy and myself which extended our ideas of the development of self within attachment relationships to the area of psychosexuality (Target, 2007; Fonagy, 2008). We noted that clinical and theoretical psychoanalysis had gradually moved away from an emphasis on sexuality toward self- and object-representations, relationships and conflicts. We suggested that sexuality is no longer assumed in psychoanalysis to be the primary basis and driver of character development and psychopathology, but rather to be a secondary or even relatively trivial aspect of most cases, or sometimes as an area of difficulty to be referred to specialist colleagues. Material about sexual behaviour, desire, erotic dreams and so on may now be thought mostly to disguise other, non-sexual self- and object-related conflicts (such as fears of intimacy based on expectations of humiliation, envious raids or corrosive contempt). Previously, interpersonal or narcissistic issues might have been thought to cover repressed psychosexual conflict or experiences. Although major theories of psychoanalysis (object relations theory, self psychology, intersubjective relational approaches) remain still clearly psychoanalytic in their focus on the dynamic unconscious, central character issues now tend to be traced to very early infantile relationships and their repercussions in the domains of interpersonal and self-experience, rather than to psychosexual fixations and conflicts which were originally the centrepiece of psychoanalytic explanation (Green, 1995; for an overview of psychoanalytic theories of development see Fonagy and Target, 2003). The classical Freudian and French schools are the main exceptions here (Green, 1997).

Object relations theories have, in part, been informed by observations and research on mother–infant interactions, with a focus on the early mother–infant bond involving feeding, holding and mirroring of affect and so on. Winnicott's work extensively illuminated the origins of emotional and creative self-development in terms of these real interactions. Bion's work – which led to a different but compatible theory of the growth of the mind and of relatedness – was also rooted in intimate caregiving interactions, but perhaps in a more metaphorical way than Winnicott's work. Winnicott's developmental model was grounded very closely in the physical experiences of the child in early relating, and the ways in which the mother's actual handling of their interactions shaped his growing mind. That model provides a broader foundation for our account of developing affect regulation and mentalization capacity, and within this a hypothesis about what makes sexuality inherently intriguing.

Some have suggested that those who focus on observation and research on the development of the self and relatedness risk forgetting 'the intrapsychic consequences of the sexual drives that do not readily lend themselves to observation' (Green, 1997: 347). Attachment theory, one of Green's bugbears, was developed by John Bowlby – a well-trained analyst but with a wider perspective and the courage of his convictions, fed by ceaseless observation and openness to neighbouring sciences. Bowlby extended the evidence and understanding of the lasting impact of very early interactions, the real behaviour of parents as a basis for preconscious templates of relating, and a framework for the action of unconscious fantasy. Bowlby, like Winnicott, thought that psychoanalysis (following Freud's shift in explaining neurosis, from trauma to psychic reality and fantasy) paid far too little attention to the crucial impact of real, observable experiences on the personality and symptomatic disorders that we treat. There is much empirical evidence to support this emphasis on real interaction, especially relational trauma and parental defences, and attachment research (much of it led by psychoanalysts) documents the decisive impact of the external, relational world on the internal world and sense of self which then develops. The links made by Freud and others between early emotional development and the drives are quite compatible with an extended model which places attachment as a foundation for later development, and I would argue recognizes the search for predictable attachment as a primary biological drive throughout human life. Bowlby's attachment theory has become influential in some psychoanalytic circles as well as well-respected in developmental and clinical psychology and relevant neuroscience. However, the theory has until very recently had little or no space for psychosexual aspects of attachment or even for the infant's aggression (Target, 2005).

I will suggest that conscious and unconscious attachment needs not only shape key aspects of personality and the capacity for emotional relating, but also set the stage for psychosexual identity, erotic fantasy and pleasure, including the capacity to combine physical and emotional intimacy. On the surface, the link between sexuality and infancy is so obvious as to be easily missed. Adult sexual relating and foreplay suggests their roots in parent–infant interaction (kissing, hugging, tickling, nuzzling, stroking, baby words, names and voices), but the direction of this relationship may not be so obvious. It is perhaps most intuitive that adult sexual intimacy re-awakens infantile feelings and makes it feel safe for adults to express the desires for closeness, holding and dependence associated with being a baby, both a desire for blissful union for oneself and the wish to satisfy that desire projected into the partner. It may also be that parents' intimate interactions with babies unconsciously incorporate elements of adult sexual excitement and closeness.

The connections between adult and infant physical intimacy have tended not to be pursued within modern psychoanalytic developmental theories, perhaps because they raise conflictual assumptions. The protective closeness of the parent and the utter dependence of a small baby makes sexual desire, with its insistence, inherent invasiveness and the ultimate selfishness of pleasure, seem brutal and alien, and indeed many couple relationships lose their erotic intensity through parenthood. Within an object relations therapeutic framework with its implicit parenting model, adult sexual experiences, associations and dreams can remain somewhat unexplored, in much the same way as the manifest content of a dream was discarded in favour of latent dream thoughts, but in the opposite direction from Freud's discoveries. In his writings, which concerned the child rather than a baby, infantile sexuality and the Oedipus complex (structured around the child's feelings of actual sexual rivalry) were fundamental and concerned real, passionate wishes, more literal than the relatively pallid, metaphorical version of much modern theory. The child's fantasies are intense, experienced as powerfully exciting and potentially frightening, hence the superstructure of defences mobilized to keep oneself acceptable to the parents, to keep the relationships safe and to maintain the possibility of feeling like a lovable and good person.

Reducing adult personality to a version of very early object relationships, as opposed to childhood sexuality, risks desexualizing it: the passion for the body of the other is in that context for the lost, loved or hated maternal object, the parent who is needed to feed and offer bodily care to a completely dependent infant. This is quite different from the oedipal model in which the young child's fantasies are around sexual interactions as between the parents, the desired bodily possession, receptiveness and penetration are as between adults not between a powerful parent and a helpless baby. However, I will argue that observations and research findings in relation to early infant development can be relevant to the development of individual sexuality as much as to other areas of relating. Object relations theories and developmental research have helped us understand the development of an emotional and thinking person within a structured attachment relationship, and they can also reach to provide a model of normal adult sexuality that may fill a gap in psychoanalytic theory. This model will be outlined in the next section. I will then consider a major way in which the experience of sexuality can become vitiated so that adult desire is pallid and 'as if', or can only be fully felt in the absence of an available partner. Some clinical cases will be described to illustrate that the healthy path of erotic development, based in muted or side-stepped early mirroring of sexual feelings which leaves a continuing search for recognition and physical engagement of a partner, may go awry. In such cases, early interactions may leave the individual alienated and excluded from his or her sexual self and from the enactment of desire.

How self-understanding develops out of primary object relationships

Previous writings have offered a bridge between psychoanalytic and empirical accounts of the development of a child's capacity to understand himself (and another) as a person motivated by thoughts and feelings (Fonagy, Gergely, Jurist, and Target, 2002; Fonagy and Target, 2006). We have argued that the ability to attribute states of mind in oneself and others ('mentalization') underpins a coherent self-structure.

The first step towards understanding the self as a psychological agent is the 'discovery' of affects through primary object relationships. Affects are not inherently known to the infant. We have proposed (consistent with Winnicott, 1960, and Bion, 1962) that they are inferred through the parent's routine attention to the baby's wishes, feelings and responses, within close interaction. Our experience of our feelings is based on internalizations of our mother's expressions as she reacts to our emotional expressions, by noticing and mirroring them (Fonagy et al., 2002; Gergely and Watson, 1996, 1999),[1] Mirroring (i.e. resonating with, reflecting on and expressing recognition of the internal state which the infant displays) is an instinctual response on the part of almost all adults (Meltzoff and Moore, 1997). Representations of internal experiences associated with primary affects are built on the mother's reflections of them. The establishment of a second order (symbolic) representation of affect states creates the substrate for affect regulation and impulse control: feelings can be manipulated and discharged internally as well as through action, they also become recognizable and possible to share.

For affect mirroring to serve as the basis for usable representations, the mother must find a way to show the baby that her mirroring responses, in particular to negative emotions, do not indicate how she herself feels, but rather her awareness of the baby's state. She may do this through exaggeration, through 'motherese' (the specific, exaggerated and playful way of talking to babies), or through contrast e.g. expressing sadness with irony. We have described this characteristic of parental mirroring as 'markedness'.

An expression that *matches the baby's state but which lacks markedness* may overwhelm him. It is felt to be the parent's own real emotion, making the infant's experience seem contagious or universal, that is even more real and powerful. This is likely to amplify rather than contain his feelings. If on the other hand the mother's responses are characterized by *markedness but do not actually mirror the infant's self-states*, the child will internalize a representation of a mismatched mental state as part of himself. This undermines the appropriate labelling of internal states which may then remain unsymbolized, confusing and hard to regulate. For example if the child's excited interest is regularly reflected as greediness or aggression, his representation of his own pleasure in the world will have the colouring and associations of greed or assault: intrusive, unwelcome, excessive, perhaps disgusting and certainly shaming. If this is his usual experience with a main caregiver, self-representations will be feebly tied to the original emotional states (liveliness and pleasurable excitement), and more strongly tied to other states (intrusive, ruthless grabbing). If his primary states have on the other hand *not been recognized at all* (even in a distorted form) by the person to whom they were most intensely addressed and who most often witnessed them, his self in that state will feel empty, uninteresting, meaningless, and later relating may feel as though it can only come from a simulated inner world.

Thus, when mirroring fails because the caregiver's expression is unmarked, inaccurate or lacking, the baby is unable to find his actual self in the other's mind and cannot gain control, understanding or enjoyment of his self states. He will only be able to build representations of his feelings from what comes through of the object's state of mind, including unconsciously repudiated aspects of herself such as unacceptable fantasies, and the defences against them such as projection and splitting. The internalization of unreflected, or mismatched/amplified mental states creates incongruence and disorganization within the self. Ground-breaking work by psychoanalyst developmental researchers such as Karlen Lyons-Ruth has brilliantly shown through parent-infant research how systematic, unconscious failures of attunement and mirroring communication do deeply distort the attachment relationship and the infant's capacities for regulation and relatedness (e.g. Lyons-Ruth and Jacobvitz, 2008). I will explore in this chapter how such systematic mismatching leaves the developing child and adult seeking physical intimacy but unable to deal with or enjoy it.

In our model, unmirrored, split-off parts of the self and incongruous identifications have been described as creating a sense of 'alien self', the presence of foreign and unacceptable qualities which feel internal yet unintegrated, qualities such as murderousness or sadism. In early development, this 'alien self' is dealt with by externalization; the infant whose attachment is disorganized has been shown to be likely to become a highly controlling and bossy toddler or bullying child, placing the unacceptable parts of his inner world on to somebody nearby. This of course often disrupts the development of later relationships, by creating a constant need for projective identification (externalization of the alien self) within relationships. As mentalization develops, the alien self can be increasingly woven into the self, creating an uneasy illusion of cohesion but around what Balint called a 'basic fault'. The capacity to mentalize will always be somewhat limited, and may feel false and threatened by the straining for a sense of integration. The person to that degree lacks an adequately authentic, organic self-image built around internalized representations of self-states. The child, and later the adult, is left with intense experiences that remain unlabelled, uncontained and not properly owned (Bion, 1962). There is a sort of vacuum within a part of the self, where internal reality remains nameless. It may be dreaded – *or exciting and mysterious*, as I will later suggest is the case in normal sexuality.

First, it is important to extend the account of how children conceive of their feelings and thoughts, beyond affect mirroring in the first year. Peter Fonagy and I with other colleagues (Fonagy and Target, 1996; Target and Fonagy, 1996; Fonagy et al., 2002) have integrated developmental research and clinical observations into a model of how mental states are experienced within the preschool years, when research shows that they cannot yet be recognized as internal and individual thoughts and feelings (mentalized). They are not felt to be states of mind, that is represented as belonging to a private perspective which nevertheless has meaningful connections to the outside. Instead there seem to be at least three main forms or modes of primitive relationship to one's own attitudes in toddlerhood (and in disturbed or normally regressed states throughout life). One mode, 'psychic equivalence', treats the internal as directly reflecting the external world; the internal world is assumed to map on to the external, which can be comforting or distressing because the projection of fantasy gives an illusion of control of the social world. In another, 'pretend' mode, mental states are experienced as omnipotent in a different sense, they are 'as if', quite separate from ordinary, serious reality – not affecting it, but also insulated from interference. The risks of 'psychic equivalence', whereby the child's thoughts may feel dangerous, are balanced by retreat into an insulated 'pretend' state of mind. The third non-mentalizing way in which mental states can be experienced is called 'teleological mode'. In this attitude, feelings and thoughts are treated not as equated with or split off from the external social world, but as though they are physical states within it. Here, states of mind can only be altered through action, not through thought. The difference may be illustrated in the context of forms of adolescent non-mentalizing. An adolescent feeling aggressive might in psychic equivalence mode believe that his hatred of his father indicates that his father actually is despicable – stupid, past it and uncaring. In pretend mode, the aggression may be expressed in the playing of violent video games, listening to music deriding the dead adult world, using sadistic pornography and so on. In teleological mode, it might feel possible to relieve the aggressive feelings only through physical rage or violence against someone blamed for the feelings, or through changing the self that has the feelings: cutting the skin, taking mind-altering substances, starving himself, may make the feelings change.

In normal development, the child integrates these modes in order to achieve *mentalization*, or *reflective mode*, where thoughts and feelings can be experienced as representations. Representations are personal, might change and are likely to be different from other people's perspectives, especially if there are other differences (e.g. girls and boys commonly become very conscious of having different typical reactions, older children are expected to have different tastes from younger, and so on). Mentalization is the conscious or preconscious recognition that behaviour is understandable given underlying mental states and intentions, that it therefore has motivation and meaning. Pleasurable and emotionally intimate sexual relationships involve both the capacity for mentalization or understanding of one's own and the other's feelings, and the ability to relinquish this mature thinking in favour of the more primitive modes of 'psychic reality', for example to feel as though one's idealization is real (psychic equivalence), that one can be taken over by and merged with the other and safe from the world (pretend), and that sexual action can obliterate self-doubt, loneliness or other frustrations in the relationship (teleological mode).

Normal failure to mirror the sexual feelings of infancy

Unlike other aspects of mother–infant interaction, the mother's reaction to a baby's sexual excitement has not been specifically researched. Peter Fonagy has reported preliminary data suggesting that mothers find it particularly difficult accurately to mirror such sexual excitement. A survey asked mothers how they responded to their 3–6 month old babies' various emotional expressions, including sexual arousal (they confirmed that they were aware of this in their babies). Almost all mothers reported responding to their babies' smiles and tears with consonant smiling or comfort, however most said that they would respond to indications of masturbation by ignoring or looking away from the baby. (We may imagine that in practice some mothers would say or do more actively discouraging things, such as scolding the child for doing that, moving their hand or strongly distracting him or her.) Psychoanalytic trainees doing infant observations rarely report maternal responses to sexual excitement, or infant sexual arousal at all. This might reflect a similar tendency to ignore or look away; while we may fairly confidently say how we might mirror a baby's distress, fear or anger, we may well find it hard ourselves to think how one would mirror infantile sexual excitement in an equally natural and appropriate way.

The perhaps surprising suggestion which I will develop is that there is a specific failure of mirroring in relation to sexual excitement, but that rather than a developmental problem, the resulting obscurity and isolation of childhood sexuality may well give necessary impetus from adolescence to look beyond family attachments for a partner with whom to express, share and potentially resolve sexual feelings. If sexual excitement is poorly reflected in the early years, one would expect it not to be well recognized, represented or integrated in the growing child's sense of his social self. The infant reacting to sexual tension in the presence of a sensitive and responsive parent would generally not be offered a congruent, metabolized representation of his or her sexual excitement or pleasure, even though other feelings may be reflected in a mostly attuned way. Without mirroring there cannot be an effective experience of containment or a sense of clear ownership of these feelings. The mother's reported response of ignoring, denying or distracting might in fact exacerbate sexual arousal rather than containing and helping the child to recognize the feelings. If this state is reflected to babies and young children at all, it may be done obscurely and ambivalently, in a way that Laplanche wrote of as enigmatic (Laplanche, 1995; see also Stein, 1998a). For example, the mother's response may either lack 'markedness' (she could seem flustered or excited herself), or be exaggeratedly marked (emphatically distancing herself from the child's state such that the resonance and identification is lost). Or an initial flutter may quickly be reversed into strong detachment, implied non-recognition or disapproval ('that's not nice, we don't want to see that' etc). This may well relate to what Laplanche described as the unconsciously seductive maternal response to the baby's desire, with an additional confusing twist of frustration. We suggest that the 'excessive' and urgent character of psychosexuality has its roots in these experiences, too early to be remembered but leaving physical and emotional feelings still needing to be resolved and reinterpreted, or at least re-enacted.

Incongruent mirroring disrupts self-coherence, generating a sense of pressure and contradiction in relation to sexual feelings. The sexually excited young child interprets the mother's responses as a mirror of his own experience and identifies with them, but since they are not mirrored 'contingently' (in a manner faithful to his own affects and experiences), they are simultaneously experienced as not his own, as alien. This sense of incongruence within the self is then associated with sexual feelings, even when in other areas the self may feel well-integrated. Sexual arousal would not then feel truly owned. Paradoxically, in this model it is only when feelings have been taken in and accepted by another that they can feel authentically part of the self. Otherwise, in favourable circumstances there will continue to be a pressure to find someone to share it with, through projection and reintrojection. The enigmatic dimension of sexuality creates an invitation that calls out to be elaborated, normally by an other. In unfavourable circumstances, depending on the way in which mirroring has been avoided, sexual feelings may feel too dangerous to share: they may for example be felt as too contagious and overwhelming to the relationship (unmarked mirroring), unacceptable (for example when there has been reflection of excitement and curiosity as aggression, or clear expression of disgust at the sexual body), or rendering the person helpless in relation to the desired other.

Laplanche's theory of psychosexuality

There are further aspects of Jean Laplanche's thinking (Laplanche, 1995; Laplanche and Pontalis, 1968) which help to elaborate our understanding of sexual experience.

Laplanche first claims that psychosexuality evolves in infancy out of non-sexual, instinctual activity. When a non-sexual instinct such as hunger and feeding, having created excitation, loses its natural object, the ego is turned in upon itself and left in a state of arousal. Laplanche terms this arousal 'an autoerotic moment' that comes to be elaborated through perception and fantasy in what he calls 'phantasmatization'. Second, this autoerotic excitement is not objectless, but its object is an internal state: the desire is for *the idea or feeling of the lost object*. This means that even if the object that is lost is the real breast, it can never be recaptured, because what is desired is no longer the actual feeding breast but the 'phantasmatic' imaginary breast, the breast elaborated through fantasy. Thus normal human sexual experience is not essentially functional, but deeply object-seeking and imbued with the memory and fantasy of feelings. Third, bodily arousal becomes sexualized: Laplanche claims that the mother's unconscious 'seduction' of the infant converts instinctual tension and excitement into an autoerotic moment. Fourth, Laplanche considers that the infant is not ready to integrate this experience with other experiences of the mother. Erotic experience is imbued with mystery (Kernberg, 1992; Stoller, 1985). The mystery may be rooted in the enigmatic quality of the mother's gestures, which initially colours the infant's experience of his excitement, then intensifies the seduction, before becoming its dominant feature.

Laplanche's model therefore focuses on the reverse situation from the failure to recognize and mirror sexual feelings and behaviour in an infant. Laplanche envisages the situation in which a mother, finding her baby in a state of tension and frustration (a loss of pleasure, peremptory need and perhaps anger), will unconsciously associate his uncomfortable clamouring with sexual arousal, which can in the more mature person produce states of mind and body which are similar. The baby's need would then be mirrored as sexual pressure or desire. If the infant were in fact in a sexually excited state, the internalization of mirroring of it would create the basis for an internal representation of the excitement, and the beginning of the establishment of a capacity to understand and manage arousal. But if the baby's struggle were not with excitement, but with the feeling of loss of the object, again the mother's mirroring would be neither fully accurate nor clearly marked.

One may imagine a number of linked reasons for this sort of misattunement. The mother may unconsciously associate frustration and insistent drive pressure from another person within a sexual relationship: the baby implores and bullies the mother in a way she may unconsciously associate with a partner in a state of sexual desire. She may confuse the baby's frustration with sexual excitement through association with a masochistic or passive colouring of her own psycho-sexuality. She may respond to the baby's frustrated need with an aggressive, teasing response through momentary feelings of power and sadism, which may in turn be rapidly, defensively covered over with sexualization, i.e. her aggressive impulse to deprive the baby is made acceptable or at least hidden by emphasizing the excitement and desire within it. She may then unconsciously sexualize distress in the infant as she might use excitement to displace sadness for herself.

In both of these situations of repeated inadequate mirroring, desexualization and sexualization of the baby's drive pressures, he may internalize a representation of his state coloured by his mother's mind especially her unconscious associations. However, the internalization will be experienced as incongruent and alien, and it will not help in regulating his future experiences of these states. Loss and frustration may become experienced as sexual frustration requiring expression with a partner, and/or sexual feelings may be felt to be incongruous and unacceptable and alien. Parts of the self which feel like that tend to be externalized. The suggestion here is that this is a normal consequence of the difficulty of mirroring this area of experience between adults and children. The resulting projection of sexual excitement, and the expectation that the other may be able to receive, reciprocate and transform it, gives sexuality its quality of transcending or transgressing personal boundaries – both physical and psychological. It is a state that presses to be experienced as part of an external relationship: because sexual excitement comes to feel incongruent with the self, excitement has to be experienced in the other and therefore with the other, at least in fantasy. The other has to be physically available or imagined to be so, if one is to experience one's excitement through them.

The pleasure of eroticism, as Ruth Stein very evocatively described (Stein, 1998a, 1998b), comes from transposing oneself into a state of mind that is felt to be the other's, and abolishing the limitations of one's separate existence (Bataille, 1957, cited by Stein, 1998b). It is not that experiencing oneself as the other is inherently pleasurable, but that one's own pleasure can only be experienced when it has been placed into the other, in fantasy. Sexual pleasure perhaps requires waves of projective identification: realizing one's own pleasure through taking control in fantasy of the thoughts and feelings of the other, possessing them momentarily, making their feelings one's own and then giving them back as one repossesses one's own desire, transformed.

Clinical illustrations: shame and loss of desire

The mental state that was originally one's own is now represented in the other, and the refinding is intensified by the release of orgasm and temporary resolution of the sense of alienation. This is seen as a core experience in normal sexuality, which of course can also be seen in distorted forms in disturbances of sex and relationships. For some, the temporary resolution does not lead to internalization of the disowned part of the self:

> Ms B was a 30-year-old prostitute who mainly picked up men in hotels. She had never had a satisfying sexual relationship with anyone other than perhaps some clients; she said she found them safer than an 'ordinary boyfriend'. She described feeling inhibited and confused about her own sexual feelings, but when she was with an aroused man, she would 'suddenly feel real'. She was fascinated by male arousal but thought the idea of women being excited and having orgasms was disgusting, and she did not really seem to believe it could happen. She would simulate excitement to excite her clients, although from her description it sounded as though she did get aroused but denied this, claiming never to have had an orgasm with or without a partner. She said that after having sex with a client she felt 'buzzy' and cheerful, not like herself. When she took a break from work, she felt depressed, flat and empty, and had on occasion picked up men and offered impersonal sex without payment. She said she did not know why she did this, except that 'it was for him, not me. I was not really interested. But afterwards I felt much better for some reason. Like I'd got something out of my system'.

Ms B was perhaps finding a way to regain something she had got out of her system, without acknowledging it.

For those who can sustain intimacy, the experience that the partner enables one's sexual self is partly internalized through a preconscious identification or even sense of merger, that gradually (over years) replaces enigma and the danger of being lost in another with familiarity and security. We could think of this as an extension of the processes of affect mirroring to the area of sexuality which were not encompassed in infancy. Underlying the gradual diminution of excitement with sexual familiarity may be a process of integration. What consciously feels like getting used to one's partner is perhaps arriving at a more integrated sense of one-self. This depletes the urgency of the need for externalization. This gives a better integrated, less troubled sense of self and the emergence of a powerful attachment relationship rooted in the experience of having been accurately reflected by one's partner. The difficulty can be that over the normal course of an adult psychosexual life, as integration increases and the driven need for intense experience with the partner is reduced, libido often fades, at least with that partner. There may of course have been other aspects of the alien self that have not been as easy to externalize or to have accepted within that relationship, which – together with a wish to re-experience the intensity of discovery and exchange with someone new – may create a restlessness for a different partner.

Mr and Mrs E presented for help as a couple; Mr E's gradual and now complete loss of sexual interest in his wife had led both of them to be dis-satisfied over the previous ten years and each had had an affair. Mr E said that emotionally he had what he wanted in his marriage ('I am completely safe and familiar with her, I am at home'), but he felt he had become 'unreal' sexually – not so much bored as non-existent. He felt that, by creating a response in a new partner, he was coming back to life himself: 'I am still "in there"'. His wife had similarly rediscovered her sexuality and felt real and alive, but, unlike him, she wanted to end the marriage and to replace it with her new relationship. Her sense of belonging and identity had become attached to her lover, while his had remained in the marriage, with his sexuality felt to be quite separate.

More tragic is when emotionally important sexual experience, with its intensity and vulnerability, is felt to be too frightening and unsafe to be enjoyable at all. This may commonly be seen in women who cannot relax or reach orgasm, with its sense of loss of control and boundaries. For men, it more commonly takes the form of separating sex and love, through casual or parallel affairs, through prostitutes, by giving up sex in favour of pornography, or rarely by giving up sex altogether.

The enjoyment of sexuality

Within this developmental approach, there seem to be some psychological pre-cursors of enjoyable, erotic sexual experiences within a relationship. First, the relationship must allow opening one's mind to another's projection; an experience of safe attachment interactions allow each partner to accept being both separate and fused with the other. Secure, playful, mutually attuned interaction with the caregiver paves the way for the intersubjectivity and creativity of creative adult sexuality. Interested, sensitive and secure parenting generates the interpersonal backdrop for erotically imaginative intercourse, while its content arises out of the adaptive mother–infant failures of attunement to the child's excitement.[2] Secondly, normal psychosexuality requires a reliable sense of the boundary of the physical self. This is blurred in intense sexual pleasure, in which the bodies may even feel merged or interchangeable, and there must be confidence that the sense of self can be restored. Thirdly, if sexual excitement is generated through increasing awareness of the excitement and fantasies of the other, genuine desire on both sides is essential. Fourthly, heterosexual excitement may be underpinned by an unconscious fantasy of also possessing/being the gender of the partner. It may be that fully expressed adult sexuality, regardless of dominant gender identity or orientation, incorporates unconscious bisexuality and blurring of the gender role of self or other. The intoxicating sense of expansion of the limits of body and mind encompasses not only actual physical bodies but also the conscious and unconscious gender identifications within the mind of each partner.

The arc of psychosexual tension is temporarily resolved after a satisfying sexual encounter by reinternalization of the projected part of the self. This reinternalization would then usually and very gradually support a strengthening attachment with many sexual experiences with the partner. The experience of alien, split-off aspects of the self having been encountered and accepted by another mind can generate intense feelings of closeness, belonging, being understood and in turn understanding, relief and gratitude.

However, what about situations in which this is not the way it seems to work? A sexual partnership may feel like the loss of self rather than a gain.

Mr A, a very successful and attractive surgeon in his forties, was anxious about getting married. He had been engaged three times to attractive and apparently appropriate women after very brief relationships, but each time he had 'gone cold'. He could not really explain why he had lost interest, or why in contrast he was so keen to get married in the abstract. The farthest he could get, in thinking about this in his consultation, was that he felt he had to 'have another half' but whenever he 'got someone' he felt as though she had taken over, he lost all sexual desire and emotional closeness. They felt increasingly like strangers.

It emerged that he became 'bored' with the woman he was with, finding her vaguely ridiculous and embarrassing, not worthy of him. Their relationship had felt empty, like going through the motions without feeling. Consciously he had decided that the woman was more stupid than he had thought, he had made a mistake, however it was not far to seek that unconsciously he thought less of the woman for settling for him, for accepting and enjoying his – to him – obviously inadequate penis and his pretensions of maturity and manliness. He angrily suspected that she was trying to make a fool of him, in pretending to want him and to be willing to marry him.

He began to remember episodes in which he had tried to impress his mother with his physical feats, and had felt her shrink from his showing off, and when he had wanted to be affectionate to his distant father, and had been told not to be 'such a sissy, no better than a girl'. He recalled episodes, for example at about ten having had an erection and feeling excited and romantic when kissing his mother, and being told sharply to leave her alone. She had – he felt – pushed him to achieve at school and in sports, but 'she only liked to see me on the honours board she didn't even come to watch'. He had ended up feeling that his successes had led him away from being close to his parents and that they had preferred it that way.

When a woman had wanted to be close to him he felt alarmed and expected to be humiliated and rejected. It emerged that he was also afraid of his anger, hatred and vengefulness becoming expressed, and that he had had increasingly clear fantasies of attacking and destroying his relationships, including by tricking his fiancées into accepting fraudulent prenuptial agreements and of secretly taking and posting intimate photographs of them online. He was ashamed of these fantasies and felt they had got worse as each relationship had become more committed. He had become sexually impotent following the engagements and felt emasculated by his partner, especially if she was understanding and accepting. By the time of his consultation he had isolated himself socially and almost given up hope of being able to marry eventually. The despair about what this said about him seemed to be a major motivation in his wish to 'find the right person' and settle down. He said after a few months that he had realized that the right person would be a blind person – someone who could not see him, someone in whose eyes he would not have to fear disgust. Although he immediately said he realized it was not really to do with eyes and seeing, there was truth in what he had said which he spent a long time considering, what it was that he 'knew' the other person would see in him, in other words the disgust he felt about himself.

Clearly Mr A's development, as for all of us, had followed a complex path since infancy and one cannot state that his parents' reactions in his earliest years had directly caused his presenting problem, but the uncovering of his fears about his own self, and his self-rejection and disgust, seemed to enable him to find a more honest and sustainable relationship outside, following two years of psychotherapy. Tellingly, he did not feel compelled to persuade this partner to marry him quickly, although after two years they did so and have had a stable relationship.

Mr H was a male homosexual banker of nearly 50, who had never been able to find a life partner despite having come out in his 20s and having had many casual 'hook ups' and short-term relationships. It emerged during analysis that he despised homosexuals, including himself, and thought they were weak, girlish and ridiculous. He was very 'straight' in appearance and manner, came from a country with a strong macho culture and strongly disliked any man who seemed gay, or who seemed straight but was in fact gay, i.e. all possibly available partners. He admitted that he thought they should all be forcibly 'retrained' and not included in polite society.

A sophisticated man, he realized that I would not be offering to 'cure his disease', and consciously he did not want to become heterosexual. He gradually realized that he wanted to be able to be a presexual child, an innocent without sin. Only then he had the right to exist. He felt sexuality to be an irreversible corruption, and that although if he had been heterosexual he would have been corrupted, at least he would have been statistically and socially normal. Being homosexual made him irrevocably unacceptable. He was attracted to but disliked and disapproved of obviously gay men, and despised their interest in him. He was unable to speak of homosexuality without visible contempt, and any sign of weakness in himself he treated with harshness close to cruelty. He said for example, after picking up a man in a seedy club, that he deserved to die and his parents had been right that all gay men are sure to die alone with a disgusting disease.

He had made a suicide attempt, the first since two in adolescence, when his workplace had asked him to act as a mentor for younger gay employees. Although he had been 'out' with his bank, he had felt much more comfortable with their earlier attitude of 'don't ask, don't tell', since he agreed with what he assumed to be their sneering and hypocritical attitude to homosexuality. He found the idea of him loving or being loved by a man ludicrous: it struck him as obscene. It emerged that his sexual experiences had consisted of furtive interactions of mutual lust infused with disgust, with little emotional meaning and quickly culminating after orgasm in visceral revulsion. He was profoundly lonely and hopeless. As he became aware of being accepted and understood in the analysis, his sexual interactions slowly changed so that he could tolerate being with a gay man and getting to know him, allowing himself to be known also. Sex became something that could cautiously take place within an emotional and social relationship, and could find its place in ordinary life.

After two years Mr H found a longer-term partner and this relationship became increasingly involved over the following two years, his lover's confidence, experience and understanding helping him to withstand his ambivalence. We were able to work through the layers of self-disgust (for his sexuality) and contempt for weakness (for his 'femininity'), as well as his underlying assumption that I found him despicable. He had taken it for granted that my aim in agreeing to treat him was – whatever I might say – to take away his sexual feelings which I must find repulsive. It is hard to make confident guesses about the origins of this fixed self-condemnation, but certainly his memory of his parents especially his mother was of a sharp, self-absorbed woman who avoided physical contact and was disdainful of her husband and son as weak men, whereas his sister was praised for her toughness, brains and beauty. My patient constantly expected and invited these attitudes from me, and for some time seemed physically afraid when telling me anything of his sexual life.

Over time it was productive to help this patient, very motivated by his suffering, to notice the ways in which he was thinking about his feelings. In terms of the modes of experience of 'psychic reality' referred to previously, in the early period, Mr H operated with split, primitive ways of experiencing his thoughts and feelings. The most striking aspects of this were (i) his 'psychic equivalence' assumption that because he was disgusted by his sexual thoughts and desires, they were universally disgusting and would destroy any relationships as soon as his partner realized what he was thinking, (ii) his solutions in 'teleological mode' were to discharge unacceptable feelings in action which temporarily abolished them, but which led to more repudiation, or to blot out his feelings through compulsive work, violent exercise or *in extremis* drug overdoses. Only action could change his toxic thoughts, which would otherwise be known to everybody and would cause irreversible disgrace. When he came to me, it was partly because he had had fantasies of mutilating his genitals in an attempt to punish himself for his thoughts, and replace his sexual feelings with so much pain that they would be blotted out for some time. Hidden behind his 'psychic equivalence' experience of his sexual desires seemed to be a pocket of 'pretend mode' thinking, of fantasy insulated from ordinary reality, that he was a small child who was innocent and would be allowed to live without guilt and pain. Many evenings would be spent looking at two photographs of himself as a very young boy, fresh and full of promise.

During analysis he became able to integrate these experiences much more, to take a perspective on his states of mind and to recognize that he had felt condemned to inescapable suffering, not necessarily because his homosexual thoughts were repulsive but because becoming an adult had separated him from his fantasy of innocence and spoiled it. He realized that he had had the idea, unconsciously, that had he been able to turn back time, he might have been acceptable to his mother, he might have made her smile with pride as he imagined she might have done when he was still a baby, without sexual feelings, or as she might have done if he had been a girl. Much of his adolescence and adulthood had been spent enacting the crime he felt she saw in him, and the punishment she would have wanted

(continued)

(continued)

him to endure. Once it became clear to him that he had treated this fantasy about his mother's attitudes concretely and applied it to everybody, then addressed himself to purging himself of his forbidden thoughts, he realized that depriving and punishing himself and having fantasies of lurid punishments had become in itself pleasurable, but had little to do with anyone else including his actual mother. He became able to find out more directly how people felt about him without assuming and reacting to his own thoughts in the 'mirror' of every other person.

Implications for the transference

It appears[3] that psychosexuality retreated from analytic focus at about the same time and rate that transference issues started to occupy the centre ground. Possibly sexuality was easier to focus on when treatment was shorter, when the relationship with the therapist was not also the central focus of analytic work, when the patient's attachment to the analyst was mostly understood to be part of their illness, and when the therapist behind the couch did not expect to get involved. With the focus on the transference and relational issues currently to the fore, the therapist is also a 'real' person whose feelings can no longer be thought of as cleanly separate from the clinical situation. The intensification of the attachment relationship and the increasing length of analytic relationships opens emotional and intersubjective channels previously kept in abeyance.

Working with – or in – the transference inevitably activates attachment feelings and the trends toward greater spontaneity, emotional engagement and self-disclosure are bound to increase transference and countertransference reactions. This can be seen most starkly throughout the literature of the relational school (see, for example, Davies, 2003). Acknowledging a 'real' as well as a 'transference' level of intersubjective experience may feel relatively comfortable, even comforting, as a quasi-parental experience, but will threaten to become much more concrete and possibly unethical in relation to sexual experience. Discussion of sexuality in sessions and in the literature may be unconsciously avoided or relabelled, as not 'really' about sex. This is reminiscent of the mother ignoring or distracting the excited child, or treating the arousal as something else, such as aggression. Resonating with and reflecting sexual arousal can be felt to risk a reciprocal building of excitement. Just as the mother unconsciously inhibits reflection of sexual excitement for fear of exacerbating the baby's arousal and focusing it on herself, so may the analyst be, rightly, very hesitant in attempting to resonate with the patient's sexual desire within the transference. But this strategy needs to be used quite consciously, perhaps as the ideal mother might, with recognition and appreciation of the feelings, and minor resonance without reciprocal excitement, but also without denial or distortion.

Dr G, an unhappy but likeable and celebrated academic of nearly 50, came to analysis because of increasing depression, impotence, and the imminent failure of his third marriage. While attractive and generally thought charming, he had the avoidance of feeling which I have encountered in many people with his history of a formal childhood mostly spent in boarding schools. Dr G had alienated his three wives and other partners with his difficulty in emotional intimacy and his mechanical sexual manner. His current wife complained that he was 'just *not there*' and like a robot following a manual when making love. When he described his experience of sex, it sounded as though he was trying to 'do it right' rather than follow any feeling of excitement. His main feeling, in contrast, was fear of rejection and blame. He would try not to look at his wife when they made love because he knew she would look irritated and disappointed. Although he described her as lively and responsive, and sexually demanding, he thought that really she did not want him or sex at all. His descriptions made it clear that he did not expect closeness, intimacy or mutual knowledge, sharing of fantasy and intense emotion, but rather sought physical release in the context of a mental blank. He seemed increasingly over time to have *needed* mental emptiness to be able to relax enough to get an erection. He acted similarly in sessions: very anxiously compliant, but also very avoidant of looking at me (though he was unable to lie on the couch because he needed to be able to look at me); he seemed wooden, and hidden, 'not there'.

However, as he felt gradually safer and somewhat confident in the analysis, although he still seemed passive and frustratingly detached, he later revealed that he had secretly begun to feel desire in the sessions, not only sexual fantasies but – still more disturbingly to him – intense longing for emotional contact, openness and intimacy. Because this was so new and unexpected it felt very overwhelming for the patient, and the intense pressure of his feelings (experienced as absolutely real and needing action rather than thought) was also unsettling for me. To resonate and reflect back his passionate feelings, even slightly, felt directly seductive (especially because this patient tended to take things literally – in psychic equivalence – even in other contexts); it felt tempting and much safer to pretend not to notice or to shift the focus. And this made sense: this transference was arguably[4] not of actual sexuality, but intense arousal stirred by a range of emotions he had fended off for many years – deep nameless need, painful excitement, loss, despair, anger, surprise, gratitude, hope and, eventually, something like love. As an adult, Dr G felt that only actual sexual contact could soothe that unbearable mixture of emotion and physical pressure, a mixture he had avoided increasingly in his relationships with women. In the analysis the compelling sense of need was raw and evident, yet to resonate to it would

(continued)

(continued)

confirm the sexualization of tension that seemed connected to these other powerful feelings. Loneliness, sadness, fear and anger were just as inexpressible to this man as were his demanding sexual feelings, in fact more so. His different tension states were not really differentiated enough for him to know what he wanted to share; sexual excitement and possession were a ready and powerful channel for a mixture of unprocessed feelings.

The analysis continued for seven years, and required me to accept and know the impact of the erotic desires and fantasies he insistently expressed, and while respecting and withstanding those feelings, to listen for others that were embedded and hidden within them, and which needed to be disentangled and thought about. The analysis needed to become a sort of testing ground for all his intense feelings, and to realize that they would be known without leading to action, either seductive or dismissive. Dr G's marriage and other relationships became much more alive (positively and negatively) and valuable to him. In analysis he had become able to express, reflect, recognize and make sense of a whole range of feelings and wishes, including unusually strong sexual longing. As with all feeling emerging in analysis, these were first experienced in 'psychic equivalence', as real and peremptory, with the pressure to action of the teleological mode. He was able to express his belief that only real sexual possession of me could make him happy, within the safe 'pretend' world of analysis which, like an adequate parenting relationship, allows oedipal feelings to be experienced without being pulled on or pushed away.

Conclusion

This chapter has focused on the difficulty of working with psychosexuality as a central human experience within current object relational psychoanalytic theories. The implicit parenting model of much contemporary psychoanalysis intensifies the problem of working with sexuality in a much more prolonged and personal analytic frame than Freud was working with. A set of ideas for thinking about the development of sexuality in infancy is suggested, based on theoretical work with Peter Fonagy. One aspect, owing much to Laplanche, concerns the sexualization of states of non-sexual arousal in the child or adult, another concerns the denial or distortion of sexuality by an adult unwilling to recognize it, a failure of mirroring which in the context of sexual feelings is normal between parent and child and very understandable between therapist and patient. However, to help our patients fully we must be aware of this potential blind-spot and find ways honestly of mirroring the heat of sexuality; it is vital that as well as doing this ethically, we can allow the strength and felt reality of the experience.

This is aided by being conscious of the different 'modes' in which states of mind are experienced by young children, and by all of us under regressive strain or in intense emotional or sexual states. The pull into concrete thinking, split-off fantasy or trying to change internal states through bodily action are understood as primitive ways of treating one's own thoughts and feelings. In normal childhood we get help from parents to step back from emotions and come to see them as states of mind in context; mentalization allows us to integrate and regulate the primitive, raw experiences within our own minds, and express them in somewhat processed ways in relationships. Sexual feelings do not become mentalized to the same extent in childhood, we have suggested because of a specific, normal failure of affect mirroring. We need later partners to help with the need for regulation and integration which only happens to a limited extent in the childhood family. For some people, this later recognition and processing of sexual feelings is obstructed by revulsion towards one's own sexuality, a rejection which is treated as externally real and inevitable, cutting the person off from developing further integration of the sense of self in adulthood, instead making him feel increasingly alienated and unacceptable, with resort only to fantasy and sporadic or stilted, self-destructive sexual interactions. In such cases, an intensive therapeutic relationship can offer a way forward. Like a sexual relationship it provides recognition of sexual feelings without rejection, but like a parental relationship it helps the patient develop, regulate and represent feelings without satisfying the desire for action.

Notes

1 I will, just to make it easier to follow, assume a female parent and male child, and later a female therapist and male patient.
2 For example a tendency for the mother to react to the girl's rubbing by encouraging some distracting energetic activity might lead to an adult female pleasure in physically active sexual 'games', while reacting to a boy's erection as though it were shocking or aggressive might lead the man to be excited by more exhibitionistic fantasies or a (perhaps playfully) coercive sexual style.
3 e.g. from the PEP database.
4 Remembering Laplanche's account of sexualization in the mother–infant context.

References

Bion, W. R. (1962). A theory of thinking. *International Journal of Psycho-analysis, 43*, 306–310.
Davies, J. M. (2003). Falling in love with love: oedipal and postoedipal manifestations of idealization, mourning, and erotic masochism. *Psychoanalytic Dialogues, 13*, 1–27.
Fonagy, P. (2008). A genuinely developmental theory of sexual enjoyment and its implications for psychoanalytic technique. *Journal of the American Psychoanalytic Association, 56*, 11–36.
Fonagy, P., Gergely, G., Jurist, E., & Target, M. (2002). *Affect Regulation, Mentalization and the Development of the Self.* New York: Other Press.
Fonagy, P., & Target, M. (1996). Playing with reality I: theory of mind and the normal development of psychic reality. *International Journal of Psycho-Analysis, 77*, 217–233.
Fonagy, P., & Target, M. (2003). *Psychoanalytic Theories: Perspectives from Developmental Psychopathology.* London: Whurr.

Fonagy, P., & Target, M. (2006). The mentalization-focused approach to self pathology. *Journal of Personality Disorders, 20*(6), 544–576.

Gergely, G., & Watson, J. (1996). The social biofeedback model of parental affect-mirroring. *International Journal of Psycho-Analysis, 77*, 1181–1212.

Gergely, G., & Watson, J. (1999). Early social-emotional development: contingency perception and the social biofeedback model. In P. Rochat (Ed.), *Early Social Cognition: Understanding Others in the First Months of Life* (pp. 101–137). Hillsdale, NJ: Erlbaum.

Green, A. (1995). Has sexuality anything to do with psychoanalysis? *International Journal of Psycho-Analysis, 76*, 871–883.

Green, A. (1997). Opening remarks to a discussion of sexuality in contemporary psychoanalysis. *International Journal of Psycho-Analysis, 78*, 345–350.

Kernberg, O. F. (1992). *Aggression in Personality Disorders and Perversions*. New Haven, CT, and London: Yale University Press.

Laplanche, J. (1995). Seduction, persecution, revelation. *International Journal of Psycho-Analysis, 76*, 663–682.

Laplanche, J., & Pontalis, J. B. (1968). Fantasy and the origins of sexuality. *International Journal of Psycho-Analysis, 49*, 1–19.

Lyons-Ruth, K., & Jacobvitz, D. (2008). Attachment disorganization: genetic factors, parenting contexts, and developmental transformation from infancy to adulthood. In J. C. P. Shaver (Ed.), *Handbook of Attachment*, 2nd Edition. New York: The Guilford Press.

Meltzoff, A. N., & Moore, M. K. (1997). Explaining facial imitation: theoretical model. *Early Development and Parenting, 6*, 179–192.

Stein, R. (1998a). The enigmatic dimension of sexual experience: the 'otherness' of sexuality and primal seduction. *Psychoanalytic Quarterly, 67*, 594–625.

Stein, R. (1998b). The poignant, the excessive and the enigmatic in sexuality. *International Journal of Psycho-Analysis, 79*, 253–268.

Stoller, J. R. (1985). *Observing the Erotic Imagination*. New Haven, CT: Yale University Press.

Target, M. (2005). Attachment theory and research: a bridge from psychoanalysis joining normal and abnormal development. In E. Person, A. Cooper, & G. Gabbard (Eds.), *The American Psychiatric Publishing Textbook of Psychoanalysis* (pp. 159–172). Arlington, VA: American Psychiatric Publishing Inc.

Target, M. (2007). Is our sexuality our own? A developmental model of sexuality based on early affect mirroring. *British Journal of Psychotherapy, 23*, 517–530.

Target, M., & Fonagy, P. (1996). Playing with reality II: the development of psychic reality from a theoretical perspective. *International Journal of Psycho-Analysis, 77*, 459–479.

Winnicott, D. W. (1960). The theory of the parent–infant relationship. *International Journal of Psycho-Analysis, 41*, 585–595.

Chapter 3

Desire and its discontents

Marilia Aisenstein and Donald Moss

The text of this chapter is the result of a serendipitous meeting. We were both on a panel on 'Desire' at the American Psychoanalytic Association meetings in January 2012. Although our contributions were written independently, they were each firmly grounded in Freud's early foundational texts, particularly Chapter 7 of *Interpretation of Dreams* (1900). This mutual grounding generates a welcome overlapping of ideas, both theoretical and clinical. In addition, though, because we come from different traditions, our contributions necessarily differ – in tone, mood and style. In this co-written chapter, we mean to illuminate the ongoing profundity of Freud's early work and its common relevance to two very different writers. Of course, we also mean to reassert the primary role of 'desire' in both the clinical and theoretical work of psychoanalysis.

Desire and its failures

Marilia Aisenstein[1]

Desire is at the heart of the human psyche and at the basis of all thought-activity. Yet we are often confronted with patients whose entire psychic life is organised against desire. I would take, as an extreme example, all forms of addictions, but also borderline patients and certain psychosomatic patients. For them, desire is lived as a narcissistic failure or as a catastrophe that puts them in danger. In this chapter I will study the question of desire in Freud's work before considering the clinical field of those patients who might be described as being 'anti-desire'. As my title indicates, I will proceed from the human relations founded on desire to all sorts of behaviours I see as their negative.

The word 'desire' makes me think irresistibly of 'love'. Which is why, before beginning to look at the Freudian theory of desire, I would like to say a few words about the love letters that the young Freud and his fiancée Martha wrote to each other during the four years of their engagement (1882 to 1886). There are 1500 letters in all, which are in the Library of Congress in Washington. Ilse Grubrich-Simitis is working on this correspondence, and has already published the first of five volumes in German under the title 'Be mine in the way that I imagine it' (Grubrich-Simitis et al., 2011).

Desire is very much present in love, along with dreaming and thinking. The theories of wishful hallucination and representation (of words and things) are already present in embryonic form in the exchanges between the two lovers. I will just give a limited sample of them here:

In June 1884, Martha wrote: 'I *welcome you in my dreams every night*, so isn't it strange that for the last few days I have been absolutely convinced that you would not come'.

Shortly after, telling her about his visit to the Notre Dame tower, Freud said: 'On each step I could have given you a kiss if you had been there, and you would have arrived at the top completely breathless and wild . . .'

There is a question of translation here that calls for comment. In French and English 'wish' and 'desire' have different meanings. We can say that a wish contains a desire, but a desire is not a wish for it implies, in addition, the notion of force, and thus of drive. Now, in German *Wunsch* and *Begierde* are synonyms. It seems that Freud employs both terms indifferently, but in English 'wish-fulfilment' should read 'desire-fulfilment'.

Freudian theory

I am going to try to summarise in simple words the schema of desire (*désir*) in Freud's work. To do this, I will refer to two fundamental works, the *Project* (1895) and Chapter 7 of the *Interpretation of Dreams* (1900). Then I will give a personal reading of the notion of 'hallucinatory wish-fulfilment', which will lead me to speak briefly about a later text 'The economic problem of masochism' (1924).

As early as 1895, in the *Project for a Scientific Psychology,* he elaborates a theory of desire beginning with the early stages of the human organism. The helpless infant is subjected to distressing stimuli, for example, hunger, which can only be alleviated by a specific external action, breastfeeding. In the infant a *memory image* is created, which associates this experience of satisfaction with the desired object. These lived experiences leave traces, which are *affects of unpleasure* and *states of wishing* (*états de désir*). These are characterised by an increase of internal tension followed by a sudden liberation. To put it differently, an experience of 'craving' creates tension in the ego, which will subsequently be associated with the investment of the object of desire. For the infant it is first the milk, and then the mother who gives him (or her) her breast. This investment is what we call a 'wishful idea' (*représentation de désir*).

Initially, this schema seems very simple but it soon becomes more complex. How does the transition from the milk to the mother (object of desire), and then to the representation of the mother, occur?

It is necessary first to differentiate between need and desire. Need is vital and corresponds to a necessity, which involves its biological root – if deprived of food, a baby dies. Desire, on the other hand, is a powerful and sometimes violent feeling, which attests to the force of the drive. It is psychic work that allows for the transition from need to desire.

For this transition to occur, the distressing stimuli must be alleviated by an 'experience of satisfaction' which is memorised. This memorisation (*trace mnésique*) will give rise to an attraction towards the object. It is this movement towards the object that we call desire. Desire arises from need. Next, the recognition of desire is the basis for recognition of the object and, consequently, the birth of the desiring subject.

In order to get a clearer idea of the Freudian conception of *hallucinatory wish-fulfilment*, I will refer to Chapter 7 of the *Interpretation of Dreams*. Freud returns to the schema described in the *Project,* and draws support for it from the clinical experience of dreams. The latter has the advantage of integrating conscious desire and unconscious wishes. The dream is a 'wish-fulfilment'. A dream exposes the facts as I would have wished them to take place.

I am not going to dwell here on this famous Chapter 7, 'The psychology of the dream processes', although it is fascinating and of great complexity. Instead, I want to place emphasis on the dream as a model of 'hallucinatory wish-fulfilment', for the latter is the basis of fantasy life and of thinking, which are characteristic of the human being as desiring subject.

Let us return to the example of the baby who is hungry. Hunger is a need, which, by virtue of the inscription of the memory trace of satisfaction, will be transformed into desire. There is a first transition: from the need for milk to desire for the breast, followed by a second transition from waiting for the breast to waiting for the object-mother. These transitions involve psychic work. As in dreams, but in the waking state, the infant who is hungry will hallucinate and imagine his mother arriving. The infant who desires thus gains access to thought. Freud writes: 'Thought is after all nothing but a substitute for a hallucinatory wish; and it is self-evident that dreams must be wish-fulfilments, since nothing but a wish can set our mental apparatus at work' (1900: 567).

This sentence is crucial and allows me to affirm that *desire is the basis of psychic work and thought.*

The masochistic structure of desire

There is one point that does not seem clear to me in Freud's text, even though I must have read it hundreds of times: how does this transition from urgent need to desire, that is, to the capacity for thinking and waiting, occur in the infant?

Here I would like to offer a personal point of view. For a long time now I have been interested in a specific form of masochism that Freud (1924) described in 'The economic problem of masochism'. I am referring to 'primary erotogenic masochism'. As far as I can see, little mention is made of this topic in North American psychoanalytic literature. And yet, in my view, this conception is fundamental for explaining the birth of desire in the infant's psyche.

Personally, I understand it in the light of the text of 1924. For Freud, this primary masochism is very early and permits the binding of contradictory impulses in the infant's ego. To put it simply: through the binding of the libido (force which pushes) and the death drive (a movement which unbinds and immobilises), primary masochism allows the capacity for waiting to be integrated. It is the mother's psychic work that makes this possible. A 'good enough' mother is one who is able to help the baby wait by saying, for example, 'Wait my little one, I'm going to take you in my arms but not right now . . . you will have your feed soon, just keep calm and wait a bit'. The mother envelops the infant with words; she gives him word- and thing-presentations. She thus helps him to wait, which suggests confidence in the object.

How is the concept of primary masochism indispensable here? Well, because if the waiting is to be tolerable, it must be 'invested masochistically'. The infant has to learn gradually that *there is also pleasure in this waiting due to the psychic work that it involves*. This investment of the delay is what lies at the basis of desire: I think about and imagine the pleasure to come. I am inclined to say that the 'structure of desire is masochistic in essence', for it is inconceivable without the renunciation of immediate satisfaction and the investment of waiting.

Someone who is in love and who is going to see the object of their desire in a week, or in a month, is able to wait because they have learnt to find pleasure in psychic work and fantasy scenarios that they create of the forthcoming encounter. This is what Freud does when he writes to Martha: 'One day you will be mine just as I imagine it'.

Use of the body in work against desire

With classical patients, whose organisations are more or less neurotic, desire and psychic work exist from the outset in the analytic treatment. The transference is based on desire. Those patients are uncertain what to do: should they follow the demands of desire or resist these demands? Excited by desire, but frightened by what they might learn and lose if they comply with it, these patients are caught between submitting to desire's demand and fighting against it.

However, many more 'difficult' patients, with borderline, psychotic, psychosomatic or 'mechanical' (*opératoire*) functioning, organise their psychic life 'against desire', thereby defending themselves against the object or against 'the Work of Desire' (Moss, below, p. 71). Moss writes: 'Those patients treat the demand as a catastrophe that must be averted, whatever the cost' (p. 71). He delineates two categories of patients, each responding differently to this demand for work. Moss introduces his paper by writing: 'I think of what follows as an extended meditation on Freud's foundational idea that drives "exert a demand . . . upon the mind for work in consequence of its connection to the body" (Freud, 1915: 121–123)'. Moreover, the notion of work also includes the idea of painful effort and thus of masochistic investment, as I argued above. The notion of masochism introduces the question of temporality – waiting – and hence that of castration by time which passes inexorably.

It is this category of patients, for whom desire is a catastrophe, that I am going to speak about now. In my view, this is a vast category that includes very different kinds of subjects: drug addicts, alcoholics, bulimic patients, but also borderline patients and certain psychosomatic patients. I would say that some resort to acting out and various forms of behavioural expression, and others to 'acting in the body or acting out through the body'. All of them appear to be fearful of forging true relationships. Joyce McDougall (2004) writes: 'Victims of addiction are all engaged in a struggle against the universal state of dependence that is characteristic of the human condition' (p. 527). This sentence is strangely reminiscent of the patient described by Moss when he says to his analyst (p. 71):

> Nothing can have impact. Nothing. That's the whole idea. If something has impact, it means you weren't perfect . . . No impact. No change . . . . I know patients are supposed to need their analysts. *Here, though, it's you who has to who need me.*

The object is experienced as a source of anxiety, and as dangerous. Every effort is made to short-circuit the psychic work engendered by the recognition of separateness or difference. Clinging imposes an ideal of absolute mastery over the object, which is not allowed any life of its own. Time has come to a standstill. What's more, these patients struggle against the work of representation. They not only struggle against the object, but *against all traces of the object within their own psyche*. They are at war against 'the work of desire'.

As an example of absolute mastery, Michel de M'Uzan (2004) describes the substance-abusing patient's encounter with toxic substances as a moment of ecstasy, because they feel they are complete and powerful. He writes: 'We are dealing with a real existential deficiency, a *lack of being,* an incapacity to have a natural sense of being oneself. It is a very different status belonging to a more archaic organisation than the classical narcissistic organisation' (p. 593). I had a heroin addict in treatment who described for me in our first session her recent encounter with heroin in very similar terms. She said the experience with heroin had been a revelation, a miraculous solution. It was a grandiose moment in which she had felt *'alive and master of the world'.* For de M'Uzan, we are dealing here with a deficiency or weakness in the 'basic tonus of identity', which originates even before the libido is attached to the drive of self-preservation, thus at the very heart of the transformation of need into desire which I have described above.

Miss C.

I would like now to relate a fragment of clinical material derived from a long psychoanalytic treatment conducted at the Paris Psychosomatic School.

Miss C. came for a consultation with me after referral by her doctors. When she was 32, she had had breast cancer; during the 18 months that followed her treatment for this, involving a mastectomy and chemotherapy, she suffered two strokes. Miss C. was a sporty-looking woman, aged 34, when

(continued)

(continued)

she began face-to-face psychoanalytic therapy with me. She told me that she had come to see me 'because she trusted her doctors, but she didn't really believe in it; she felt she didn't have any problems, any anxieties, or depression'. She said she didn't dwell on herself too much; she *'didn't like thinking and much preferred action'*. In fact, she was a professional sportswoman, and had no social or erotic life. She didn't try to make friends because she quickly felt 'invaded' by the presence of other people. Her very ascetic life revolved around her exhausting training sessions, though she had no complaints about that.

Her whole life was organised to *avoid thinking, desire, and relationships*, and discharging tensions through exhausting physical exercises.

From a psychosomatic point of view, the sequence that I qualify as 'somatic disorganisation', manifesting itself in the form of a cancer and two strokes, had followed a serious fracture that had immobilised her and deprived her of the outlet of sports for more than six months, thereby barring her usual path of discharge. If it were possible to identify all of the causes that converged to result in the appearance of these particular illnesses, cancer and strokes, in this unique patient at a specific time in her life, I would guess that there are a million factors involved, including biological, genetic and environmental ones. But I do know that in her case, her usual route of psychic discharge through exercise had been blocked about one year before her cancer and strokes manifested. So while I remain uncertain about the causal role that her mental state played in the appearance of her illnesses, I believe her psychic life influenced the timing and course of these illnesses.

For reasons of space I cannot give an account of this long, intensive, but fascinating treatment.[2] The clinical sequence I am referring to took place towards the end of the seventh year, at a time when C. had come to terms with desire, her body and her femininity. She had just undergone reparative surgery, which she was very pleased with. Before that, for years, her scar had not bothered her; she hadn't even noticed it. She thought now she might like to have a child or else might think of adopting one.

In this context, one Friday, during a session, she told me in a cold and somewhat flippant tone that she had received a visit from her mother who had insisted on seeing her 'new breast'. She further insisted on having the name and address of the plastic surgeon because she wanted 'to have hers done in the same way'. I felt shocked and appalled. I asked her what she had felt, if she was angry.

'No, I felt nothing, and feel nothing', C. said.

I was worried about what I saw as a regression, a return to past times when her affects had been totally frozen. I thought again about her abusive mother who used to beat her violently. Her father had died in a car accident when C. was 12 years old, and it was shortly after this that C. found that she couldn't feel anything anymore, neither pain nor sensations of hot and cold.

This sensory 'anaesthesia', which later spread to the whole of her emotional life, had been the object of years of work with me.

The following Monday morning the secretary told me that C. had left a message to cancel her session; she had had violent pains in her belly and had gone to see a gynaecologist. A second message on Tuesday told me that she had been hospitalised for a cyst in the uterus. Given her medical past, an extemporaneous biopsy was planned for that Thursday. So she had cancelled her sessions for about 15 days. I was terribly worried, fearing the worst.

On Friday morning, a third message was waiting for me at the hospital: in fact, C. had not had the operation, had left the hospital, and wanted to resume her sessions on Monday; she would explain then . . .

Between the initial scan on Monday and the second one on Thursday, the cyst had been resorbed; in fact, it was one of those rare cases of 'functional cysts'. C. was smiling and felt completely reassured; however, a series of sessions followed in which she exploded with unprecedented rage against her mother. I now learnt about something she had kept from me up until then, not because she had forgotten about it but 'because she felt ashamed'. It seemed that her mother had been something of a nymphomaniac, bringing men home with her several times a week with whom she would have sexual relations in front of her daughter or with the latter shut in the kitchen. C. went on to tell me about the way her mother would subject her to 'inspections' to see if she was still a virgin.

At this point she brought a dream:

There were three of us in my office. She was sitting on the couch, her mother was in the armchair, and I was in my usual place. So we formed a sort of equilateral triangle. I was leafing through a big book on my knees and said that we were going to review all her dreams since her father's death. I started reading. C. was fighting against drowsiness and finally lay down on the couch and fell asleep. She dreamt (within the dream) that her mother wanted to wake her up and that I was opposing this, violently telling her, 'No, you're going to traumatise her again; get out of here'. The mother left and the patient continued her dream in which a little boy sat down on the edge of the couch. She finally woke up and we were alone. Still in the dream, she apologised for her impoliteness.

This clear yet elaborate dream, containing a dream within a dream in which she represented the presence of a child after I had sent her mother packing, seemed to me to be a mark of the resumption of good mental functioning. Moreover, it was during the months that followed this dream that the patient initiated official adoption proceedings.

For C. to be able to discover and accept desire, affect and psychic work, it had been necessary for her to make a long detour involving a lengthy and painful period of work during which, thanks to the transference, she was able to reconcile herself with the work of thinking and representation, and thus with desire and the object.

I have chosen this short fragment from the end of an analytic treatment to illustrate what I have called 'acting out through the body', which is very different from the processes of somatisation described in the literature of the Paris Psychosomatic School. It is also different from hysterical conversion, because there is clearly a functional somatic symptom aimed at short-circuiting psychic elaboration and the feared emotional storm.

Joyce McDougall (1984) has spoken about the role of addictive behaviour as an analgesic. I would say the same thing about many 'anti-thinking' behaviours. I would prefer to compare this role to the massive consumption of analgesic drugs for preventive purposes, even though the outcome is often fatal. I have tried to give my own psychoanalytic viewpoint (Aisenstein, 2006) on questions that require a multi-disciplinary approach, although it would be folly to disregard the biological, genetic, histological components, among others, which are also part of our search for truth.

The work of desire/the work of being desired

Donald Moss

> No, I don't like work. I had rather laze about and think of all the fine things that can be done. I don't like work – no man does – but I like what is in the work, the chance to find yourself. Your own reality – for yourself, not for others – what no other man can ever know. They can only see the mere show, and never can tell what it really means.
>
> (Joseph Conrad (1899), *Heart of Darkness*: 71–72)

I think of what follows as an extended meditation on Freud's foundational idea that drives exert a demand 'upon the mind for work in consequence of its connection to the body' (1915, p. 121).

Desire

Imagine the moment: you are at rest, still and quiet, when suddenly your self-sufficiency comes to an end. You are aroused, you want something; you and your body are infiltrated. The arousal is abrupt, unwelcomed and unbidden. You now feel yourself under the pressure of an exigent force, an imperious demand. You feel mobilised, your rest disturbed – you are alert, intent and focused. Your aim is to find your way to an object – one with the power to both relieve and refuse you. With your body, you must do something with/to this object. While the object's power is enhanced, yours is diminished. A moment ago you were resting in a secure present tense. Now, you are thrust into the uncertainties of temporal life. The present tense is deficient; you are now looking to the future to find the object that might – only might – restore the stillness and satisfaction that you have just lost. Better put, it is you yourself and not the present tense that is deficient. You lack what you must have. Uncertainty and risk have displaced comfort and rest.

Through no fault – no decision, even – of your own, you now face the prospect of potential satisfaction but also of potential despair. You cannot set the terms nor foretell the outcome. This, I think, is desire in action. Its invariant demand, then: Find the object. Do what you must. Get to work. Work means the abandonment of the present in favor of the future, the abandonment of timelessness for temporality, of certainty for contingency, of stasis for movement.

I mean to delineate two categories of patients now, each responding differently to this demand for work:

1   The first category treats the demand as a catastrophe that must be averted, no matter the cost.
2   The second category is uncertain what work to do: the work demanded by desire or the work of resisting this demand. Excited by desire's promise of satisfaction while terrified by what they might learn and lose if they comply with it, these people are caught: submitting to desire's demand for work while also working against it.

Category I: Desire as catastrophe

I think we can empathise with this substantial group of patients who, like Melville's infamous Bartleby the Scrivener, live lives oriented around the anthem of 'I would prefer not'. Unlike Bartleby, though, these patients' refusal of desire's demands for work will rarely seem to us the product of a calmly stated 'preference'. Instead, these patients' voices will contain an undertone of urgency. For them, the demands made by desire are unbearable; to submit to them, to work at their behest, would 'drive me crazy', 'I would fall apart', 'I could not stand it'.

It is important to realise that it is not the object of desire that these patients refuse; rather, it is the work of desire. The work of desire demands that the object, before being found, be kept in mind. Such work insists on delay, on a unit of time when the worker, though lacking the object, must nonetheless preserve its representation. He/she must suffer the painful awareness that representation is not identical to possession. For this group of patients, such suffering is unbearable. For them, the quantitative falloff from physical immediacy to psychic representations, from contact to memory, is so steep as to make it seem to them that psychic representation is utterly useless, that in demanding this work of them, desire – and you, desire's agent – might as well be asking them to find their requisite calories by remembering yesterday's meal. As one patient recently said, 'I hate language. It just reminds you of what you don't have'. She also explicitly names the task she sets herself in relation to desire: 'It's been a battle from the beginning here; you work to name things, I work to un-name them'.

Another example – a man in his 60s in analysis four times per week:

> 'Impact? Nothing can have impact. Nothing. That's the whole idea. If something has impact, it means you weren't perfect. It means you could be better, you could change for the better. You could want something. You will never

have an impact on me. I will never want something from you. Never. I've lived in New York for 36 years. It's never touched me. I don't want to become a man. I don't want to become anything. Once you say you're becoming something it means that you weren't already where you want to be. I'm where I want to be. Perfect. I know it's crazy. I'd never stand up in Hyde Park and say this. People would walk away. They'd say the guy is crazy. This is different, telling you. The difference is that you can't walk away. You're here forever. Me and you like this forever. No impact. No change. The same. We're stuck together permanently. I have you. That will never change. Why should it? It's perfect. Time doesn't matter then. Nothing matters. That's the way I want it. I know patients are supposed to need their analysts. Here, though, it's you who has to need me. I'm a patient, a case, an example, a study. You want to succeed. You need me in order for you to be successful'.

This patient's notion of effortless desire, of desire apparently always satisfied, a desire that knows no past or future but only a 'perfect' present, seems to present us with an oxymoron. The oxymoron falls apart, though, if, for this patient, we simply posit a peculiar and non-commonsensical object: a desire whose aim and object are identical; a desire that aims directly – without mediation – at finding and obliterating itself, aims, that is, at pure self-sufficiency, a desire for 'nothing'.

We can give a name to this patient's object of desire – we can call it 'nothing'. He seems to submit to one demand only, the one driving him to maintain himself as 'perfect'. If 'perfect', he is permanently 'exempt' (a word he often applies to himself) from the work of looking for an object; he always already has his – 'nothing'. This patient means to maintain himself in a state resembling the uninterruptable calm of Bartleby's 'I would prefer not' – a fullness that lacks nothing, a present tense forever sufficient unto itself. Or, as Stefan George (1907) beautifully puts it in his poem, 'Litany', this patient's desire is to 'kill the longing, close the wound'. To permanently 'kill the longing' – to end the work, to retire, this is the aim of patients like these, for whom longing is unbearable.

The work of desire necessarily takes place in time. Desire commemorates what has been lost and pursues the possibility of re-finding its semblance. These patients want no hint of time. They aim to obliterate all markers of past, present and future: nothing missing, nothing wanted, nothing possible.

Long ago now, my patient's father phoned him to say that he wanted my patient's help, that he wasn't feeling well. Hearing this, my patient felt triumphant and cruel. He told his father he was too busy to talk right then. He hung up the phone. 'I gave him nothing', he later said to me. That evening the father killed himself. It was shortly after that that my patient began his treatment with me. From its inception, that treatment has been marked by the patient 'preferring not to'.

Only if the analyst can preserve – first for himself and then, perhaps, for the patient – a sense of meaningful time, a differentiated past, present and future, can work with these patients be bearable. Lose a sense of time, as I often do with this patient, and I feel the threat of something like being buried alive, entombed. At moments like those, I want to destroy the patient who seems then devoted to destroying me. I momentarily join him, then, in a shared desire whose aim, whose work, is mutual obliteration.

Occasionally, rarely, this patient is able to speak in a language infiltrated with time: a past, a present and a future. 'When I think back', he once said, 'I don't deserve to live. I'm in solitary confinement for life. No brothers, no sisters, no parents. No one. I'm the end of the line. We will all vanish. We all deserve to vanish'.

This, then, is the work of his desire – not 'nothing' really – but rather to join his parents in a permanent and obliterated unity – no traces left, no present, no past, no future – no more work.

Category II: Do the work demanded by desire, or work against it?

My patient here clearly states the conflict between the work demands associated with unbearable desires in one direction and those directed toward a more bearable alternative: 'shutting things down', as this patient puts it.

> *Everything is a dream or fantasy and maybe if I say it there will be nothing left to say or to think about. I think I'm trying . . . think I'm trying to shut things down, to stop talking. The first time I'm starting to think . . . maybe I really don't have interest in a lot of things because they're scary, inconvenient, will cause me problems . . . It's not . . . I find myself in a situation . . . Not comfortable having things out in the open . . . Or . . . Difficult to even get them out, even say them, even if they're right in the front of my mind . . . bothering me . . . I won't say it . . .*
>
> *Just seems really frightening. Like it's such a late . . . So much willpower to do it . . . so much in my nature that goes against it . . . god damn it . . . the thing I'm thinking about today . . . in my mind . . . know it . . . don't want to say it . . . another step in . . . certain direction . . . in what direction . . . homosexuality? . . . I don't want . . . I want to control it . . . don't want that to be my direction . . . I don't know . . . again embarrassed . . . what I thought about . . . almost like I'm going to confess something . . . there it is . . . now let me leave . . . sin no more . . . don't do it anymore . . . I was gonna say . . . two instances in last six months when I was masturbating in the shower . . . penetrated myself with my fingers . . . felt good . . . pressure . . . I don't know . . . felt good . . . twice . . . sometimes when I'm in the shower now I think about it but don't do it . . . when I was . . . I haven't thought about it at all . . . this really isn't process material . . . I think I just boxed that out . . . don't know . . . don't know if it means anything . . . my relation to it now is that it can't mean anything . . . a different feeling . . . different . . . just different . . . don't know . . . just I always*

thought that would be the worst thing, last thing, never happen and it did happen . . . I did it to myself and that's . . .

I feel uncomfortable talking about this to you, to another person . . . the fear that keeps popping into my head . . . pre-empt it, apologise . . . what if telling something like that turned you on . . . I don't think that . . . why would . . . do I want that? . . . I have no idea . . . just had that fear . . . don't want to have that . . . I think that's true . . . I do not want to have a sexualised relation to you . . . sex would make it bad, you know . . . really want this to be a neutral relationship . . . because I'm trying to sort out what I'm thinking . . . can't do that if I'm sexualizing you . . . not because you're a man . . . I think I'm doing it . . . look at the bike, the dreams . . . that's what I'm afraid of in the dream . . . sometimes I don't know . . . the image pops into my mind . . . sexual . . . and then they . . . just take them out . . . lying here . . . you came over, got on top of me . . . just a flash . . . not like . . . don't want that to happen . . . just take them out . . . be done . . . be done .

The anguish given voice here is reminiscent of Samuel Beckett. This patient's every sentence – the means, in analysis, by which he takes up drive's demand to work – seems to swallow itself, starting in the direction of a desired aim and a desired object and finishing in the direction of the erasure of both that aim and object as well as of the sentences that housed them. The work vector turns around, mid-job, so to speak, aiming to obliterate itself and the demand that instigated it. We can again almost hear Beckett when the patient, in response to conflicting work demands that cannot be reconciled, concludes his hour with a plaintive cry: 'be done', 'be done'. This, I think, is the emblematic phrase of these patients for whom desire's demands for work are tempting enough to maintain themselves in consciousness while at the same time terrifying enough so that they must be resisted, worked against, with a force that turns out to be equal to, but not greater than, desire's.

Being desired

You are his analyst and it's you he wants – your face, your body, your voice, your ideas, your possessions, the way you smile, your strength, your weaknesses, your marital status, your professional vulnerabilities, your omniscience, your lapses – he wants all of it, loves all of it, admires all of it. He is certain that you are the object he has long desired and until now had abandoned hope of finding. He has found in you all that he has found lacking in himself. This finding makes you tense. The patient, with certainty, sees in you what you, with equal certainty, know is not there. What you know as shadow he knows as substance. You are enveloped in his desire. Whatever you say confirms him in his certainty. Your status as a separate person is under threat. You feel stalked. Your experience resembles that of an aggressively interrogated suspect, whose every denial and every silence are treated as signs of guilt. Your every effort to say, in effect, 'I think', is heard as an indirect affirmation of 'We are'. And it is here, in the gap between your powerless 'I think' and the patient's tenacious 'We are' that you experience the unremitting demand for work made on your mind as a consequence of being desired.

A representative example:

The patient is a 35-year-old man, whose professional successes have won him international acclaim. He is in the second year of his analysis, initiated by his doubts regarding his own capacity to love and, more generally, his capacities for anything good. He feels his acclaim and the apparent affection of family and friends are the products of fraud, easy to achieve – people can be fooled. The only figure whom he cannot fool is the analyst. The premise of the analysis is this, that his goodness is false, that his 'rottenness' is the only enduringly true baseline. There is no disturbing this baseline. Two years of experience with him has provided the analyst with many opportunities to experience what he means by the baseline's durability.

From a recent session:

The patient is berating himself about his way of being in analysis. He can't even say what he's doing here. If someone were to ask him what he talks about, he would be unable to tell. What an idiot he is. All this time and he still doesn't know what he's talking about. I said to him that the question as he poses it is both cruel and ill-informed, that it's designed to be unanswerable and to make its recipient feel himself a failure. I was meaning to illuminate the cruelty lurking in the hour.

His response was to agree, to express amazement, to wonder why he didn't see the cruelty that I saw, and then to shift his attention now to how useless he is in the analysis if he can't even see cruelty when it's right in front of his face.

I said that what I said seemed to confirm what he was feeling, because he hadn't thought it himself. If he hasn't thought it, what good is he?

He then spoke of how he is unable to really appreciate what I do, because when I do something good it just reminds him of his incapacity to do what I've just done. That no matter how much he tries he is unable to really use and appreciate what I offer him.

I said that I thought that in speaking harshly about himself he, in fact, was also indirectly showing his appreciation of me.

He then said that this was the most 'profound' sense of understanding he'd ever experienced, that no matter what he did to me I could always find

(continued)

(continued)

a way to point out something useful to him, that I wasn't blocked in by his ways of seeing me and that my capacity not to be blocked was what allowed him to proceed so successfully with his own life and that he himself would never, could never, achieve that capacity.

At this point in the session, I gave up and was silent for the rest of the hour. Lurking in that silence was a failure to properly work as an analyst. Feeling encaged by my patient's desire, all of my thoughts seemed useless. My capacity to even imagine an exit from this cage seemed to have reached its limit. I could neither effectively resist nor actively confirm my patient in his certainty that he had, indeed, found the object of his desire. I experienced as obliterating violence what the patient was experiencing as satisfied desire. The work I was unable to do here was to create, on my own, an imagined object – neither me nor the patient – whose vital constituents would have included the unstable, but nonetheless, viable mix of love and violence so palpable in the session, an object toward which, if I could only hold it, would provide me with evidence of my own functional separateness and provide the patient with a beacon toward which some day he might be able to aim his desire.

Like the work of desire, the work of being desired, then, resembles what I think Loewald (1960) had in mind when he wrote:

> We must have an image of that which needs to be brought into its own . . . an image that the analyst has to focus in his mind, thus holding it in safe keeping for the patient to whom it is mainly lost.
>
> (p. 18)

Loewald here is, in essence, simply situating psychoanalytic work within the broader genre of the work of desire. For it is the generic function of both the work of desire and the work of being desired to incarnate and to 'hold in safe keeping' a possibility, in the form of an object, that would otherwise be enslaved to desire's relentless demand to obliterate the future and turn the present into a state of permanent satisfaction.

Reflections: Aisenstein on Moss

I find Moss's idea of 'two categories' of patients illuminating. It allows us to draw a very clear line of demarcation between two different clinical fields: on the one hand, what Freud described as the 'neuro-psychoses of defence' and, on the other, all those patients who, in my view, led him to revise his first theory of the drives and, consequently, in 1923, his topographical conception. I think that it was the clinical failures, namely, the negative therapeutic reaction, deadly masochism and the traumatic neuroses, that forced him to rethink his metapsychology and to write *Beyond the Pleasure Principle* (1920). Moss's Category II corresponds to patients who, under the aegis of the pleasure principle, are struggling with their desires. The others are *beyond the pleasure principle*. Their struggle does not consist of intrapsychic conflicts between agencies; rather, they are struggling against the 'work of desire', under the aegis of pure repetition-compulsion. This theoretical understanding has considerable clinical implications.

It is worth noting that Moss does not refer here to the classical and over-worked question of 'analysability', which has been debated at length by Fenichel, Greenson, Sandler, Lowenstein and others, but that is not what is involved here. Not only are the patients of Category I analysable but – and I really believe this – only analysis can help them. It seems to me that a large part of André Green's work is concerned with showing this (Green, 1983,1990).

On the other hand, taking them into analysis implies a theoretical and clinical revision of our conceptions of the transference and modes of interpretation. Analysis is a 'talking cure' and interpretation of the latent contents rests on the method of free association.

What do we do with patients who tell us that they do not want to think or who, like the one mentioned by Moss, affirm: 'I hate language, it just reminds you of what you don't have . . . It's been a battle from the beginning here; you work to name things, I work to un-name them'. Here the question of the counter-transference acquires its full significance; it is a question of the analyst surviving psychically while keeping 'a sense of meaningful time' (this volume, p. 72), even though he is confronted with a discourse that is not, or is no longer, 'alive' because it is 'actual', without history. The mode of psychic functioning is often 'mechani-cal' (*opératoire*), and there is an apparent absence of affects. Psychic energy is not worked over and manifests itself through acts or, as in the case of Miss C., through the soma. We do not detect resistances or off-shoots of the repressed or compromise formations; it is as though there were no conflicts between opposing psychic forces.

Often the only guiding thread is anxiety – the affect of anxiety, as Freud calls it. An affect of unpleasure, anxiety is a flight in the face of the libido of which it is at once an outcome and an alteration. I cannot enter here into the complex relations between anxiety and the agencies, but will simply say that the locus of anxiety, and of affect, is the preconscious, and then, in principle, the ego. A rudiment of unconscious affect seeking to break through can thus appear in the form of anxiety. The work of analysis and the interplay of the transference/countertransference can qualify it and attribute to it the status of true affect. Such work is profoundly psychoanalytic but based on a different metapsychology. It seems to me that Moss's clinical vignettes and my own illustrate this clearly.

The question of the transference

I have stressed the importance of the countertransference, but with these patients the transference remains enigmatic. One may wonder why and how patients who do not want to desire or to think or to imagine, and who are dead scared of dependency, can transfer? Why do they accept coming several times a week for years? What do these patients, who are in the actual, the present, refusing to be in time and history, transfer?

Yet they do transfer, they invest the psychoanalyst massively, for there exists, I believe, in each human being, a 'compulsion to transfer'. Small children fall in love with a toy, a doll, a lorry – now these are already transferences. Transference exists in life and the analytic setting helps to organise it and interpret it.

But is it the same transference as in the neuro-psychoses of defence? I am not convinced it is. To understand this I think we need to remember that there are already two theories of transference in Freud's work, the first of which is clearly set out in 1912 in 'The Dynamics of Transference': the motor of the transference is the constantly repeated need for instinctual satisfactions within the context of the pleasure principle. Transference is pure desire transferred on to the analyst.

But I think that we can detect a second theory between the lines, the seeds of which were present as early as 1914 when Freud discovered the compulsion to repeat. After 1920, the transference can be understood as a fundamental tendency to repeat which is 'beyond the pleasure principle'. As the traumatic situation has led to an unbearable degree of tension, the patient no longer transfers under the sign of the quest for pleasure but at the behest of an innate tendency to repeat.

These two conceptions of the transference are not in contradiction and they often co-exist. They nonetheless have their origins in different clinical situations. Thanks to the 'compulsion to transfer' (*compulsion au transfert*) even patients who struggle against 'the work of desire' will be able to gain access to it through analytic experience.

Reflections: Moss on Aisenstein

Aisenstein quietly makes an elegant and profound point when she notices that 'primary erotogenic masochism' commands little attention in the North American psychoanalytic literature. She then aims precisely at that point of absence in our literature when she writes 'the structure of desire is masochistic in its essence'. This simple declaration, then, addresses what can easily be thought of as the most important clinical/theoretical problem we all face – the problem of 'delay'.

When Freud writes about 'delay' in Chapter 7 (1900), he refers to the educative force of 'bitter experience' – in the search for satisfaction, 'delay' results if and only if immediate impulse fails. There is something unsatisfying about Freud's formulation, something too rationalistic. We're asked to picture an emerging infant capable of what – for Bion, say – is the most demanding possible task: namely, learning from experience. Aisenstein brilliantly corrects this unlikely claim. For her, the infant is not, in fact, 'learning' at all. That is, the infant is not submitting to the demands of reality, readjusting its operations accordingly. No, Aisenstein pictures the contrary. The infant turns 'reality' on its head and essentially finds satisfaction in what reality offers as satisfaction's denial. In the struggle over immediacy, apparent 'delay' becomes, for the infant, an indirect – masochistic – form of immediacy. In going through the motions of 'delay', the infant finds immediate masochistic satisfaction. From the point of view of theory, then, delay no longer need present us with such a puzzling problem. 'Delay' is not necessarily a higher form of functioning at all. Instead, it represents a subtle, indirect, covert means of finding immediate satisfaction while only apparently waiting for it.

This conceptual move offers us North Americans the possibility of real theoretical clinical relief. We can breathe easier. The huge, and almost always insurmountable, problems posed by trying to account for the emergence of 'higher' functions – each of which depend upon mobilizing tactics of delay – can be put aside. These 'higher' functions, Aisenstein implies, can instead be thought of as the result of an indirect subtle employment of 'lower' ones – i.e. erotogenic masochism.

The resulting tension is not between immediacy and delay but rather between the satisfactions available when the object is present and those available when it is not. Either way, the subject in question – infant or adult – is finding its way toward satisfaction. Desire will tolerate nothing less. Now or later is not the proper dichotomy. For desire, it's always now. Desire works like a martial artist works. It takes what you give it. Give it what it wants and it's satisfied. Deprive it of what it wants and it satisfies itself with your deprivation.

No matter what, desire wins.

Notes

1 Translated by Andrew Weller.
2 I have spoken at length (Aisenstein, 2013) about this patient in *Transference and Countertransference Today* (see Oesler, Ed., 2013), and another sequence is reported here.

References

Aisenstein, M. (2006). The indissociable unity of psyche and soma. *Int. J. Psychoanal.*, *87*: 667–680.
Aisenstein, M. (2013). Countertransference with somatic patients. In R. Oesler (Ed.) *Transference and Countertransference Today*. London: Karnac.
Conrad, J. (1899). *Heart of Darkness*. Portland, OR, and Brooklyn, NY: Tin House Books (2013), pp. 71–72.
Freud, S. (1895). *Project for a Scientific Psychology*. *S.E., 1*. London: Hogarth, pp. 281–397.
Freud, S. (1900). *The Interpretation of Dreams*. *S.E., 4–5*. London: Hogarth: pp. 1–600.
Freud, S. (1912). The dynamics of transference. *S.E., 12*. London: Hogarth: pp. 99–108.
Freud, S. (1915). Instincts and their vicissitudes. *S.E., 14*. London: Hogarth, pp. 117–140.
Freud, S. (1920). *Beyond the Pleasure Principle. S.E., 18*. London: Hogarth, pp. 1–64.
Freud, S. (1924). The economic problem of masochism. *S.E., 19*. London: Hogarth, pp. 157–179.
George, S. (1907). Litany, in *Der siebente Ring* (The Seventh Ring), also in *Poems*, Trans. & Ed. C. North Valhope and E. Morwitz. New York: Pantheon, 1946.

Green, A. (1983). *Narcissisme de vie, Narcissisme de mort.* Paris: Minuit. [*Life Narcissism, Death Narcissism,* A. Weller (Trans.). London: Free Association Books, 2001].

Green, A. (1990). *La folie privée, psychanalyse des cas-limites,* Paris : Gallimard.

Grubrich-Simitis, I., Fichtner G., and Hirschmüller, A. (Eds.) (2011). *Sei mein, wie ich mir's denke: Brautbriefe.* Frankfurt am Main: Fischer.

Loewald, H. W. (1960). On the therapeutic action of psycho-analysis. *Int. J. Psychoanal., 41:* 16–33.

McDougall, J. (1984). The 'dis-affected' patient: Reflections on affect pathology. *Psychoanal. Q., 53:* 386–409.

McDougall, J. (2004). Economie psychique de l'addiction. *Revue Française de Psychanalyse* (Addiction et Dépendance), *68:* 508–527.

M'Uzan, M. de (2004). Addiction et problématique identitaire. *Revue Française de Psychanalyse* (Addiction et Dépendance), *68:* 590–597.

Oesler, R. (Ed.) (2013). *Transference and Countertransference Today.* London: Karnac.

Chapter 4

Disrupting Oedipus

The legacy of the Sphinx

Nicola Barden

Introduction

Analytic theory presupposes a heterosexual norm. This is not surprising in terms of its original context. What is surprising is what might be seen as the tenacity of the profession's attachment to this presupposition and the security of its position in the analytic canon, to this day.

Perhaps this statement raises eyebrows. Of course, it could be said, heterosexuality is the norm, just look around. But psychoanalysis was not built on norms; it was built on shattering them and disrupting the idea of normality altogether. Where has the disruption gone? Sexual conservatism is an odd centre for a profession originating in sexual radicalism. Yet analytic theory persists in centring itself to a position that keeps homosexuality at a comfortable distance, at the far end of a sexual spectrum which takes heterosexuality as its starting point.

This chapter presents the case for disturbance, not through altruism or kindness or even equality but because hetero-normativity is a poor basis on which to build theory about gendered as well as sexualised identities and a fundamentally inadequate tribute to Freud's work and spirit.

Analysis is of course not alone in taking a hetero-normative stance – it is a worldwide phenomenon. But the lack of a reflective position on this is notable in a profession built on the capacity to self-reflect. Nor has the stance been a neutral one – psychoanalysis has been both follower and promoter, without apparent pause for thought.

This chapter aims to provide such a pause and to offer a consideration of the constraints of oedipal theorising on sexuality and gender through a broad over-view of the literature. If sexuality and gender are interdependent then not only are they both constrained by hetero-normativity, but a change in approach to sexuality might axiomatically require a change in approach to gender. Homosexuality carries a burden on gender's behalf and the implications for a change in position may upset more than the sexual order.

Problems with Oedipus

> Psychoanalysis and homosexuality are both late 19th century inventions.
>
> (Ratigan, 2010: 9)

Freudian theory was embedded in nineteenth century Europe with its Enlighten-ment emphasis on reason and individualism. Rational thought and scientific drive led progress. Philosophy focused on the meaning of individual lives (Whyte, 1979). Civilisation rested on the triumph of the mind over the instincts and the relationship between mind and body was a preoccupation of philosophers and moralisers alike. Freud was part of this milieu (Quinton, 1972) and embraced a scientific approach to the irrational, placing it in the unconscious and sifting it with logic, a psychic archaeological dig. The irrational was not a discard but a clue, a nonsense poem with personal meaning that analysis could decode. Freud challenged dualism and sought the join between mind and body: 'The relation between body and mind (in animals no less than in human beings) is a reciprocal one' (Freud, 1905a: 284).

Freud's forensic interest in the creation of identity was set in the dawn of a new era for homosexuality in Europe. A compassionate move away from sin (Karlen, 1971) and towards constitution began to combine with a more individu-alistic philosophy in moving activity to identity – sexuality was not just what you did but who you were. This created space for a new moral neutrality that was at the forefront of the radical dialogue that engaged Freud, who supported the decriminalisation of homosexuality. Early approaches (Ulrichs, 1864, Krafft-Ebbing, 1886) cast homosexuality as a gender conundrum – a male homosexual had a female spirit in a male body – making same sex desire comprehensible by framing it as a psychologically heterosexual pairing, academically neither normal nor perverse. Some congruence in Freud's thinking with the work of this movement is plain to see, from his reference to Ellis and his use of the term inversion (Ellis, 1900) to his ease with the equation of cross gender identification and same sex desire.

Defining sexuality against a stable gender framework (putting the blame on gender) also helped with the conundrum of de-pathologising homosexuality within an evolutionary framework – sex and reproduction remained joined up, even if only in phantasy. Anchoring homosexual development within a hetero-sexual norm gave the destabilising potential of the oedipus complex safe passage through the Darwinian imperative of survival.

Adhering to the notion of a normal outcome in terms of gender and sexual iden-tity, at least in terms of functioning, Freud upturned the notion of a simple organic process and illuminated the precarious psychic journey the child undertakes in order to become an adult. 'Natural' sexuality was excavated into separate pieces of drive, aim and object; polymorphism only fell into its heterosexual resolu-tion through a complex pathway of identification and desire, stimulated by the recognition of sexual difference. Family constellations presented natural dilem-mas. Both genders had the mother as their first love object; both genders valued and wanted the penis; only one gender had to shift the object of desire. Picking a pathway towards mature heterosexuality took the route of rivalrous, anxious renunciation for the boy, as his castration anxiety was resolved through male iden-tification and desire of the female; and envious, resentful compromise for the girl, whose penis envy caused her to reject and then re-identify with the mother as she resolved her castration complex through desire of the male.

The oedipal resolution has consequences for theories of sexuality and gender identity that require further consideration.

Firstly, for homosexuality. 'One of the tasks implicit in object choice is that it should find its way to the opposite sex. This, as we know, is not accomplished without a certain amount of fumbling' (Freud, 1905b: 229). The various processes and outcomes in the oedipal resolution required desire and identification to be separate; to confuse them resulted in the disaster that was unresolved oedipus, bound to an infantile state, unable to turn outwards from the maternal coupling towards the world and its adult opportunities. Homosexuality in this scenario must be a developmental inhibition, a variation or diversion from the norm: a fumble.

Secondly, for gender. Psychic bisexuality found its way to a clear gender identity through heterosexual normativity. Men became men through defining their relationship with women, that is, through castration anxiety; women became women by defining themselves in relationship to men, through penis envy. Their cast-off parts were accessible through relationship with the other, and this cemented sexuality's role as a container for gender identity.

And yet – while laying these conditions down, Freud also indicated his discontent with them. He did not press the neurotic aspect of homosexuality as many of his followers did; he was in the forefront of its normative advancement. He de-pathologised homosexuality while at the same time being unable to theoretically normalise it. For homosexuality to be a mature sexuality that goes beyond a fumble the implicitness of the object choice can no longer be taken for granted. Responding to this is not just a matter of reshuffling the Kinsey spectrum; Freud made gender and sex into closely woven concepts that cannot be altered independently of each other in the current oedipal construct. Homosexuality is a casualty of this solution – and so is gender.

While sexual difference was fundamental to Freud – 'for the psychical field, the biological field does in fact play the part of the underlying bedrock' (Freud, 1937: 252) – he was never content with its definition. He acknowledged his discomfort with the terms masculine and feminine. He resisted their description as active versus passive, finding it reductive and simplistic, yet continually revisited the adjectives for the want of an alternative. As descriptors of gender,

> Freud clarified their uselessness [but] ... returned to the erroneous terms [masculine and feminine] with the fascination of a man who could not see his way through them as terms, as though ... he had come to an understanding of their meaning which surpassed them.
>
> (Mitchell, 1990: 46)

As we shall see, it is difficult to think freely about gender when so much rests on its demarcation lines.

The oedipal legacy

Twentieth-century analysis has continued down the road more travelled in relation to sex and gender, perhaps mistaking familiarity for stability when looking for foundations on which to build its otherwise radical theories of the development of identity. While it is 'ungrateful' (Dinnerstein, 1976: xi) to judge Freud on the basis of his milieu, it is legitimate to consider how its repercussions have been passed down onto subsequent generations of theory and practice, and at what cost.

It will not be lost on the reader that so far only male homosexuality has been spoken about, and mostly by men, and this will continue to be the case. Indeed, by 1998 there were fewer than one hundred analytic accounts of female homosexuals in the analytic canon (Downey and Friedman, 1998). Freud acknowledged his uncertainty about women's psychology and female analysts tried to redress the balance. They critiqued the male-centredness of the castration complex, Horney (1926) calling in to view the particular privileges of pregnancy and motherhood from which men were excluded and about which they may experience unconscious envy. Male depictions of childbirth seemed somewhat idealised (Ferenczi, 1938) and Horney stopped short of this, although she and other female analysts were restricted in considering broader interpretations of female creativity that later focused on the world outside motherhood (Izzard, 2001; Raphael-Leff, 2001). Where Freud had suggested an absence of genital experience for women, Horney reinterpreted castration anxiety as an implicit knowledge of feminine genitality with its inferred desire for the penis, and insisted on equality of sexual pleasure for both genders.

Deutsch likewise affirmed a body-based femininity but focused this more around motherhood than genital pleasure. The '*magnificent satisfaction*' of motherhood (Deutsch, 1930: 60 italics in original) was compensation for the societal and mental restrictions of femaleness, its nature made weaker by the continual burden of menstruation and childbirth and its focus continually inward-looking (1925), mirroring the reproductive energy that was so different from the phallic outward thrust. The clitoris was a reminder of the absent penis and so envy was again present, although for both sexes.

While edging towards a more equal female experience, both Horney and Deutsch were constrained by a biological essentialism that rooted experience in the body while analysing it through the contextual mind. The trauma of childbirth made women weaker; knowledge of the vagina and clitoris led to a more significant awareness of the absent penis around which gender therefore continued to be constructed. The mental structure for femininity was hung on the physical framework of reproduction. Female homosexuality was immature as it was not fully genital (Deutsch, 1932) nor did it engage with the maturity of the maternal state, in phantasy or reality.

Riviere's 1929 paper 'Womanliness as Masquerade' did engage with developing the meanings of gender rather than finding different-but-equal paths to it. She suggested that excessive femininity could be a disguise for masculine strivings, raising the possibility that gender behaviour was not natural but a play – foreshadowing later ideas of gender as performance (Butler, 1990). The disguise was necessary because some strivings were forbidden, and women analysts generally moved towards acknowledging that women's position in society was influential in the development of female gender identity. This view took a long time to gain significance, however, and was reinvigorated by Mitchell (1971) who gave consideration to penis envy as the literalised translation of the envy of phallic power, thus relating oedipus to the contextual reality of women's place in the world and to a more universal psychological family constellation rather than a literal nuclear one. This incorporated meaning into difference – it was not just about being sexed, but what being sexed meant – which did not solve it but did make more sense of it. It was later still that the parallel of gay identity being influenced by heterosexual hegemony entered analytic thinking.

Klein repositioned the oedipal complex into the oral stage, reinforcing an infantile awareness of bisexual genitality through projections into the mother's body. The breast was the primary object of love and hate through which the boy experienced castration anxiety – biting off the breast/penis and fearing retaliation just as the girl feared punishment for harbouring desires to possess as well as receive the penis/breast. The much earlier stage of these processes meant that cross gender identification was a normal part of them and it was not until the phallic stage that the reality of physical difference overwhelmed the omnipotent bisexual phantasy and mature gender and sexual identities were achieved. The girl held on to her wish to take in the penis above her wish to possess her own; the boy's phallic aim emphasised the penetrative over the incorporative and so maintained a female love object; a heterosexual resolution was found. A non-heterosexual resolution inferred an inability to engage with the reality of the body, with a developmental trajectory halted at the more infantile stage of bisexuality and multiple identifications.

Klein's resolution to gender difference was therefore through the already familiar oedipal pattern of heterosexual complementarity, resting on the separation of identification from desire. The body is the incontrovertible container and exhibitor of difference. A continued identification with both male and female becomes an indication of an inability to face reality rather than a psychic concept of bisexuality that can continue alongside an appreciation of difference. The reproductive imperative is called down as justification for this – but with a rigidity that Blechner (1995) suggests amounts to a fetish in its insistence on creating a completeness to gender difference that is not so purely borne out in lived lives.

While Klein attempted to enter the whirling confusion of the infant part-object world in a way that possibly no clinician has bettered, the overlay of adult cognition is in some ways a problem. The infant cannot literally imagine a penis and a vagina; Stoller (1975) knew that the infant mind simply did not have this capacity, and object relations highlighted how long it took for the infant to develop a capacity to conceive of another at all. The inchoate swirling of the infant mind's interpretations of its bodily experiences is beautifully drawn by Klein but it confuses the picture to imagine them as forerunners of its later interpretations of difference.

When a three-year-old's play with bricks is interpreted as a replay of the primal scene (Klein, 1945) the positioning of this interpretation within a societal context that expected heterosexuality and an analytic context that expected oedipus can no longer be ignored.

In animal and human worlds the implicitness of object choice is questionable. Species have survived with multiple variations of sexual behaviours, pairings and groupings and indeed 'sexualities' (Bagemihl, 1999) throughout history; constancy of object choice can and does exist independently of sexual aim or reproductive necessity. This is as much a fact as physical difference. Yet reproduction has been claimed by psychoanalysis with a possessiveness that begs meaning to be made of it, just as analysis makes meaning of difference: the 'something special about a man and a woman making a baby' (Mendoza, 2007: 340); the 'wondrous act of creativity that is denied to (homosexuals)' (Sandler, 2006); a promotion of repro-duction that seems be staking some sort of claim rather than stating a fact. The body seems unquestionable, yet using biology as the *sine qua non* of gender iden-tity is a short cut too convenient. It is surely delusional to ignore the possession of a penis or vagina as bedrock, and yet the gender conundrum is just this – that the body is not ignored and yet does not answer the question of identity. The physical in this sense is hijacked by the metaphorical; a body cannot be inhabited for itself apart from the meanings accrued to it. To possess a male or female body (and recognising the many fine distinctions that must combine to facilitate such an assured definition, as a quick look at the rules for gender authentication in sport will evidence) is to inhabit something predestined, and so attempts to learn what the body might teach about the psyche have been continually hampered by precisely the expectation that its teachings will be fundamental.

There is a natural link between Klein and object relations through her conviction that relationship was essential to drive satisfaction. This tended to get lost in analytic accounts of homosexual relationships which were rather tied down to the 'essentials' – what physical parts go where and with whom. Even after object relations theorists had brought the relational perspective solidly into drive theory, in homosexuality they were separated out again. Discussions of 'successful' analytic treatment of homosexuals focused on the achievement of sexual restraint as if the accompany-ing emotional restraint would naturally follow, placing a bolster in the bed between homosexual acts and relational intimacy. This reductionism is particularly peculiar given the analytic account of homosexuality growing out of complex relationships.

Jung's concepts of anima and animus gave scope for a different theory building around gender. As gender archetypes (Samuels et al., 1986) they recognised a feminine principle in men (anima) and a masculine principle in women (animus) that gave a framework for both to include aspects of the other in their own per-sonas without perversion or neurosis. Holding these aspects in continual tension and balance was the essence of healthy creativity and this could have allowed for some recognition that soft men are still real men, for example. However, caught up in the expectations of complementarity, Jung's archetypes were constrained by too literal interpretations of content and a conservatism on what constituted balance that ran perilously close to contemporary ideals of men and women. Real men could only be so soft. Freer expression of the self was eluded when disputatious women were being too animus-ridden, and timid men were being too anima-fuelled, and each gender was left no closer towards ownership of human expression on its own gendered terms. Intimacy between men remained hostage to the accusation of homosexuality, or acceptable through the distance of an anima function that avoided disruption of the masculine ethos. Intimacy between women was not problematised but independence was; acceptable independence rested on a healthy animus, therefore was still owned by the masculine principle; unacceptable independence indicated an over-dominant or unintegrated animus – the woman was too much a man for her own good. The *coniunctio* of male and female, symbolic of the coming together of opposites and creation of new life, was symbolised only heterosexually and was not theorised into a generality that would allow homosexuality to be equally symbolic. Androcentrism and misogyny, as Wehr (1988) boldly stated, distorted Jung's accounts of gender and, by implication, of sexuality. Heterosexuality was constructed through a wholesome balance of archetypal gender; homosexuality was an attempt to correct an imbalance, but always remained representative of it (Jacobi, 1969).

Relationship and drive

Winnicott addressed drive and relationship, looking beyond the *existence* of a relationship to its *quality*. This connected phantasy and reality in a new way, less through the body and more through emotional experience. Infants did not experience themselves as gendered but their caring environment did, and many meanings of gendered existence were communicated to the infant prior to its own conscious apprehension of this. Winnicott was no liberal on the desired outcome of gender identity – homosexuality signalled a return to a pre-oedipal state and a flawed cross gender identification (1964) – but he did prepare for the possibility of gender identity being built up from complex relational experiences that included but were not limited to the oedipal. Simply redirecting the sexual drive was by implication an insufficient resolution to homosexuality; the relational aspect must also be addressed. As perversion became not just what you did but who you were, that is, a relational concept, so homosexuality was more than just an act.

Object relations theory developed as society was changing. Stoller (1985) concluded that unequivocal gender-affirming responses to the child from its parents contributed to an unshakeable gender identity, established by three years of age. Such certainty, once achieved, could overcome even body-based dysphoria, for example where external genitals did not match assigned gender identity (Money and Ehrhardt, 1972). It followed that children with uncertain or opposite gender identifications were suffering in part from inadequate role modelling in the parents and had been presented with inadequate identificatory opportunities. Treatment focused on rectifying this. Heterosexuality was an indicator, a sign of a successful outcome in terms of adaptation to a re-assigned gender identity.

More recent accounts of transgender identities have used the opportunity it offers to illuminate the many functions of gender (Harris, 2009). The traditional analytic account is phallically preoccupied; how to interpret the wilful giving up of the penis, or the illegitimate gain of it, becomes the focal point in a welter of mutilation and perversion. Psychological identity is delegitimised if not corresponded to by the body, as if the body is the only dependable source of gender identity. Ironically, transgender can also be a flag-waver for 'proper' identity as the conviction of transgender requires great certainty of the binary divide between male and female. The body is at once integral and peripheral, and transgender sits within a context that can only support its contradictory relationship with binary certainty. Transitioning often comes with the essential task of learning the gender traits appropriate to the other sex in a way that simultaneously highlights their conformity. McClosky, a male to female transgendered woman, describes the endeavour as '"deeply" superficial, a performance, something that must be studied and learned . . . Like method acting' (1999: 83–4). In this she touches the conundrum that Freud foresaw, the necessity and impossibility of gender.

It seems a greater transgression for men to cross gender norms than women (Zucker and Lawrence, 2009), up to the point at which female masculinity appears to move from admiring envy to castrating possession. Feminine boys are more likely to be expected to become homosexual than masculine girls, although studies disprove such a linear link (Coates and Wolfe, 1995). Kaftal suggested that 'homosexual panic' (1991: 325) was actually about male terror of emotional vulnerability that can otherwise be projected into women and underpinned by heterosexual pairing. Homosexuality demands male to male intimacy that feels unmanning and it is dishonestly avoided by heterosexual complementarity, even in analysis, 'creating a situation in which the male analyst can, as it were, hide behind the skirts of the internalised mother and fail to connect emotionally with his male patient' (Kaftal, 1991: 322). Female intimacy is less problematic; 'Boston marriages' (platonic lifelong female partnerships) were well tolerated. It is the usurping of the phallic position by women that causes controversy; it is the sex in lesbian relationships that is the problem.

Oedipal constraints

This chapter suggests that unwavering adherence to the oedipal model makes it difficult to think creatively about sex and gender. The heterosexual norm is the fulcrum on which oedipal identity balances. At one end is complementarity – the sexes being made whole by their combination in relationship – and at the other is homosexuality, the challenge to complementarity that is defeated by making it a defect of proper gender alignment. Clinical treatment of homosexuality aligned it with other gender identity disorders (transvestism, transsexualism). Gender change should therefore result in a balancing change in sexual orientation – yet this is not always the case, as male to female lesbian transsexual Jennifer Spry wrote, 'It is not my sexuality that was crossed, but my gender' (1997: 2). Consideration was and is given to forms of treatment for, and explanations of, homosexuality through ovary and testes transplants (Freud, 1905b), hormone replacements, brain development and other idiosyncratic pieces of research that pop up from time to time. All these possibilities rely on a link between feminisation/masculinisation and homosexuality; if the individual could be made more fully male/female, the sexual identity would revert to its proper place. Yet Gershman (1970), agreeing that poorly formed gender identity was the root of perversion, did acknowledge that while hormones might influence libido they had no sway over object choice; and Coates and Wolfe (1995) agreed that although hormones might influence gender-typical *behaviours*, any inference of gender identity *disorder* was more to do with the interpretation of gender appropriate play than a causal link with GID. What is interesting about more recent analytic practice that holds far less rigidly to the cross gender/cross sexuality link is that treatment has often moved on without a simultaneous revision of theory, so it is possible to practise without conscious gender or sexual discrimination while thinking from a theoretical foundation based on it.

It is almost as if analysis was prevented from doing what it does best and thinking the unthinkable in relation to gender and sexuality because it was simply too unthinkable to do so.

External challenges

The removal of homosexuality from the list of mental disorders in the United States, and from the classification of criminality in the UK, was a challenge to psychoanalysis. In the UK it accepted that decriminalisation at least put the disorder in the realm of treatment rather than punishment (Ryan, 2008) and offered some support to the 1957 Wolfenden Report (preparatory to the 1967 Sexual Offences Act) recommending decriminalisation. In contrast the American Psychoanalytic Association opposed the removal of homosexuality as a sexual deviation and mental disorder from the DSM III (APA, 1980) as it believed homosexuality to be treatable and therefore disordered. The analytic world seemed confusingly unaware of its own bias. Bieber et al.'s 1962 study of aetiology concluded that male homosexuality was related to over-close mothering and ineffective fathering. Macintosh's 1994 survey of psychoanalysts concluded that they did not hold prejudicial attitudes because they did not believe that homosexuals could and should change orientation; however, remarks such as '*I do not doubt that they both long for or may even engage in homosexual experiences . . . but their heterosexual marriages have endured*' (1994: 1192 italics in original) stood as evidence of successful change. Nevertheless, between 1999 and 2009 the American Psychoanalytic, American Psychiatric and American Psychological Associations had all made public statements on the ineffectiveness and undesirability of reparative therapy.

Changes in psychoanalytic theorising about homosexuality reflected external events. Decriminalisation, declassification, Stonewall, equal pay and equal rights for women – these gathered pace from the 1960s onward. Friedman, who was involved in supporting the DSM III declassification, suggested that Freud's work was influenced by its time and had been generalised without sufficient regard to context. He questioned the bar to gays/lesbians training and practising as analysts as there was insufficient evidence to make 'a necessary relationship between homoerotic feelings or acts and psychopathology of any type' (Friedman et al., 1976: 58).

In 1996 Isay became the first openly gay man in the American Psychoanalytic Association (1996). He retheorised accepted doctrines and opened the door to considerations that homosexuality existed independently of gender disturbance; there was no problem identifying as a man and desiring a man. It was more society's wish to leave gender undisturbed that was the problem. But this view struggled to gain ground. McDougall (1995), investigating (at last) female homosexuality initially linked it with gender as an unconscious wish to belong to both sexes, to continue a phantasy of omnipotent bisexuality that allowed a woman to have her oedipal cake and eat it too. To be a woman and to want a woman was to identify as a man. Bisexuality must give way to a heterosexual resolution which disallowed multiple identifications.

The feminist movement began to impact on psychoanalysis in consideration of the politics of relationships. Chodorow (1978) returned the emphasis to the mother and expanded Mitchell's reading of the oedipal situation as metaphor. Female analysts brought new perspectives to bear on gender and sexuality that were at once radical and conservative. Eichenbaum and Orbach (1983) considered mothers' identifications with their daughters and erotic connections between mothers and daughters as well as sons. Fast emphasised the 'undifferentiated and overinclusive' (1984: 13) early gender experience which required a later adaptation to loss as gender restrictions were revealed – but she treated the limitations as intrinsic and missed reflecting on their culturally bound nature; she also saw their resolution in the reciprocity of a heterosexual relationship, which again required homosexuality to be the repository of unintegrated difference. Brennan took up the inequality of Freud's gender trajectories which could only lead to the conclusion of penis envy, whether understood metaphorically or literally. Gendered 'self containment' (1992: 221) – masculinity and femininity keeping themselves to themselves – was illusory and again left only a resolution of complementarity.

Clinical challenges

New ground was broken by O'Connor and Ryan in 1993 when they critiqued the assumption of heterosexual complementarity as the resolution to gender difference and as the '*necessary* organising principle of desire' (1993: 270 italics in original). They challenged the demarcation line between identification and desire – that it was not possible to identity with and desire the same gender and have a healthy oedipal outcome – because this led inevitably to homosexuality's outcast position. They noted that even feminist theorising was hampered by this single limitation: 'sexual orientation is conflated with gender identity . . . and . . . femininity is collapsed within heterosexuality' (Schwartz 1998: 19). As Miller (1986) had challenged autonomy as the goal of maturity, O'Connor and Ryan challenged heterosexuality as the mature sexual goal. If identification and desire could be released from mutual exclusion it opened the way for homosexuality to be an equally valid developmental outcome – but this could not be done without retheorising the oedipal reliance on precisely this opposition.

Chodorow (1992, 1994) concluded that it was sexuality as a whole rather than homosexuality as a specific that was problematic: the idea of unproblematic identity was the falsehood. To examine deviance without examining norm rather missed the point of trying to examine all the possible components of sexual and gendered identity – anatomy, culture, inter- and intra-psychic constellations.

Benjamin retheorised the relationship between identification and desire. Following Fast's lead she saw identification with the mother as present in both girls and boys in the overinclusive pre-oedipal phase (1995a). However, she reconsidered Fast's solution to this and suggested that the father acted as container for the girl's desire for externality, the outside world, otherness; her identification with him was a healthy identification with her own desire, not a cross-gendered mix-up. Only if the father/other were unavailable would penis envy develop; otherwise, it was met in his welcoming of her phallic desire. Before she turns to him in object love, the girl finds in him subject love (1995b). There was no need for cross gender identification to be renounced; in fact the homoerotic component of identificatory love underpinned heterosexuality and gender. Identification was a necessary result for post-oedipal development, an 'important base of the love of the other' (Benjamin, 1991: 277). This offered a non-pathologising route for same sex desire, and an answer to O'Connor and Ryan's critique.

Benjamin referred to the philosophical zeitgeist which at this point was moving towards postmodernity. Just as the problem of 'woman' had dogged feminism – how to articulate anything meaningful when unifying such a vast constituency – so postmodernism worried at the heels of the single identity. Although not always warmly received by psychoanalysis (Massicotte, 1999), postmodernism has allowed for a recasting of identity that has left room for precisely the sort of deconstruction required to find more meaningful concepts of sexuality and gender.

The Lacanian perspective, as it moved the debate from the biological to the linguistic (Breen, 1993), is an important reference for some postmodern thought. Lacan's concept of phallus as signifier of unfulfilable desire, of the lack found at the core of both masculinity and femininity, attributed to the former the false hope of equating penis with phallus, to the latter the false phantasy of appropriating a penis/phallus through heterosexual desire. As the penis was the image for the phallus it was left to femininity to stand for its absence – yet again constructing the female body ego around the male (Irigary, 1990). Homosexuality was similarly false and additionally narcissistic as it replaced desire for the other with desire for the mirrored self (Lacan, 1949).

The oedipal scenario was thus translated into linguistic form and gender into a symbolic state, theoretically unattached to the body. However, the freedom of thought this could have led to remained hampered by the underpinning attachment of phallus to penis. Gender as a construct remained untouched; the apparent mobility of the signifier in reality seldom moved it, and the cultural heft of the symbol to which it was attached – its phallic weight – seemed invisible. The phallus remained bound to the body (Moi, 2004) and the sexes remained bound to each other. Irigary concluded that, as discourse is already gendered, siting gender in language is not of itself liberating; Lacan stating that the phallus was ungendered did not make it so. It has, however, left room for freer theorising about the meaning of both gender and sexuality. 'Gender needs to be embodied, and sex needs to be symbolised' (Gherovici, 2010: 247) – even if it is never achievable.

It is this unachievability that leads the way in Butler's (1993) engagement with Lacanian and Foucauldian ideas. Butler separated gender from sex and sex from the body – the categories had meaning through tradition and expectation but of themselves consisted entirely in the realm of discourse. Where analysis might read cross gender identification as indicative of pathology, Butler might suggest such a reading revealed the pathology of analysis, or of the society in which analysis was co-created. The forbidden nature of homosexual eroticism (Butler, 1995) led to a foreclosure of desire for the same sex parent which, because it was unacknowledged, converted into identification; in this analysis gender identity was the product of loss, and homophobia a result of unconscious envy – not of the penis, but of the achievement of the foreclosed desire. The more heterosexuality relied on the diminishment of homosexuality the more it was held hostage by it, creating the phantasy of a natural order that then restricted gendered experience. In Butler's perspective gender is a product of heterosexuality, and heterosexuality as it exists is a product not of the body but of the homosexual taboo that denies the body. For Butler there is no elemental 'natural', not even the body, as one cannot stand outside of context and discourse.

By casting identity as a verb rather than a noun – a performance rather than a place – Butler lifts gender identity out of its role as anchor for heterosexuality and leaves both with a capacity to float, unsettling in some ways, but freeing in others. If homosexuality's position was liberated then gender's was too and, by implication, heterosexuality, which came in on gender's coat tails.

Gender as performance facilitated clearer identities. Frosh et al. (2002) noted in interviews with secondary school boys in London that not only were their masculine identities multiply formed by particular combined circumstances of race, class, ethnicity and family – there was no such thing as 'a boy' – they were also multiply expressed depending on circumstances – the sort of boy they were at school was different to the sort of boy they felt themselves to be at home, for example. Each boy was a plural. Yet the ubiquitous fear of a homosexual label cut them off from owning any aspects of masculinity that could be cast as feminine, reinforcing homosexuality as the container of unwanted aspects of gender. Weakness, effeminacy, softness, artistry in men; forthrightness, ambition, ruthlessness in women: all shared the homosexual space. Not only did this crowd the space, it also denied to these and other boys and girls the capacity to be fully themselves without the spectrum of self becoming experienced as part of a disorder.

The element of construction in gendered and sexual identities is set into relief by the anxiety over their transgression. Psychoanalysis perches hawk-like on the fence, ready to swoop down over irregularity as if without constant vigilance, constant repair, the edifice will fall apart. This evidences a lack of faith in precisely that which it purports to believe – the natural beneficence of correct gendered and sexual identities. Yet out of all sorts of family constellations boys and girls are produced with the capacity to experience a knowledge of who they are. Speaking of working with boys raised by single parents and lesbian mothers – configurations psychoanalysis has warned against as particularly risky for raising boys – Corbett has noted 'while I have observed with considerable interest that their masculine subjectivities reflect the relational contours of their families, the degree to which their experience of masculinity links up with that which is considered normal has been remarkably unremarkable' (Corbett, 2009: 79). The individual is both subject to gender and participant in it. Predetermining gender sets up the possibility of not recognising it, and as long as homosexuality is pathologised the straightjacket that ties proper gender to proper sexuality will stay, as will the predestination of gendered fates. Gendered and sexual identities are paradoxically most secure when they are most free.

Meeting the challenges

When gender identity is linked to homosexuality via effeminacy the consideration of how gender identity can be so precarious in the first place is obscured. The narrowness of gender's boundaries contributes to the fragility of its possession. Retheorising gender so that it is not wrapped up with homophobia is a significant psychoanalytic challenge.

If gender is thought of as performance, multiple expressions become possible without being exclusive or contradictory. Butch lesbians can feel both female and masculine; butch heterosexual women likewise. It is the 'density' of experience (D'Ercole, 1996: 147) that gathers it into a sense of personhood; as experience shifts so does identity, stabilised by its very impermanence. Gender is no longer sufficiently categorised as the psychological and cultural delineation of biological sex. Dimen considers it a 'force field' (1991: 335), attracting to itself varying differences and definitions that are too complex to be reduced to biology. With gender no longer a standard performance from a sexed body, and sex no longer heterosexually organised, homosexuality can be part of a successfully gendered self, whatever that is, and equally open to question in terms of its own definitions.

Such fluidity raises anxieties. Postmodernism seems to ask one to exist without certainty, almost without identity, to lose a necessary coherence. Facts, like norms, are in part relational, an expression of context and viewpoint. The heterosexual norm comes in part from numerical certainty. But the numbers count definitions, opportunities, prohibitions, anxieties, confusions, sanctions, political environment and meaning – all the things that surround the end result of object choice – not just the thing itself. This is surely Freud's point, that identity is contingent. To argue simply for a homosexual norm would miss the more fundamental opportunity of re-examining the relationship of psychoanalysis to the 'normal', and therefore to its own position on gender and sexuality as a whole. The need for order, for and against, one or the other, is as Lévi-Strauss (1963) noted, a human tendency. Where might deconstruction end? What chaos might it lead to? Difference needs articulation (Maguire and Dewing, 2007) and postmodernism can seem to attempt a deconstruction that takes it beyond the liveable. How much this is the case, though, depends rather on how liveable life has been previously. The compromises made by those on the outside to gain some place on the inside – without which the world becomes an object of hatred rather than love, which is even less liveable (Nevins, 2008) – are rendered invisible by the cloak of tolerance and acceptance. Gay men and lesbians have long made the adjustments required to belong to the world while having no real place in it. Psychoanalysis has shielded itself in Izzard's 'vacuum' of the consulting room (2002: 11). The emphasis on privacy, individuality and internality has allowed analysis to theorise as if it is untouched by context, whereas 'Citizenship, class, ownership, wealth and debt, gender community, the social relations between men and women, ethnicity and race, forms of power and so on – all these features of the social world are found *in* the Oedipus complex' (Brenkman, 1993: 245 italics in original).

Guss questions the psychoanalytic transference to homosexuality: 'It is interesting to note that a field that conceives of psychic states as multiply determined will find a need for bedrock, and that rock is found in bed' (2008: 364). If psychoanalytic control of homosexuality is in compensation for the instability of heterosexuality, then the subsequent political and social deregulation of desire must cause resistance and anxiety in the field. Non-pathologised gay and lesbian identities are challenges to gender whether or not they want to be.

Breaking the chain

Breaking the link between gender and sexual identity has brought forth some rich theoretical veins from gay and lesbian analysts and therapists in particular. Different pictures of identity have emerged, such as Harris's notion of 'softly assembled' foundations (2009: 160), or Drescher's 'mosaic' (1996: 175), moving away from Kinsey's spectrum with its unconnected ends. The energy for taking this forward comes predominantly from the gay/lesbian and feminist communities, who are extending the theorising to heterosexuality too. For example Drescher reflects on the emphasis placed on receptivity as a gay male trait and how it belies the activity involved in 'reception' (something that Freud sensed from the beginning) while consigning receptivity in heterosexual men to an anxiety-ridden place of homosexuality/castration. Again following Freud, Drescher (1998) urges a move away from aetiology, which has been an analytic preoccupation with homosexuality, towards meaning – what does it mean to live as a gay- or lesbian-identified person in the world? How is that negotiated, and with what consequences in the psyche? One might ask the same for living heterosexual lives – how is that psychically negotiated, with the repudiation of aspects of the gendered self, the projection into otherness, it requires? Are heterosexual models of partnership idealised? Is 'promiscuous' gay male sex a viable alternative or a striving for paternal recognition denied by parental rejection? Or both? Slowly the agendas for working with gay and lesbian clients are becoming visible, finding their way out of the analytic closet. By and large they do not contain worries about gender identity. In fact an acceptance of gender confusion is a positive starting point, as a gay patient says: 'You know, the more I stop trying not to be a girl, the easier it is for me to be a boy. Whatever in the hell that is' (Corbett, 1996: 460).

This brings challenges to psychoanalysis. Much of the new theorising is finding its home outside the more traditional analytic institutes. They do not wait for, nor are particularly interested in, the institutional hierarchies that are so much a part of the history of psychoanalysis in Europe. The pragmatism of the American approach has driven change more powerfully and more swiftly than the more orthodox allegiances of European institutions have allowed. On a smaller scale a similar pattern can be seen in the United Kingdom, where analytic institutions are still not leading in the development of theory in the field. As the domination of evidence-based practice in the NHS has forced an acceptance of the necessity of analytic engagement with research, so the equality agenda has the potential to force psychoanalysis into rethinking its theory into a position of equality on sexuality and gender. As Lewis made clear in 1995 the shift in attitude up till that point had neither resulted in nor stemmed from a real shift in theory: 'The analytic community has adopted this new point of view, but it has not yet adequately examined how consistent such new ideas are with the general body of analytic theory' (Lewes, 1995: xlv). Psychoanalytic theory continues to remain at risk of becoming simply irrelevant in this field unless it recognises what is now required of it. What then is to be done with oedipus?

One option is to consider that, while contextually relevant at origin, oedipal theory is simply no longer viable or valuable as an account of gendered and sexual identities and can be left behind without loss to the progress or heart of psychoanalytic thinking. If gender and sexuality are linked through the opposition of identification and desire, embedding the impossibility of a non-pathological view of homosexuality into the fabric of the oedipal resolution, then there is no reasonable way forward from there. Salvage attempts cannot escape from the consequences of this basic flaw, and it is best left behind as new pathways are forged that are responsive to today's contexts and understandings. Alternatively, it can be considered that the underlying oedipal framework is robust and can be expanded from within to account for homosexuality alongside heterosexuality as a normal, or at least equally pathological, developmental outcome. The oedipal scaffold of drive and aim, identification and object choice, hosts as many homosexual as heterosexual outcomes (Lewes, 1995) and structurally need not be homophobic. Or again, it can be seen that oedipal theory includes crucial developmental points that remain valid, and gender and sexual identity can be stripped out while retaining these important aspects. Freud was continually reworking his ideas on sexuality and there is capacity to continue working on them today. The oedipal movement from a dyadic to a triadic relationship as a negotiation of otherness is just as relevant without gender demarcations; the mark of oedipal phantasies on future relationships may mark the nature of intimacy without affecting the nature of gender or sexuality.

Underlying these options is a broader reconsideration of the ontology of psychoanalysis, its method for conferring authority on knowledge and its own position in that process. Much of the new thinking about gender and sexuality has drawn on phenomenological approaches, perhaps from a need to address that space between theory and speculation and to re-assert the legitimacy of experience in the face of interpretive dominance. From this perspective there is an analytic redress required that cedes authority back to the patient, and this challenges the nature of the relationship assumed between analyst and analysand – an added complication to retheorising oedipus.

Conclusion

To find a home for homosexuality in psychoanalysis requires something further than just hunching up on the sofa to make room for one more.

O'Connor and Ryan suggest that the compulsory heterosexuality of the oedipus complex, on which so much of this rests, is itself an imperialistic visitation of a universalist approach, and that 'a psychoanalytic position which allows for different and more diverse views of homosexuality would involve a rethinking of the status of the Oedipus complex within that theory' (1993: 268). Analysis has instead kept its back to the wall, 'still frightened that a homosexual attack will rob it of its masculine potency' (Barden, 2010: 100) – whereas in a parody of such fears it has in fact tied its potency up in the oedipal apron strings. The most liberating current theorising for both sexuality and gender takes place not only where homosexuality is normalised but also when the notion of normality is scrutinised. The point is not to rehabilitate homosexuality but to think about the analytic space that has been built for gender and sexuality and to grasp its points of discomfiture for both. The mainstream UK field tends not to stray far beyond the middling compassion that Denman (1993) criticises as condescending; in the USA there is often more vocal passion at each extreme. In a way the motivation of self interest is inevitable; one cannot think from a position one does not inhabit, even if one can think about it, and homosexuality must fight its own corner as long as it is pushed in to it. But restricted gender experience is a price that everyone pays for the current position. While the payment is made less painful by devaluing the currency, the diet remains poor.

Through the oedipal metaphor Freud spoke to a negotiation of universal themes of human development: power, desire, fear, growth, gain, loss. Although Freud's theorising came through the media of sex and gender it is clear that these are not required for oedipal relevance. Core oedipal concepts have since been elaborated either without reference to them or in a refreshed frame of reference that undoes the conflation of sexuality with gender. This has enlivened the oedipal debate and brought new ways of thinking and practising. But the legacy arguably remains to be dealt with as complementarity remains a gendered and sexual expectation in much of psychoanalysis whether housed in the body or the mind. The freeing of oedipal developments from the ties of sex and gender has not resulted, for the most part, in the freeing of sex and gender from oedipal complementarity. In that sense mainstream psychoanalysis does no worse than the rest of society, but it is curious that it is slow in meeting the challenge to do better.

The question of the Sphinx will always remain: what are we, and how do we inhabit the span of human life? Freud's answer in Oedipus is theoretical, not sacred, and psychoanalysis can only benefit from engaging itself with the divisions and dilemmas that homosexuality has brought to it. Freud established a good tradition of disruption; it would be a shame to lose it.

References

APA (American Psychiatric Association) (1980) *Diagnostic and Statistical Manual of Mental Disorders (DSM III)* (3rd ed.). Washington DC: American Psychiatric Association.

Bagemihl, B. (1999) *Biological Exuberance: Animal Homosexuality and Natural Diversity.* London: Profile Books.

Barden, N. (2010) *Divided Selves: Psychoanalytic Conceptualisations of Sexuality and Gender.* University of Leicester: Department of Lifelong Learning Vaughan Paper 45.

Benjamin, J. (1991) Father and Daughter: Identification with Difference – A Contribution to Gender Heterodoxy. *Psychoanalytic Dialogues*, 1: 277–299.

Benjamin, J. (1995a) Sameness and Difference: Toward an 'Overinclusive' Model of Gender Development. *Psychoanalytic Inquiry*, 15: 125–142.

Benjamin, J. (1995b) *Like Subjects, Love Objects: Essays on Recognition and Sexual Difference.* New Haven, CT and London: Yale University Press.

Bieber, I., Dain, H.J., Dince, P.R., Drellich, M., Grand, H., Grundlach, R., Kremer, M., Rifkin, A., Wilbur, C. and Beiber, T. (1962) *Homosexuality: A Psychoanalytic Study of Male Homosexuals.* New York: Basic Books.

Blechner, M.J. (1995) The Shaping of Psychoanalytic Theory and Practice by Cultural and Personal Biases about Sexuality, in T. Domenici and R.C. Lesser (eds.) *Disorienting Sexuality: Psychoanalytic Reappraisals of Sexual Identities.* London: Routledge.

Breen, D. (ed.) (1993) *The Gender Conundrum: Contemporary Psychoanalytic Perspectives on Femininity and Masculinity.* London: Routledge.

Brenkman, J. (1993) *Straight Male Modern: A Cultural Critique of Psychoanalysis.* New York and London: Routledge.

Brennan, T. (1992) *The Interpretation of the Flesh: Freud and Femininity.* New York and London: Routledge.

Butler, J. (1990) *Gender Trouble: Feminism and the Subversion of Identity.* New York and London: Routledge.

Butler, J. (1993) *Bodies that Matter: On the Discursive Limits of Sex*. New York and London: Routledge.

Butler, J. (1995) Melancholy Gender: Refused Identification. *Psychoanalytic Dialogues*, 5: 165–180.

Coates, S.W. and Wolfe, S.M. (1995) Gender and Identity Disorder in Boys: The Interface of Constitution and Early Experience. *Psychoanalytic Inquiry*, 15: 6–38.

Chodorow, N. (1978) *The Reproduction of Mothering: Psychoanalysis and the Sociology of Gender*. Berkeley: University of California Press.

Chodorow, N. (1992) Heterosexuality as a Compromise Formation: Reflections on the Psychoanalytic Theory of Sexual Development. *Psychoanalytic Contemporary Thought*, 15: 267–304.

Chodorow, N. (1994) *Femininities, Masculinities, Sexualities*. London: Free Association Books.

Corbett, K. (1996) Homosexual Boyhood: Notes on Girlyboys. *Gender and Psychoanalysis*, 1: 429–461.

Corbett, K. (2009) *Boyhoods: Rethinking Masculinities*. New Haven, CT, and London: Yale University Press.

D'Ercole, A. (1996) Postmodern Ideas about Gender and Sexuality: The Lesbian Woman Redundancy. *Psychoanalysis and Psychotherapy*, 13: 142–152.

Denman, C. (1993) Prejudice and Homosexuality. *British Journal of Psychotherapy*, 9 (3): 436–358.

Deutsch, H. (1925) The Psychology of Women in Relation to the Functions of Reproduction. *International Journal of Psychoanalysis*, 6: 405–418.

Deutsch, H. (1930) The Significance of Masochism in the Mental Life of Women. *International Journal of Psychoanalysis*, 11: 48–60.

Deutsch, H. (1932) On Female Homosexuality. *Psychoanalytic Quarterly*, 1: 484–510.

Dimen, M. (1991) Deconstructing Difference: Gender, Splitting and Transitional Space. *Psychoanalytic Dialogues*, 1: 335–352.

Dinnerstein, D. (1976) *The Mermaid and the Minotaur: Sexual Arrangements and the Human Malaise*. New York: Harper and Row.

Downey, J.I. and Friedman, R. (1998) Female Homosexuality: Classical Psychoanalytic Theory Reconsidered. *Journal of the American Psychoanalytic Association*, 46: 471–506.

Drescher, J. (1996) Across the Great Divide: Gender Panic in the Analytic Dyad. *Psychoanalysis and Psychotherapy*, 13: 174–186.

Drescher, J. (1998) *Psychoanalytic Psychotherapy and the Gay Man*. Hillsdale, NJ: The Analytic Press.

Eichenbaum, L. and Orbach, S. (1983) *Understanding Women*. Harmondsworth: Penguin.

Ellis, H. (1900) *Studies in the Psychology of Sex*. New York: Random House.

Fast, I. (1984) *Gender Identity: A Differentiation Model*. Hillsdale, NJ: The Analytic Press.

Ferenczi, S. ([1938] 1989) *Thalassa: A Theory of Genitality*. London: Karnac.

Freud, S. ([1905a] 2001) Psychical (or Mental) Treatment, in J. Strachey (ed.) *The Standard Edition of the Complete Psychological Works of Sigmund Freud* Vol. VII. London: Vintage, Hogarth Press and the Institute of Psychoanalysis.

Freud, S. ([1905b] 1953) Three Essays on the Theory of Sexuality, in J. Strachey (ed.) *The Standard Edition of the Complete Psychological Works of Sigmund Freud* Vol. VII. London: Hogarth Press and the Institute of Psychoanalysis.

Freud, S. ([1937] 1964) Analysis Terminable and Interminable, in J. Strachey (ed.) *The Standard Edition of the Complete Psychological Works of Sigmund Freud* Vol. XXIII. London: Hogarth Press and the Institute of Psychoanalysis.

Friedman, R.C., Green, R. and Spitzer, R.L. (1976) Reassessment of Homosexuality and Transsexualism. *Annual Review of Medicine*, 27: 57–62.

Frosh, S., Phoenix, A. and Pattman, R. (2002) *Young Masculinities: Understanding Boys in Contemporary Society*. Basingstoke: Palgrave.

Gershman, H. (1970) The Role of Core Gender Identity in the Analysis of the Perversions. *American Journal of Psychoanalysis*, 30: 58–67.

Gherovici, P. (2010) *Please Select Your Gender: From the Invention of Hysteria to the Democratizing of Transgender*. New York and Hove: Routledge.

Guss, J.R. (2008) in D.F. Glazer, J.R. Guss, A. D'Ercole and S. Masters, Homosexuality and Psychoanalysis III: Clinical Perspectives. *Journal of Gay and Lesbian Mental Health*, 12 (4): 355–379.

Harris, A. (2009) *Gender as Soft Assembly*. New York and London: Routledge.

Horney, K. (1926) The Flight from Womanhood: The Masculinity-complex in Women, as Viewed by Men and Women. *International Journal of Psychoanalysis*, 7: 324–339.

Irigary, L. (1990) The Sex Which Is Not One, in C. Zanardi (ed.) *Essential Papers on the Psychology of Women*. New York: New York University Press.

Isay, R.A. (1996) *Becoming Gay: The Journey to Self-Acceptance*. New York: Pantheon Books.

Izzard, S. (2001) Creating Space: Women without Children. In S. Izzard and N. Barden (eds.) *Rethinking Gender and Therapy*. Buckingham: Open University Press.

Izzard, S. (2002) Deconstructing Oedipus. *European Journal of Psychotherapy, Counselling and Health*, 5 (1): 1–12.

Jacobi, J. (1969) A Case of Homosexuality. *Journal of Analytical Psychology*, 14: 48–64.

Kaftal, E. (1991) On Intimacy between Men. *Psychoanalytic Dialogues*, 1: 305–328.

Karlen, A. (1971) *Sexuality and Homosexuality: A New View*. New York: W.W. Norton & Co., in G.H. Weideman (1974) Homosexuality, a Survey. *Journal of the American Psychoanalytic Association*, 22: 651–696.

Klein. M. (1945) The Oedipus Complex in the Light of Early Anxieties. *International Journal of Psychoanalysis*, 26: 11–33.

Krafft-Ebing, R.F. von ([1886] 1965) *Psychopathia Sexualis*. New York: Stein and Day.

Lacan, J. (1949) The Mirror Stage as Formative of the Function of the I as Revealed in Psychoanalytic Experience, in D. Birksted-Breen, S. Flanders and A. Gibeault, (eds.) (2010) *Reading French Psychoanalysis*. London: Routledge.

Lévi-Strauss, C. (1963) *Structural Anthropology*. New York: Basic Books.

Lewes, K. (1995) *Psychoanalysis and Male Homosexuality*. Northvale, NJ, and London: Jason Aronson Inc.

Macintosh, H. (1994) Attitudes and Experiences of Psychoanalysts in Analyzing Homosexual Patients. *Journal of the American Psychoanalytic Association*, 42: 1183–1205.

Maguire, M. and Dewing, H. (2007) New Psychoanalytic Theories of Female and Male Femininity: The Oedipus Complex, Language and Gender Embodiment. *British Journal of Psychotherapy*, 23 (4): 531–545.

Massicotte, W.J. (1999) Psychoanalysis, Science, and Postmodernism. *Journal of the American Psychoanalytic Association*, 47: 544–547.

McCloskey, D. (1999) *Crossing: A Memoir*. Chicago and London: University of Chicago Press.

McDougall, J. (1995) *The Many Faces of Eros: A Psychoanalytic Exploration of Human Sexuality*. New York and London: W.W. Norton.

Mendoza, S. (2007) Adversity and Perversity. *British Journal of Psychotherapy*, 23 (3): 329–341.

Miller, J.B. (1986) *Towards a New Psychology of Women* (2nd ed.). London: Penguin.

Mitchell. J. (1971) *Woman's Estate*. Harmondsworth: Penguin.

Mitchell, J. (1990) *Psychoanalysis and Feminism*. London: Penguin.

Moi, T. (2004) From Femininity to Finitude: Freud, Lacan and Feminism, Again, in I. Matthis (ed.) *Dialogues on Sexuality, Gender and Psychoanalysis*. London: Karnac.

Money, J. and Ehrhardt, A.A. (1972) *Man and Woman, Boy and Girl: The Differentiation and Dimorphism of Gender Identity from Conception to Maturity*. Baltimore, MD: Johns Hopkins University Press.

Nevins, P. (2008) How *Not* to be a Happy Homosexual. *Sitegeist: a Journal of Psychoanalysis and Philosophy*, 1: 45–57.

O'Connor, N. and Ryan, J. (1993) *Wild Desires and Mistaken Identities: Lesbianism and Psychoanalysis*. London: Virago.

Quinton, A. (1972) Freud and Philosophy, in J. Miller (ed.) *Freud: The Man, His World, His Influence*. London: Weidenfeld and Nicolson.

Raphael-Leff, J. (2001) Emotional Experiences of Becoming a Mother, in S. Izzard and N. Barden (eds.) *Rethinking Gender and Therapy*. Buckingham: Open University Press.

Ratigan, B. (2010) Second Forward, in N. Barden, *Divided Selves: Psychoanalytic Conceptualisations of Sexuality and Gender*. University of Leicester: Department of Lifelong Learning Vaughan Paper 45.

Riviere, J. (1929) Womanliness as Masquerade. *International Journal of Psychoanalysis*, 10: 303–313.

Ryan, J. (2008) The Privacy of the Bedroom? Fifty Years on from the Wolfenden Report Reforms. *Sitegeist: A Journal of Psychoanalysis and Philosophy*, 1: 13–27.

Samuels, A., Shorter, B. and Plaut, F. (eds.) (1986) *A Critical Dictionary of Jungian Analysis*. London: Routledge and Kegan Paul.

Sandler, A.M. (2006) Commentary on Friedman, in P. Fonagy, R. Krause and M. Leuzinger-Bohleber (eds.) *Identity, Gender and Sexuality: 150 Years after Freud*. London: International Psychoanalytical Association.

Schwartz, A.E. (1988) *Sexual Subjects: Lesbians, Gender and Psychoanalysis*. New York and London: Routledge.

Spry, J. (1997) *Orlando's Sleep: An Autobiography of Gender*. Norwich, VT: New Victoria.

Stoller, R. (1975) *The Transsexual Experiment*. London: Hogarth Press.

Stoller, R. (1985) *Presentations of Gender*. New York and London: Yale University Press.

Ulrichs, K. ([1864] 2001) *The Riddle of 'Man-Manly' Love*, in J. Drescher (ed.) *Psychoanalytic Therapy and the Gay Man*. Hillsdale, NJ: The Analytic Press.

Wehr, D.S. (1988) *Jung and Feminism: Liberating Archetypes*. London: Routledge.

Whyte, L.L. (1979) *The Unconscious before Freud*. London: Julian Friedmann.

Winnicott, D.W. (1964) *The Child, the Family and the Outside World*. London: Penguin.

Zucker, K.J. and Lawrence, A.A. (2009) Epidemiology of Gender Identity Disorder: Recommendations for the *Standards of Care* of the World Professional Association for Transgender Health. *International Journal of Transgenderism*, 11: 8–18.

Acknowledgements

Bernard Ratigan, a man who knows a great deal about Freud and wisdom.

Chapter 5

No maps for uncharted lands

What does gender expression have to do with sexual orientation?

Vittorio Lingiardi[1]

> None of us want to be in calm waters all our lives.
>
> (Jane Austen, *Persuasion*)

Our sexualities and genders are developmental and relational constructions: simultaneously biological and social, inventive and defensive. They result from genetic and hormonal predispositions, family expectations and social pressures, conflicts and defences, fantasies, identifications and counteridentifications, projections and introjections. They arise from the incessant attempt to come to terms with one's own pleasures, anxieties, identities and compromising solutions. Does the orientation of our *sexuality* have to do with the construction and expression of our *gender*? The multiplicity of meanings contained in those two embodied concepts is a definite obstacle for a full understanding of the relationship that unites and separates them.

So, the *first* answer should be no – everybody knows that gender expression and sexual orientation are two independent dimensions. Rather, for a long time, psychoanalytic theorisation about homosexuality has overlapped male homosexuality with 'femininity' and female homosexuality with 'masculinity'. This overlapping, based on a binary and stereotyped idea of 'masculine' and 'feminine', has nevertheless delayed the theorisation both on gender and sexual. Homosexual men, for example, have been thought of as 'failed women', a sort of 'sub-gender', losing the inevitable weave of their sexualities, cultures and personal styles. Instead of using 'homosexuality' as a way of de-binarising gender categories, also revealing the inadequacy of the category of 'heterosexuality', it has been used as a way for confirming gender binarism (Lingiardi, 2007). Rather than exploring the experience of homosexuals to broaden the categories of gender, psychoanalysts 'have restricted the possibilities of gender to the conventional heterosexual masculine/feminine binary' (Corbett, 1993: 346).

The *second* answer should be yes, and in any case – homosexuals or heterosexuals. The relationship between gender and sexual orientation is a topic too often approached in a polarised way; we should be able to understand it with a more dialectical attitude. They cannot overlap completely or be separated categorically, and they cannot be read wearing only one type of glasses: biological, psychological or social. 'The challenge is neither to essentialize gender nor to dematerialize it' (Dimen and Goldner, 2012: 135).

Sexual orientation and gender are not connected in a forced and predictable way. Personal histories and cultural inscriptions influence the gender shadows by which the individual expresses her/his desires. We know that there is no gender that is 'expressed' by actions, gestures, or speech. Rather, its performance was precisely that which retroactively produces the illusion that there was an inner gender core (Butler, 1990, 1999). So, when thinking about gender, we cannot make reference to a template. Gender is something we do rather than something we are. Even the idea of a 'natural body', pre-existent to its discursive productions and cultural inscriptions, is illusory. Gender can be culturally forced, but it is also individually shaped and personally interpreted. Why do some people appear more *gendery* (Sedgwick, 1990) than others?

Homosexuality has so many different shapes that trying to hold them together in a comprehensive theory succeeds only at the cost of a grave distortion of the differences which exist between homosexual individuals: 'an act that could in the extreme constitute "intellectual genocide"' (Bollas, 1992: 152).

While aware that categorisation runs the risk of flattening the sexual discourse, I'll try to reflect on the various combinations between sexual orientation and gender expressions. I will stress my attention on male homosexuality because I am more familiar with the male side of this story. This and other topics will be mainly discussed from the perspectives of clinical psychoanalysis. Addressing the uncertain findings from empirical research in this field is beyond the scope of this article.[2]

Finally, the hypothesis that '*gender is a kind of imitation for which there is no original*', an 'imitation that produces the very notion of the original as an *effect* and consequence of the imitation itself' (Butler, 1991: 21, italics in the original) will challenge my reflections.

All that masculinity refuses

1   [My father] loved power tools and guns, old Cadillacs, pickup trucks, and campers. I didn't. He liked to build houses, hunt deer, and tinker with engines, and he would have enjoyed having me working and playing at his side, but while he was out in the shop painting, plumbing or rewiring, I was lying on the living room floor, listening on the radio to Milton Cross narrate Texaco's 'Saturday morning at the Opera'.

2   I grew up in the projects with a small group of friends, and we spent all of our time thinking, talking, and playing sports . . . [My father] taught me how to throw a curve, and he often got us bleacher seats for Red Sox games at Fenway Park. These games were the most exciting part of my youth . . . I felt I belonged in the game. It was as if somebody had injected baseball into my veins, and from then on it was always in my blood.

If a random sample of readers read these two autobiographical extracts (in Le Vay, 2011: 82–83) – both belonging to two gay adults – they would probably ascribe the first one to a gay man and the second one to a straight man (these ascriptions would be more likely twenty years ago than today as gays are generally perceived as more *masculine*). Because of the strong socio-cultural dissonance, the further a behaviour is from traditional gender roles, or better, the closer it is to the female dimension in the boy and to the male dimension in the girl, the more it is considered pathological in the eyes of all. However, cross-gender attitudes in feminine boys were less acceptable than in masculine girls (Bergling, 2001; Blakemore and Hill, 2008; Freeman, 2007; Kane, 2006; McDermott and Schwartz, 2013).

Freud (1910) describes Leonardo da Vinci's homosexuality saying that he has been 'robbed of a part of his masculinity' and left 'to play the part of women'. Sixty years later, Charles Socarides (1968, 1989) attributed male homosexuality to 'a lifelong persistence of the original primary feminine identification with the mother, and a consequent sense of deficiency in one's masculine identity'. Reflecting on women striving after the possession of a male genital (envy of the penis) and men's struggle against their passive or feminine attitude towards other men (masculine protest), Freud observes (1937):

> We often have the impression that with the wish for a penis and the masculine protest, we have penetrated through all the psychological strata and have reached bedrock, and thus our activities are at an end. This is probably true, since, for the psychical field, the biological field does in fact play the part of the underlying bedrock. The repudiation of femininity can be nothing else than a biological fact, a part of the great riddle of sex.
>
> (p. 252)

He adds that they look different but are connected: 'Some factor common to both sexes is forced, by the difference between them, to express itself differently in the one and in the other'. The 'factor common to both sexes' is the 'repudiation of femininity'.

The discovery that women do not have a penis affects the two sexes differently, explaining the difference between them. Therefore, the fear of lack and the trauma of lack become the founding moment of, respectively, male and female gender identity.

Freud's idealisation of phallic activity[3] not only made femininity an emerging category from the negative (*all that masculinity refuses*), 'but also delayed a theorization of masculinity in all its specificity and multiplicity' (Dimen and Goldner, 2012: 137). Any maleness that doesn't 'measure up' jumps the gender binary, becoming 'effeminacy' – a degraded varietal of femaleness. Hence, understanding homosexuality as a challenge to the heteronormative binary categorisation male/female is too shallow. How does a homosexual man experience his gender?

Rather than draw upon the homosexual's experience to open up the categories of gender, Freud removes the homosexual male from the realm of masculinity and recasts him as counterfeit woman following the equation: male homosexuality = passivity = femininity (Corbett, 1993). According to Freud, 'it is not for psychoanalysis to solve the problem of homosexuality' (1920: 171). But the issue here is not only unsolved, it is 'displaced'.

The adhesion of the 'traditional' male homosexual to a feminised gender expression has been interpreted using cultural, environmental, psychological, genetic and temperamental factors, in a circle (between virtuous or vicious) between heteronormative expectations and spontaneous imitation, in an oscillatory game of request ('be a woman') and adhesion ('I am a woman') (Herek, 2002).

The last decades of historical, philosophical, psychoanalytic, literary, social deconstruction of genders have relaxed their binary constraints, helping to break stereotypes and prejudices that conditioned the relationship between homosexualities and genders, and thus widening the multiple dimensions of gender.

Most of the gay people I know (friends, colleagues, patients) describe their experience of gender, past and present, as 'mixed', even when they identify themselves as 'males'. They relate it to the impossibility of polarised masculinity and femininity to catch all the 'remains of gender' of the homosexualities.

Tomboys and girlyboys

I remember the first time it dawned on me that I might be a homosexual. I was around the age of ten and had succeeded in avoiding the weekly soccer practice in my elementary school. [. . .] That lucky afternoon, I found myself sequestered with the girls, who habitually spent that time period doing sewing, knitting, and other appropriately feminine things. [. . .] Then a girl sitting next to me looked at me with a mixture of curiosity and disgust. 'Why aren't you out with the boys playing football?' she asked. 'Because I hate it', I replied. 'Are you sure you're not really a girl under there?', she asked with the suspicion of a sneer. 'Yeah, of course', I replied, stung, and somewhat shaken. It was the first time the fundamental homosexual dilemma had been put to me so starkly. It resonated so much with my own internal fears that I remember it vividly two decades later. Before then, most of what I now see as homosexual emotions had not been forced into one or the other gender category. I didn't feel as a boy or a girl; I felt as me.

(Andrew Sullivan, *Virtually Normal*)

Mickäel was a ten-year-old girl with short hair, shorts and sneakers. (S)he is very good at football. During the summer holidays, (s)he moves with her family to a new neighbourhood where (s)he makes friends with other children and, especially, winds her/his way into Lisa's heart, her contemporary. But the 'real' name of Mickäel is Laure, a female name. The 'deception', staged with her sister's help, is soon discovered by their mother, who forces Mickäel/Laure to be dressed as a female when with her friends. Mickäel cannot 'pretend' to be herself. Mickäel must be Laure and appear like her. This is the story of the protagonist of *Tomboy*, a film of 2011 by Céline Sciamma, winner of the Teddy Award at the Berlin Film Festival.

Deliberately, the director asks questions she leaves unanswered. She provides no explanation of Mickäel/Laure's behaviour, nor tells us what will happen to her/him. A young gender-outsider, a 'tomboy', as in the title of the film? A prelude to a future transgender? Or a young explorer in search of models that help her to organise the signs of a homosexual orientation in a rigidly heteronormed context?

Teens struggling with the discovery of sexuality are always concerned about the complicated interplay between gender identity and sexual orientation (Rivers and Barnett, 2011/2013). A compulsory gender binary often casts some boys/girls in the realm of 'gender nonconformity', obscuring the possibility of reading 'mixed gender feelings' that a gay patient describes as follows:

> I know that my father wanted me to be a man, and I knew that I was not being a man like him. I was not being a woman, but I was not being a man within his definition of it.
>
> (Corbett, 1999: 121)

Many homosexual adults recall growing up with an internal feeling of being sexually different or with behaviours and interests that are discrepant from those of their peers (Cohen and Savin-Williams, 2012). Two of the neologisms coined to designate them, *girlyboys* (Corbett, 1999) and *tomboys* (Craig and Lacroix, 2011; Harris, 1991, 2005), make me think about the aspects, both indecipherable and self-evident, of the developmental trajectories that are waiting for them on the border of gender/sexual orientation. And at the patient rhythm of indifference, observation, decoding and support that caregivers, or eventually psychologists, must be able to sustain moving between dimensions of gender dysphoria (Cohen-Kettenis and Pfäfflin, 2003; Drescher and Byne, 2012; Saketopoulou, 2014; Wallien and Cohen-Kettenis, 2008), atypical gender identity organisation (Di Ceglie, 1998, 2013; Wilson, Griffin and Wren, 2005) or more simply of gender nonconformity or variance (American Psychiatric Association, 2013; Drescher, Cohen-Kettenis and Winter, 2012; Levounis, Drescher and Barber, 2012; Mathy and Drescher, 2009).

Ludovic. I borrowed this pseudonym from the young hero of Alain Berliner's film *Ma Vie en Rose* (1997). When we first met, Ludovic was 22 years old and having difficulty with his male gender role. He was still suffering from the gender confusion he first had in childhood, when he wanted to wear his mother's skirt to school. At the start of his analysis with me he used some painful and inefficient strategies to deal with his inner tangle: *bodily,* he has dysmorphophobia that has led him to undergo a series of small surgeries; *romantically,* he has been having nearly passionless heterosexual relationships; and as far as his *desires* are concerned, he was afraid of turning into a ridiculous outsider. He has failed identifications with his father; a secret and private idealisation with his mother; and he feels deep shame at not meeting other people's expectations. He has post-traumatic memories of being insulted and beaten by his classmates. It is not my intention to trace the whole course of Ludovic's analysis (see Lingiardi, 2007), but I'd like to briefly mention one of its crucial moments. Unable to stand the tension between feminine and homosexual and still unable to find a space – psychically and relationally – where he could develop his own personal take on the passive aspect of masculinity, Ludovic suffered the pain of rejection from every recognised category, and this slowly drove him toward the only world that would have him: the world of self-hatred, with all its narcissism and destructiveness. The arc of his gender identity can be traced roughly like this: gender non conformity ⇔ interest in passivity ⇔ equation homosexuality-femininity ⇔ social stigmatisation ⇔ shame and anger ⇔ refusal of homosexuality ⇔ (internalised) homophobia ⇔ misogyny.

In the analytical dialogue with Ludovic, the psychic issue was not gender *per se*, but how rigidly and concretely it was being used in an individual mind or family context. The question was whether he experienced himself as personally investing gender with meaning or whether gender was a meaning happening to Ludovic.

We often see *nonconforming gender* behaviour in a child facing his homosexual attraction and forced to conform simultaneously to social gender rules and to his parents' heterosexual expectations (Drescher, 1998). And I would add that having experienced nonconformity in gender identification and in the objects of romantic or affective fantasies softens the pre-existing borders of the gender dichotomy and leaves him open to mixed resolutions. The attachment context will determine whether this greater fluidity leads to the construction of positive or punitive solutions. Experiences of secrecy and outsider identity will be inevitable, and they will inevitably be traumatic regardless of attachment context.

> *When I was ten* – Ludovic recalls – *my feelings couldn't be classified according to gender: they didn't match those of my male classmates or my female classmates . . . When I was with other kids I was stuck in a paradox – I felt both included and rejected.*

Ludovic learned that male and female have to unite and in order to unite they must be in opposition. Male–male attraction, which is contradictory and not permitted by social norms, becomes an anomaly that cries out for a feminine polarity to bring the two universes back to stability and cast aside the multiple solutions (male–female, male–male, female–female) offered by Plato.[4]

The same process that superimposes the male homosexual with the female gender, and the female homosexual with the male gender, is at work in the psychology of the child *and* in the psychology of the social fabric. Male and female are the social containers that Ludovic has to deal with. Activity is masculine, passivity is feminine. The child Ludovic asks the same question that Freud asked; he viewed the homosexual person's gender experience as a kind of crisis category and asked: to what gender can we assign these mysterious individuals? (Corbett, 1999).

At the start of the analysis, his life precisely mirrored his relational conflicts: *secretly homosexual, but homophobic; heterosexual in public, but a misogynist.* And this split destroys any possibility of change, any search for his own idiomatic outcome.

This is the first dream that Ludovic told me.

> *I'm at the zoo with my parents and my sister. A violent thunderstorm breaks. We have to run to our camper for safety, but my father says that the animals also have to be carried to safety. I begin running; I'm very scared. While my sister is collecting two turtles, I notice three soaking-wet puppies and I run to get them. I hear my father saying: 'Three is too many, leave one behind!' His voice is threatening. I don't know which puppy to sacrifice. I leave the middle one on the ground, the spotted one, and I see the water slowly carrying it off. It drowns.*

Ludovic says that this dream reminds him of the *Final Judgement*. I call it the *Noah's Ark dream* because it touches on the normative principle that generally conditions the way we talk about sex: things go together two by two. Obviously there are a million ways to read this dream (the passage from two to three immediately recalls Oedipus; the concepts of emergency and sacrifice, etc.), but what strikes me about Ludovic's associations is the impossibility of saving the third one; Ludovic interiorised the obligation to make an agonising choice between only two options: *tertium non datur*.

There are many systems of psychoanalysis, even if sometimes they have spoken with one voice (Lingiardi and Capozzi, 2004). Those that do not want to be confused with the heteronormative moral and formulate commandments and curses now take on multiple and relational perspectives (Caviglia and Lingiardi, 2014; Lingiardi and Federici, 2014). As a consequence, they are becoming increasingly aware that each of us constructs our own gender identity and recognises the two big differences of human life – adults/children and males/females – with their transition from dual to triangular relationships, following highly variable combinations.

As psychoanalysts, we will be working more and more often in a space that is wildly crowded with new identities and visions replacing, adding to, and interacting with the traditional ones.

We're not obliged to bring the opposites together: we can simply accept them as they are . . . and often we have no other choice. Refusing forced binaries doesn't mean defending the grey area equidistant from the two extremes, nor does it mean inventing a new normality that, this time, is politically correct. The idea is not to idealise the middle values of a Kinsey Scale of masculinity and femininity, but to respect whatever idiomatic placement we encounter. We must simply ensure that the underlying psychological and social dangers of the splitting are revealed. Indeed, splitting inevitably hinders the recognition of a third option, demonstrates the limits of a lack of reflective function, and strengthens the implicit binary hierarchy, with all that it brings: active is better than passive, male is better than female, tall is better than short, white is better than black, heterosexual is better than homosexual, and so on.

The splitting process informs the dominant constructions of gender in the attempt to acquire a coherent or culturally approved identity. We are also made of what gets split and then repressed or dissociated. If we forget it, a part of us 'proliferates', as Freud (1915) would say, 'in obscurity'.

Bearness as a masquerade

Awareness of cultural disapproval can lead to a number of responses – often shame and attempts at passing, although hiding traits that are disapproved of is not often easy or optional. Quentin Crisp (1968: 28) described his own rebellious response to cultural disapproval and ridicule of his movements, in particular the flutter of his hands and his voice. But he wanted everybody to know that he was not ashamed, and so he decided to be more demonstrative: he even started to wear make-up (Cohler and Galatzer-Levy, 2013).

We can consider the cultural phenomenon of gay 'bears' as a 'case' for studying the relationship between (male) homosexuality and (masculine) gender expression and for deepening the hypothesis that gender can also be seen as a symbolic resource that not only affects us, but that we can also set up.

So, the question 'how does gender work?' implies the following: 'how we run it?' As Butler wrote (1990):

> If gender attributes and acts, the various ways in which a body shows or produces its cultural signification, are performative, then there is no preexisting identity by which an act or attribute might be measured; there would be no true or false, real or distorted acts of gender and the postulation of a true gender identity would be revealed as a regulatory fiction.
>
> (p. 141)

We can apply the theory of Butler, and her example of the drag queen as performative impersonator of the female gender, to the example of the bear as performative impersonator of the male gender (generated by its own performance). In fact, the bear figure could be considered an example of *subjectivity in drag*, where the reproduction/invention of the stereotype is also the occasion of its ridicule or the mockery of the mechanisms that regulate it.

In the mid-1980s, a group of gay Californians decided to call themselves bears. Enlisting under the bear paw was a way to emphasise their happiness and pride for being fat, hairy and gay. The bears soon decided on a group code articulated in aesthetic roles – *little bear, teddy bear, chubby bear, muscle bear, daddy bear*, etc. (Donahue and Stoner, 1997; Wright and Fritscher, 2001) – that eventually iconified, and inevitably marketed, the original idea.

A spontaneous cultural creation, and also, inevitably, an imitation of gender, the bear figure reveals how masculinity is a mythology with its own pantheon, and how the concept of naturalness is far from nature. There are many more or less seductive dreams of natural masculinity, from marble athletes, bearded deity, tawny vikings, chubby wrestlers, leather bikers, police officers and sailors to the Tom of Finland, wood-men for Whitman, proletarians for von Gloeden, knaves for Genet, Sebastians for Mishima, young suburbanites and black primitives for Pasolini, magnetic Arabs for Lawrence of Arabia right up to the cowboys of Brokeback Mountain.

> I am enamoured of growing outdoors, Of men that live among cattle or taste of the ocean or woods, Of the builders and steerers of ships, of the wielders of axes and mauls, of the drivers of horses, I can eat and sleep with them week in and week out. [. . .] The scent of these arm-pits is aroma finer than prayer.
>
> (Whitman, 1855: 21, 29)

But, if we reduced the psychic meaning to the literal meaning of the gender per-formance we would make a mistake. In fact, psychoanalysis insists that

> the opacity of the unconscious sets limits to the exteriorization of the psy-che. [. . .] What is exteriorized or performed can be understood only through reference to what is barred from the performance, what cannot or will not be performed.
>
> (Butler, 1997b: 144–145)

Like any other theatre, the bear scene is also populated by ghosts. The first ghost evoked by bearness could be a compensatory reactivity in comparison with overly effeminate personifications of male homosexuality (Green, 1987). The second one could be the idealisation of 'natural' and archetypal masculinity, however victim of the inevitable sisyphean condemnation to imitation. The third one could be manifest as a choice of 'wearing' powerful masculinity as a defence from the expectation of being stigmatised as a gay man. Finally, the fourth one could be taken as an attempt to exorcise the trauma of the AIDS season and eroticise the vitality of a thriving and robust body to counteract the thinness and the pallor of the sick body.

Compared with the traditional model of masculinity, bearness shows a double attitude of challenge and recognition: a mixture of traditional and reinterpreted, halfway between repetition and transformation. The bear figure could be inter-preted as a compromise formation between the reappropriation of the symbols of masculinity (to remove it from the heteronormative control) and the imitation of an idealised masculinity (identification with the aggressor? Batesian mimicry?[5]) to defend itself from the stigma associated with the equalisation of Faggot = Loser (Corbett, 2001).

The ideal of a male 'natural' body and the associated symbolic and affective constructions have played a central role in the formation of homosexual desire, since they have often matched the 'natural' with the 'heterosexual'. The history of magazines such as *Physique Pictorial* (pansies in a swoon for photographs of sailors, farmers, gas station attendants and any other archetype of manliness) tells very well how, for a good first half of the century, 'homosexual' stood for 'weak' and 'heterosexual' for 'strong' (Bergling, 2001; Lingiardi, 1997/2002; Mosse, 1996; Theweleit, 1977). Every desire 'hallucinates' a desirable body, shaping its gender stereotype. If we wrote a history of the 'homosexual body' we should highlight, along with its cultural malleability, as in many cases it has reflected and at the same time produced, a conviction of its own inadequacy, enhancing the erotic appeal of the heterosexual Übermensch and minimising their own.

Gay bodies, *but* hypertrophic and masculine; gay identities, *but* not feminised; Gay subjectivities no more graceful, *but* hirsute and overweight (Moskowitz et al., 2013) – bear identity constitutes itself in a negative sense: 'bear is not woman, not straight, not faggot' (Hennen, 2005: 34). But gay bear is not only a male response to previous pathologised models and a specific response to the stereotype of the effeminate gay; it is also an attempt to conceptualise and spread a 'masculinity for homosexuals' just when the gay body wins new followers to the cosmetics market, and then to the gym and then to the tattoo (Lemma, 2010; Lingiardi and Luci, 2011).

With impressive acceleration times and fuel consumption, over the last thirty years the gay imaginary (and marketing business) have staged a great parade of sexual personae of manhood – many of which are prefigured in brilliant synthesis from the Village People: as the group's leader, Victor Willis, said, 'the group performs a masculine show'. This very visible diversity makes it all the more incredible that there are still some who see fit to attribute fixed characteristics of gender to homosexuality. In the early 1970s, when gay culture came out of the closet, new types of homosexuals appeared on the scene – for example, macho men, leather men and the denim clones – opening the so-called 'masculinization of gay culture' (Altman, 1982). The news was not so much that gays idealised virility, but that they represented it in public. Until that time, the 'manly homosexual' was an oxymoron. The visibility of gay people, either by choice or by force, could rarely rescind from a camp dimension in which they lost the boundaries between temperamental femininity, cultural femininity, disguise and provocation.

Being hypermasculine was to protect themselves from the fear of not being masculine enough. Making themselves feminine was to unknowingly join in the demands of the heteronormative binary rules. Gender constructs trap: because a core gender does not exist (Butler, 1991), as soon as we try to reproduce it, it goes up in smoke.

Not only in gay contexts, but also in heterosexual ones, male gender does not necessarily reflect the cultural requirements of the sex, i.e., what men are expected to do differently from women.

Male identities, straight or homosexual as they exist, can be embodied and expressed in different types of masculinity (Moss, 2012; Reiss and Grossmark, 2009) revealing the negotiation and cultural construction between Western codes and heteronormative requirements (McNamara, 2013; Page and Peacock, 2013). For example, outside of Western culture, especially in India, the category 'men who have sex with men' (MSM – nongay-identified men who have regular ongoing sex with other men) seeks to include men with such diverse sexualities as 'masculine' men who prefer women but may have sex with other men to satisfy their sexual desires or for social activity; men with masculine identities who strictly prefer sex with other men; men with 'feminine' identities who prefer sex with men; and biological men who may identify with the female gender (Dube and Kamath, 2013).

Certainly, queer masculinity for straight men raises new questions: what is the attraction of moving outside the hetero-masculine norm? What is gained? Is there a difference between queer experiences by straight males that take place in private space versus public space? What does it mean when self-identified straight people perform gay or queer masculinities? Is this an honouring of queerness or a use of queerness for another purpose (Heasley, 2005)?

The idea of 'homosexualising' heterosexuals goes back to Frank Rich's 1987 *Esquire* article in which he called it 'the most dramatic cultural assimilation of our time' (quoted in Buckland, 2002: 142). In 1994, the journalist Mark Simpson coined the term '*metrosexual*', referring to

> [a] single young man with a high disposable income, living or working in the city (because that's where all the best shops are), [that] is perhaps the most promising consumer market of the decade. In the Eighties he was only to be found inside fashion magazines such as *GQ*. In the Nineties, he's everywhere and he's going shopping.

Over time, the label resists any exclusive definition (see Anderson, 2009; Anderson, Adams and Rivers, 2010; McCormack and Anderson, 2010) and indicates, in turn, fluidity of gender expression, bisexuality, occasional situations in which straight men entertain homosexual relations (Peterson and Anderson, 2012).

The concept of 'metrosexuality' is interesting as it highlights the emergence of new male narratives and gives men a long-awaited popular justification for the ability to associate with femininity and to cross previously stigmatised boundaries of homo-sociality. It has therefore served as a mediating factor in the manner in which homophobia has traditionally policed gendered boundaries.

In 2011, Simpson adds:

> Contrary to what you have been told, metrosexuality is not about flip-flops and facials, man-bags or mascara. Or about men becoming 'girlie' or 'gay'. It's about men becoming *everything*. To themselves. In much the way that women have been for some time. It's the end of the sexual division of bathroom and bedroom labour. It's the end of sexuality as we've known it.

All of these forms of masculinity represent something much more than just men who are 'nontraditional'. They are not just gender-bending. They create a language for queer-straight males. They suggest a masculinity and male heterosexuality that extend the reach of societal perceptions of either, and one that for each of these males allows the potential for evolving a broadened definition. They reveal the inadequacy of gender categories for heterosexual experiences, and expand norms and expectations for straight men who are whatever they can do and say.

Gender expression and sexual orientation: divided but always united

> À partir du moment où une realité nouvelle prend corps,
> où elle existe, la psychanalyse [. . .] doit la penser, l'interpréter
> et la prendre en compte, et non pas la condamner,
> car cela reviendrait à l'exclure ou à la dénier, et donc
> à transformer une discipline en code de déontologie
> et à faire des praticiens des censeurs ou des procureurs.[6]
> (Derrida and Roudinesco, *De Quoi Demain . . . Dialogue*)

> I was not ladylike, nor was I manly. I was something else altogether.
> There were so many different ways to be a beauty.
> (Michael Cunningham, *A Home at the End of the World*)

Psychoanalytic practice cannot be separated from sexual identities theory, since our states of mind escape any attempt at categorical enclosure, often justified with forced pretexts to anatomy. However, the body itself is the place of maximum transformability, as well as representation[7] and performativity. When we try to use it as the unique parameter and landmark for the construction of our identity, it makes any presumed certainty illusory.

No one is born and develops outside a system of norms, but at the same time no one develops as a simple mechanical reiteration of such norms (Butler, 1997a, 2004; Corbett, 2001, 2008, 2009; Layton, 1997), and no norm is a norm if it does not also consider what remains outside. Talking about *what remains outside*, we can refer to Butler's melancholy identification (1990, 1997b). For each accomplished identification there is at least one loss.

Clinical practice reminds us that binary option allows a defensive reaction on the part of a conscious search to force order on the chaotic overinclusiveness of the unconscious. Taking it as a distinct identity and singular position keeps us away from the deep understanding of the psychic experience.

A binary code can help to simplify the reading of reality, but for living in it one needs more solutions. We need to deconstruct gender and then be able to reassemble it. Many patients have taught us that it's necessary to go beyond the dominating gender binaries, and have asked us to help them build new, amalgamated positions. Others – drowning in issues ranging from role confusion to gender dysphoria – have asked us for actual certainties, with literal and often even biological anchoring points.

As others have so eloquently noted, the concept of gender must thus be understood as a paradox built on the tensions of its components: 'a force field (of dualism) . . . consisting not of essences, but of shifting relations among multiple contrasts' (Dimen, 1991: 343); 'a necessary fiction' (Harris, 1991); 'a real appearance' (Benjamin, 1995, 1998); and 'a false truth' (Goldner, 1991). As we see from these metaphors, our gender, although not an essence, is still nevertheless a 'core experience' of identity. It's a gradient, the measure of disparity, that challenges us neither to essentialise it nor to dematerialise it.

As Adrienne Harris (1991) notes, in any one person's experience gender

> may occupy both positions. Gender may in some contexts be thick and reified, as plausibly real as anything in our character. At other moments, gender may seem porous and insubstantial. Furthermore, there may be multiple genders or embodied selves. For some individuals these gendered experiences may feel integrated, egosyntonic. For others, the gender contradictions and alternatives seem dangerous and frightening and so are maintained as splits in the self, dissociated part-objects.
>
> (p. 212)

The only option is to seek idiomatic solutions, to seek ideographic assemblages that are still anchored to the nomothetics of gender tropes offered by our life-paths and our cultural, familial and biographical backgrounds.

Committed to grasp what is most similar and obvious in human sexual development, psychoanalysis paid little attention to the variable and multiple elements with which each subject organises his/her sexuality. Bodily experiences, erotic desires, sexual practices, sexual object choices take us away from the idea that coherence really exists. Internal worlds, affective tonalities, relational biographies untie us from the impossibility of positioning ourselves within or beyond a single axis of sameness-difference. As Corbett says:

> Too often analysts have looked at variance and called it illness. Too often analysts have failed to note the ways in which the pain of fragmentation is simultaneously the variant construction of a way out. Too often we have looked upon the trauma of difference and sought to cure it through the clumsy application of similarity.
>
> (2008: 851)

More than scouts in the borderlands of gender (McKenzie, 2010), psychoanalysts have positioned themselves as gender border guards (Kulish, 2010), forgetting that there are no identities and sexual orientations in the unconscious (Dean, 2010).

'We still are not in possession of an adequate model of mind to account for the great variety that marks the relationship between gender, psychological equilibrium, and the indistinguishable work of cultural regulation' (Corbett, 2008: 849).

However, when psychoanalysis also focused on *cultural studies* and *queer theory* (Dimen and Goldner, 2010, 2012), it considered the idea of a multiplicity of developmental outcomes, embracing a more complex and less polarised gender conceptualisation.

For some of us, gender is a ghostly alternation; for others, it is a vital source of growth; for others still, it is sublimated and seamlessly transmuted into self-experience. There are gender divides in each of us, but the boundaries we draw vary in meaning, intensity, and function.

> The concept of soft assembly offers the potential for thinking about particular forms of gender life or desire that may be either rigid or flexible. The soft-ness in soft assembly does not necessarily mean flexible or fluid. The terms describe a process of development, not a particular character of psychic struc-ture. Gender can be a rich playground or a desert, a stark cartoon or highly elaborated spaces in mind, body and life [. . .] Gender may be softly assem-bled, but it is also a work in progress.
>
> (Harris, 2005: 151, 173)

Gender as 'symbolic resource' (Gagnon, 1991) and 'personal idiom' (Bollas, 1989) is inseparable from the interpersonal fields in which it is embedded. Expressions revealing flexible and controversial gender meanings are constructed and reconstructed all life-long (Chodorow, 2012). Body is just one of the elements of gender expression.

What about sexual orientations? We all have a 'closet' in which we hide our gender ghosts. Since gender identity is a psychic before bodily reality, gender takes variable meanings, a variability that generates instability. We do not know what precisely links gender and sexual orientation, but we have to recognise their recip-rocal influence, the way to stand on the sexual scene in a performative dialogue.

For some, gender expression and sexual orientation are each dependent on the other, in a linear, consciously consistent and sexually appropriate concep-tion of themselves. For others, they may contradict each other in a deeply personal, ambiguous and constantly changing experience of themselves.

Lynch (Chapter 7, p. 139) points out that similarities and differences overlap, and reminds us with the apt words of Sedgwick (1990) of the opportunity for psy-choanalysis to encompass enormous complexity due to its assortment of physical zones, developmental stages, representational mechanisms, and levels of con-sciousness, although it sometimes reduces complexities to reified entities such as '*the* mother, *the* father, *the* pre-oedipal, *the* oedipal, *the* other or Other'.

As clinicians, we have the possibility of not only helping people to recognise and follow the directions of their own desires, but also to compose the absolutely personal sense of identity between gender, sexual orientation and social culture. We have to work for the integration of the fluid and flexible components of iden-tity with those components needing stability and shared definitions.

The challenge ahead lies in capturing the different states of mind without dropping that '-s'. Considering potentially healthy and potentially pathological instability as well as rigidity. Assimilating variance without repudiating same-ness. Admitting the *tension* between what we have and what we are missing.[8] Grasping the singularity of each condition and, at the same time, recognising the contingencies that qualify that condition, making it plural.

What's needed is a continuous process of *solve et coagula*,[9] as an alchemist would say. Everything permanent, everything that belongs to the hardening of our habits, must be made fluid; everything volatile and uncertain must be anchored and solidified. Tension – the oscillation between relative and absolute – will guide us on the search for idiomatic pathways that can sustain our creations of gender. It is in this capacity, both individual and social, to be 'standing in the spaces' (Bromberg, 1998) of genders, that we determine whether we are working on an idiomatic solution or an exile from ourselves.

Notes

1 Vittorio Lingiardi, M.D., psychiatrist and psychoanalyst (IARPP, IAAP), is Full Professor and Director of the Clinical Psychology Specialization Program at the Department of Dynamic and Clinical Psychology, Faculty of Medicine and Psychology, Sapienza University of Rome, Italy. The author thanks Dr. Nicola Carone for his collaboration in the writing process of this paper.

2 In a short note, we can summarise that both retrospective methods (Alanko et al., 2009; Alanko et al., 2010; Bailey and Zucker, 1995; Blanchard et al., 1983; Cardoso, 2005, 2009; D'Augelli et al., 2008; Isay, 1999; Landolt et al., 2004; Lippa, 2003, 2008; Plöderl and Fartacek, 2008; Zucker et al., 2006) and prospective methods (Bailey, Dunne, and Martin, 2000; Bartlett and Vasey, 2006; Bell, Weinberg, and Hammersmith, 1981; Drummond et al., 2008; Green, 1987; Rieger et al., 2008; National Children's Study, 2009; Wallien and Cohen-Kettenis, 2008) have found that gay men and lesbians report greater childhood gender nonconformity than do heterosexual adults (although this difference is considered substantial for both sexes, it is more relevant for the so called pre-gay than pre-lesbian children). However, these studies do not provide information about how and to what degree the children were *gender outsiders* (Thomas and Blakemore, 2013) and how their solutions were ego-syntonic or ego-dystonic. Starting from the pioneering study by Terman and Miles (1936), other studies have tried to identify the causes for a specific sexual orientation (Bem, 1996, 2008), what kind of connection exists between gender nonconformity in childhood and sexual orientation in adulthood (see Bailey and Zucker, 1995; Corbett, 1999; Green, 1987; Sandfort, 2005, 2008), and if children who become gay adults (pre-gay children) differ from children who become straight adults (pre-straight children) (see Le Vay, 2011). The most accepted hypothesis now states a combination of biological and cultural factors, but no study has (yet?) managed to discover the specific role of each factor (Ashley, 2013; Burri et al., 2011). According to Le Vay (2011), 'the association between sexual orientation and other gendered traits arises because all these traits differentiate under the influence of a common biological process – the sexual differentiation of the brain under the influence of sex hormones'. But, he concludes, 'obviously, this point of view carries a risk of stereotyping' (p. 74).

3 Many commentators have pointed out the existence of at least two Freuds – the radical and the bourgeois: heteronormative in the text and revolutionary in the footnotes (Lingiardi, 2007; May, 1986). 'It's impossible to make a statement about Freud being right or wrong since he is always both' (Marcus, 1975, XLI). We can see an example of this when he states that gender splitting is necessary for procreative purposes while also maintaining that 'every individual . . . displays a mixture of the character traits belonging to his own and to the opposite sex; and he shows a combination of activity and passivity whether or not this tallies with their biological ones' and that there is nothing to inherently distinguish the 'procreative' form from other kinds of sex (Freud, 1905: 220 footnote).

4 It's interesting that both Freud and Jung cite the myth of Aristophanes in Plato's *Symposium* selectively: they seem to want to skip past the explicit reference to same-sex couples (see also Lingiardi, 1997/2002: 163).
5 According to the Batesian mimicry, the animals belonging to harmless species can take the typical colors, or other morphological characteristics, of dangerous species in order to increase the probability of being avoided from predators.
6 'From the moment a new reality takes shape, where it exists, psychoanalysis [. . .] must think, interpret and consider it. Must not condemn, because this would lead to exclusion or denial and, in so doing, would turn a discipline into a code of ethics, and practitioners into censors or prosecutors' (translation mine).
7 As Breen (1993) observed: 'The body for Freud is always representation of the body' (p. 22).
8 One patient pointed out to me that his personal construction of gender was representing his genitals not just as a hard object – tough, defensive and offensive, like a pistol or a dagger (as suggested by his father and friends, pornography and popular culture) – but also a fragile, soft, delicate object, like a flower or a baby chick.
9 'Dissolve and coagulate' (in Latin: 'solve et coagula'), 'separate and join together'. The alchemical motto, often quoted by C.G. Jung, seems to imply analysis of a substance into its components before synthesising the desirable elements into a new substance.

References

Alanko, K., Santtila, P., Harlaar, N., Witting, K., Varjonen, M., Jern, P., Johansson, A., von der Pahlen, B., and Kenneth Sandnabba, N. (2010). Common Genetic Effects of Gender Atypical Behavior in Childhood and Sexual Orientation in Adulthood: A Study of Finnish Twins. *Archives of Sexual Behavior*, *39*, 81–92.
Alanko, K., Santtila, P., Witting, K., Varjonen, M., Jern, P., Johansson, A., von der Pahlen, B., and Kenneth Sandnabba, N. (2009). Psychiatric Symptoms and Same-Sex Sexual Attraction and Behavior in Light of Childhood Gender Atypical Behavior and Parental Relationships. *Journal of Sex Research*, *46*, 494–504.
Altman, D. (1982). *The Homosexualization of America*. Boston, MA: Beacon Press.
American Psychiatric Association (2013). *Diagnostic and Statistical Manual of Mental Disorders* (5th ed.). Washington, DC: American Psychiatric Publishing.
Anderson, E. (2009). *Inclusive Masculinity: The Changing Nature of Masculinities*. New York and London: Routledge.
Anderson, E., Adams, A., and Rivers, I. (2010). 'You Wouldn't Believe What Straight Men Are Doing with Each Other': Kissing, Cuddling and Loving. *Archives of Sexual Behavior*, *41*, 421–430.
Ashley, K.B. (2013). The Science on Sexual Orientation: A Review of the Recent Literature. *Journal of Gay and Lesbian Mental Health*, *17*, 2, 175–182.
Bailey, J.M., and Zucker, K.J. (1995). Childhood Sex-Typed Behavior and Sexual Orientation: A Conceptual Analysis and Quantitative Review. *Developmental Psychology*, *31*, 43–55.
Bailey, J.M., Dunne, M.P., and Martin, N.G. (2000). Genetic and Environmental Influences on Sexual Orientation and Its Correlates in an Australian Twin Sample. *Journal of Personality and Social Psychology*, *78*, 524–536.
Bartlett, N.J., and Vasey, P.L. (2006). A Retrospective Study of Childhood Gender Atypical Behavior in Samoan Fa'afafine, *Archives of Sexual Behavior*, *35*, 6, 659–666.

Bell, A.P., Weinberg, M.S., and Hammersmith, S.K. (1981). *Sexual Preference: Its Development in Men and Women*. Bloomington: Indiana University Press.

Bem, D.J. (1996). Exotic Becomes Erotic: A Developmental Theory of Sexual Orientation. *Psychological Review, 103*, 320–335.

Bem, D.J. (2008). Is There a Causal Link Between Childhood Gender Nonconformity and Adults Homosexuality? *Journal of Gay and Lesbian Mental Health, 12*, 1/2, 61–79.

Benjamin, J. (1995). *Like Subjects, Love Objects*. New Haven, CT: Yale University Press.

Benjamin, J. (1998). *Shadow of the Other. Intersubjectivity and Gender in Psychoanalysis*. New York: Routledge.

Bergling, T. (2001). *Sissyphobia. Gay Men and Effeminate Behavior*. New York: Harrington Park Press.

Blakemore, J.E.O., and Hill, C.A. (2008). The Child Gender Socialization Scale: A Measure to Compare Traditional and Feminist Parents. *Sex Roles, 58*, 192–207.

Blanchard, R., McConkey, J.G., Roper V., and Steiner, B.W. (1983). Measuring Physical Aggressiveness in Heterosexual, Homosexual, and Transsexual Males. *Archives of Sexual Behavior, 12*, 511–524.

Bollas, C. (1989). *Forces of Destiny. Psychoanalysis and the Human Idiom*. London: Free Association Books.

Bollas, C. (1992). *Being a Character. Psychoanalysis and Self Experiences*. London: Routledge.

Breen, D. (1993). *The Gender Conundrum. Contemporary Psychoanalytic Perspectives on Femininity and Masculinity*. London: Routledge.

Bromberg, P.M. (1998). *Standing in the Spaces: Essays on Clinical Process, Trauma and Dissociation*. Hillsdale, NJ: Analytic Press.

Buckland, F. (2002). *Impossible Dance: Club Culture and Queer World-Making*. Middletown, CT: Wesleyan University Press.

Burri, A., Cherkas, L., Spector, T., and Rahman, Q. (2011). Genetic and Environmental Influences on Female Sexual Orientation, Childhood Gender Typicality and Adult Gender Identity. *PLOS ONE, 6*, 7, 1–8.

Butler, J. (1990). *Gender Trouble. Feminism and the Subversion of Identity*. New York and London: Routledge.

Butler, J. (1991). Imitation and Gender Insubordination. In D. Fuss (Ed.), *Inside/Out. Lesbian Theories, Gay Theories* (pp. 13–31). New York and London: Routledge.

Butler, J. (1997a). Response to Lynne Layton's 'The Doer behind the Deed.'. *Gender and Psychoanalysis, 2*, 515–520.

Butler, J. (1997b). *The Psychic Life of Power. Theories in Subjection*. Stanford, CA: Stanford University Press.

Butler, J. (1999). Preface. In *Gender Trouble. Feminism and the Subversion of Identity* New York and London: Routledge.

Butler, J. (2004). *Undoing Gender*. New York: Routledge.

Cardoso, F.L. (2005). Cultural Universals and Differences in Male Homosexuality: The Case of a Brazilian Fishing Village. *Archives of Sexual Behavior, 34*, 1, 103–109.

Cardoso, F.L. (2009). Recalled Sex-Typed Behavior in Childhood and Sports' Preferences in Adulthood of Heterosexual, Bisexual, and Homosexual Men from Brazil, Turkey, and Thailand. *Archives of Sexual Behavior, 38*, 726–736.

Chodorow, N.J. (2012). *Individualizing Gender and Sexuality. Theory and Practice.* New York: Routledge.

Cohen, K.M., and Savin-Williams, R.C. (2012). Coming Out to Self and Others. Developmental Milestones. In P. Levounis, J. Drescher, and M.E. Barber (Eds.), *The LGBT Casebook* (pp. 17–33). Washington, DC: American Psychiatric Publishing.

Cohen-Kettenis, P.T., and Pfäfflin, F. (2003). *Transgenderism and Intersexuality in Childhood and Adolescence: Making Choices.* Thousand Oaks, CA: Sage Publications.

Cohler, B.J., and Galatzer-Levy, R.M. (2013). The Historical Moment in the Analysis of Gay Men. *Journal of the American Psychoanalytic Association, 61,* 1139–1173.

Corbett, K. (1993). The Mystery of Homosexuality. *Psychoanalytic Psychology, 10,* 3, 345–357.

Corbett, K. (1999). Homosexual Boyhood: Notes on Girlyboys. In M. Rottnek (Ed.), *Sissies and Tomboys: Gender Nonconformity and Homosexual Childhood* (pp. 107–139). New York: New York University Press.

Corbett, K. (2001). Faggot = Loser. *Studies in Gender and Sexuality, 2,* 1, 3–28.

Corbett, K. (2008). Gender Now. *Psychoanalytic Dialogues, 18,* 838–856.

Corbett, K. (2009). *Boyhoods. Rethinking Masculinities.* New Haven, CT: Yale University Press.

Craig, T., and Lacroix, J. (2011). Tomboy as Protective Identity. *Journal of Lesbian Studies, 15,* 4, 450–465.

D'Augelli, A.R., Grossman, A.H., and Starks, M.T. (2008). Gender Atypicality and Sexual Orientation Development among Lesbian, Gay, and Bisexual Youth: Prevalence, Sex Differences, and Parental Responses, *Journal of Gay and Lesbian Mental Health, 12,* 1/2, 95–119.

Dean, T. (2010). Scouts in the Borderlands of Gender: Response to Susan McKenzie and to Barry Miller. *The Journal of Analytical Psychology, 55,* 125–129.

Di Ceglie, D. (1998). Reflections on the Nature of the Atypical Gender Identity Organization. In D. Di Ceglie and D. Freedman (Eds.), *A Stranger in My Own Body: Atypical Gender Identity Development and Mental Health* (pp. 9–25). London: Karnac Books.

Di Ceglie, D. (2013). Care for Gender-Dysphoric Children. In B.P.C. Kreukels, T.D. Steensma, and A.L.C. de Vries (Eds.), *Gender Dysphoria and Disorders of Sex Development: Progress in Care and Knowledge* (Focus on Sexuality Research) (pp. 151–169). New York: Springer.

Dimen, M. (1991). Deconstructing Difference: Gender, Splitting and Transitional Space. *Psychoanalytic Dialogues, 1,* 335–352.

Dimen, M., and Goldner, V. (Eds.) (2010). *Gender in Psychoanalytic Space: Between Clinic and Culture* (2nd ed.). New York: Other Press.

Dimen, M., and Goldner, V. (2012). Gender and Sexuality. In G.O. Gabbard, B.E. Litowitz and P. Williams (Eds.), *Textbook of Psychoanalysis* (2nd ed.) (pp. 133–154). Arlington, VA: American Psychiatric Publishing.

Drescher, J. (1998). *Psychoanalytic Therapy and the Gay Man.* Hillsdale, MI: Analytic Press.

Drescher, J., and Byne, W. (Eds.) (2012). *Treating Transgender Children and Adolescents.* New York: Routledge.

Drescher, J., Cohen-Kettenis, P.T., and Winter, S. (2012). Minding the Body: Situating Gender Identity Diagnoses in the ICD–11. *International Review of Psychiatry, 24,* 6, 568–577.

Drummond, K.D., Bradley, S.J., Peterson-Badali, M., and Zucker, K.J. (2008). A Follow-up Study of Girls with Gender Identity Disorder. *Developmental Psychology*, *44*, 34–45.

Dube, A.R., and Kamath, J. (2013). Social Constructions of Male Sexual Identity: Translational Limitations of Western 'Homosexuality' in an Indian Male Patient. *Journal of Gay and Lesbian Mental Health*, *17*, 3, 352–360.

Freeman, N.K. (2007). Preschoolers' Perceptions of Gender Appropriate Toys and Their Parents' Beliefs About Genderized Behaviors: Miscommunication, Mixed Messages, or Hidden Truths? *Early Childhood Education Journal*, *34*, 357–366.

Freud, S. (1905). Three Essays on the Theory of Sexuality. In J. Strachey (Ed. and Trans.), *The Standard Edition of the Complete Psychological Works of Sigmund Freud* (Vol. 7, pp. 130–245). London: Hogarth Press, 1953.

Freud, S. (1910). Leonardo da Vinci and a Memory of his Childhood. In J. Strachey (Ed. and Trans.), *The Standard Edition of the Complete Psychological Works of Sigmund Freud* (Vol. 11, pp. 59–137). London: Hogarth Press, 1957.

Freud, S. (1915). Instincts and Their Vicissitudes. In J. Strachey (Ed. and Trans.), *The Standard Edition of the Complete Psychological Works of Sigmund Freud* (Vol. 14, pp. 109–140). London: Hogarth Press, 1957.

Freud, S. (1920). The Psychogenesis of a Case of Homosexuality in a Woman. In J. Strachey (Ed. and Trans.), *The Standard Edition of the Complete Psychological Works of Sigmund Freud* (Vol. 18, pp. 145–172). London: Hogarth Press, 1955.

Freud, S. (1937). Analysis Terminable and Interminable. In J. Strachey (Ed. and Trans.), *The Standard Edition of the Complete Psychological Works of Sigmund Freud* (Vol. 23, pp. 209–254). London: Hogarth Press, 1964.

Gagnon, J. (1991). Commentary on Goldner's 'Toward a Critical Relational Theory of Gender'. *Psychoanalytic Dialogues*, *1*, 273–276.

Goldner, V. (1991). Toward a Critical Relational Theory of Gender. *Psychoanalytic Dialogues*, *1*, 3, 249–272.

Green, R. (1987). *The 'Sissy Boy Syndrome' and the Development of Homosexuality*. New Haven, CT: Yale University Press.

Harris, A. (1991). Gender as Contradiction. *Psychoanalytic Dialogues*, *1*, 3, 197–224.

Harris, A. (2005). *Gender as Soft Assembly*. Hillsdale, NJ: Analytic Press.

Heasley, R. (2005). Queer Masculinities of Straight Men. A Typology. *Men and Masculinities*, *7*, 3, 310–320.

Hennen, P. (2005). Bear Bodies, Bear Masculinity: Recuperation, Resistance, or Retreat? *Gender and Society*, *19*, 1, 25–43.

Herek, G.M. (2002). Gender Gaps in Public Opinion about Lesbians and Gay Men. *Public Opinion Quarterly*, *66*, 1, 40–66.

Isay, R.A. (1999). Gender in Homosexual Boys: Some Developmental and Clinical Considerations. *Psychiatry*, *62*, 2, 187–194.

Kane, E.W. (2006). No Way My Boys Are Going To Be Like That! *Gender and Society*, *20*, 149–176.

Kulish, N. (2010). Clinical Implications of Contemporary Gender Theory. *Journal of the American Psychoanalytic Association*, *58*, 2, 231–258.

Landolt, M., Bartholomew, K., Saffrey, C., Oram, D., and Perlman, D. (2004). Gender Nonconformity, Childhood Rejection, and Adult Attachment: A Study of Gay Men. *Archives of Sexual Behavior*, *33*, 117–128.

Layton, L. (1997). The Doer behind the Deed. *Gender and Psychoanalysis*, *2*, 515–520.

Le Vay, S. (2011). *Gay, Straight, and the Reason Why*. New York: Oxford University Press.

Lemma, A. (2010). *Under the Skin: A Psychoanalytic Study of Body Modification*. London: Routledge.

Levounis, P., Drescher, J., and Barber, M.E. (Eds.) (2012). *The LGBT Casebook*. Washington, DC: American Psychiatric Publishing.

Lingiardi, V. (1997/2002). *Compagni d'amore. Da Ganimede a Batman. Identità e mito nelle omosessualità maschili*. Milano: Raffaello Cortina. English Translation: *Men in Love*. Chicago, IL: Open Court.

Lingiardi, V. (2007). Dreaming Gender: Restoration and Transformation. *Studies in Gender and Sexuality, 8*, 4, 313–331.

Lingiardi, V., and Capozzi, P. (2004). Psychoanalytic Attitudes towards Homosexuality: An Empirical Research. *International Journal of Psychoanalysis, 85*, 1, 137–158.

Lingiardi, V., and Luci, M. (2011). La piel que habito. Introduction to the Italian edition of A. Lemma (Ed.) (2010), *Sotto la pelle. Psicoanalisi delle modificazioni corporee* (*Under the Skin. A Psychoanalytic Study of Body Modification*) (pp. vii–xxvi). Milano: Raffaello Cortina,.

Lippa, R.A. (2003). Handedness, Sexual Orientation, and Gender-Related Personality Traits in Men and Women. *Archives of Sexual Behavior, 32*, 103–114.

Lippa, R.A. (2008). The Relation between Childhood Gender Nonconformity and Adult Masculinity-Femininity and Anxiety in Heterosexual and Homosexual Men and Women. *Sex Roles, 59*, 684–693.

Lynch, P.E. (in this volume). Intimacy, Desire and Shame in Gay Male Sexuality, Ch. 7.

Marcus, S. (1975). Introduction. *Three Essays on the Theory of Sexuality*. By Sigmund Freud. Trans. James Strachey (pp. xix–xli). New York: Basic Books,.

Mathy, R., and Drescher, J. (Eds.) (2009). *Childhood Gender Nonconformity and the Development of Adult Homosexuality*. New York: Routledge.

May, R. (1986). Concerning a Psychoanalytic View of Maleness. *Psychoanalytic Review, 73*, 179–194.

McCormack, M., and Anderson, E. (2010). 'It's Just Not Acceptable Any More': The Erosion of Homophobia and the Softening of Masculinity at an English Sixth Form. *Sociology, 44*, 5, 843– 859.

McDermott, R.C., and Schwartz, J.P. (2013). Toward a Better Understanding of Emerging Adult Men's Gender Role Journeys: Differences in Age, Education, Race, Relationship Status, and Sexual Orientation. *Psychology of Men and Masculinity, 14*, 2, 202–210.

McKenzie, S. (2010). Gender and Sexualities in Individuation: Theoretical and Clinical Explorations. *The Journal of Analytical Psychology, 55*, 91–111.

McNamara, S. (2013). Gay Male Desires and Sexuality in the Twenty-first Century: How I Listen. *Journal of the American Psychoanalytic Association, 61*, 2, 341–362.

Moskowitz, D.A., Turrubiates, J., Lozano, H., and Hajek, C. (2013). Physical, Behavioral, and Psychological Traits of Gay Men Identifying as Bears. *Archives of Sexual Behavior, 42*, 5, 775–784.

Moss, D. (2012). *Thirteen Ways of Looking at a Man: Psychoanalysis and Masculinity*. New York: Routledge.

Mosse, G.L. (1996). *The Image of Men. The Creation of Modern Masculinity*. New York: Oxford University Press.

National Children's Study, The (2009). *What is the National Children's Study?* Available at http://www.nationalchildrensstudy.gov/Pages/default.aspx; accessed July 30, 2013.

Page, A.D., and Peacock, J.R. (2013). Negotiating Identities in a Heteronormative Context. *Journal of Homosexuality, 60*, 639–654.

Peterson, G.T., and Anderson, E. (2012). The Performance of Softer Masculinities on the University Dance Floor. *The Journal of Men's Studies*, *20*, 1, 3–15.

Reiss, B.E., and Grossmark, R. (Eds.) (2009). *Heterosexual Masculinities. Contemporary Perspective from Psychoanalytic Gender Theory*. New York: Routledge.

Rieger, G., Linsenmeier, J.A.W., Gygax, L., and Bailey, J.M. (2008). Sexual Orientation and Childhood Gender Nonconformity: Evidence from Home Videos. *Developmental Psychology*, *44*, 46–58.

Rivers, C., and Barnett, R.C. (2011/2013), *The Truth about Girls and Boys: Challenging Toxic Stereotypes about Our Children*. New York: Columbia University Press.

Sandfort, T.G.M. (2005). Sexual Orientation and Gender: Stereotypes and Beyond. *Archives of Sexual Behavior*, *34*, 6, 595–611.

Sandfort, T.G.M. (2008). Preface. In R.M. Mathy and J. Drescher (Eds.), *Childhood Gender Nonconformity and the Development of Adult Homosexuality* (pp. xxi–xxiv). New York: Routledge.

Sedgwick, E.K. (1990). *Epistemology of the Closet*. Berkeley, CA: University of California Press.

Simpson, M. (2011). *Metrosexy: A 21st Century Self-Love Story*. CreateSpace Independent Publishing Platform.

Terman, L.M., and Miles, C.C. (1936). *Sex and Personality: Studies in Masculinity and Femininity*. New York: McGraw-Hill.

Theweleit, K. (1977). *Männerphantasie*. München: Piper Verlag.

Thomas, R.N., and Blakemore, J.E.O. (2013). Adults' Attitudes about Gender Nonconformity in Childhood. *Archives of Sexual Behavior*, *42*, 399–412.

Wallien, M.S.C., and Cohen-Kettenis, P.T. (2008). Psychosexual Outcome of Gender-Dysphoric Children. *Journal of the American Academy of Child and Adolescent Psychiatry*, *47*, 1413–1423.

Whitman, W. (1855). *Leaves of Grass* (1st ed.). Brooklyn, NY: Rome Brothers.

Wilson, I., Griffin, C., and Wren, B. (2005). The Interaction between Young People with Atypical Gender Identity Organization and Their Peers. *Journal of Health Psychology*, *10*, 3, 307–315.

Wright, L.K., and Fritscher, J. (Eds.) (2001). *The Bear Book II: Further Reading in the History and Evolution of Gay Male Subculture*. New York: Harrington Park Press/ Haworth Press.

Zucker, K.J., Mitchell, J.N., Bradley, S.J., Tkachuk, J., Cantor, J.M., and Allin, S. (2006). The Recalled Childhood Gender Identity/Gender Role Questionnaire: Psychometric Properties. *Sex Roles*, *54*, 469–483.

Part III

Homosexuality

Part III

Homosexuality

Chapter 6

A scientific theory of homosexuality for psychoanalysis[1]

Peter Fonagy and Elizabeth Allison

We will begin this chapter with a brief history of writings on homosexuality, trying to provide an epistemological understanding. We will then examine homosexuality from the perspective of post-modernism, and in doing so will return to a classical psychoanalytic perspective that focuses on the body.

The past

When gender and sexuality are in question, there has been a historical tendency to think in terms of mutually exclusive *binaries*, usually the opposition of male vs. female, but equally homosexuality vs. heterosexuality, and perhaps also trans-gender vs. cis-gender. Homosexuality has often been conflated with gender identity. For example, in the mid-nineteenth century, Ulrichs (1864/2001) explained what he viewed as the riddle of 'manly love' by theorizing that some men were born with a woman's spirit trapped inside their bodies. Understanding homosexuality as a manifestation of femininity has led to some paradoxical consequences in modern society, as Drescher (2007) pointed out. For example, the Islamic Republic of Iran hosts more sex reassignment surgery than any other nation except Thailand. There are over 150,000 transsexuals in Iran, a country where homosexuality is a capital offence (it is outlawed in the Qur'an) but sex change operations are not. Those who feel the need to live with other men feel pressured to become transsexual.

Drescher (2002) refers to this habit of thought as '*binary thinking*'. From a Kleinian-Bionian perspective, the imposition of categorical either-or distinctions on a continuum of phenomena might be termed paranoid-schizoid. From a neuroscientific perspective, we might describe it as a result of failure of the mentalizing capacity normally supported by the prefrontal cortex which is caused by discomfort with the phenomena under consideration. When mentalizing goes offline, self-coherence has to be achieved by means of more primitive strategies, such as locating any disturbing elements firmly in the other: this can lead to conceptualizations of homo- and heterosexuality as different in kind. Whatever name we give to this type of thinking, it flourishes in the social and scientific discourse of communities dominated by fundamental, empirically untestable assumptions. In these social groups aspects of human subjectivity appear not to be a legitimate domain of inquiry. Sadly, such rigid binary thinking has underpinned many of the theories historically propounded about the meanings and causes of homosexuality. The narratives accompanying these theories reveal underlying moral judgments and 'malignant prejudices' (Fonagy and Higgitt, 2007) loosely interwoven with speculations concerning aetiology.

The 'causes' of both heterosexuality and homosexuality are shrouded in mystery, but because heterosexuality is the dominant narrative it has rarely been felt to require any explanation. However, in the *Three Essays*, Freud specifically emphasized that 'the exclusive sexual interest felt by men for women is also a problem that needs elucidating and is not a self-evident fact based upon an attraction that is ultimately of a chemical nature' (1905: 145–6).

Three types of narratives with aspirations to scientific status have accompanied both psychoanalytic and extra-psychoanalytic theories about the nature of homosexuality (see Drescher, 2002). These imply no specific theory of causation and take largely overlapping perspectives about the nature of the *actual* cause, be that nature or nurture.

1   Theories that consider homosexuality as a naturally occurring phenomenon reflecting *normal variation*. Variation would prototypically be considered genetic in origin, with a trait-like bimodal distribution like the one character-izing handedness, which is similarly associated with past stigma. But now, broad-minded as we are, we have learned to accept left-handed people as simply different, accepting that they are after all just part of the overarching construct of human variation.

2   Theories that view homosexuality as *a pathology*. Homosexuality is seen as a deviation from heterosexual development where any atypical gender behav-iour is viewed as a symptom of an underlying disease process. Such theories may hold external pathogenic agents responsible or blame an internal, con-stitutional defect. For example inter-uterine hormonal exposure, particular types of parenting and even sexual abuse have been considered as causes. Often these theories pathologizing homosexuality shade into the moralistic (e.g. Bergler, 1956: 28–9).

3   Theories of *immaturity* see homosexual attitudes and actions as a normal part of the emergence of adult heterosexuality. Homosexuality is seen as a normal phase that is expected to be outgrown unless a developmental arrest brings about permanent immaturity and adult homosexuality. In this context, homosexuality carries fewer malignant meanings, but is considered an imma-ture mode of functioning. For example, Otto Kernberg (1975) in *Borderline Conditions and Pathological Narcissism* argued that the highest level of psychological development any homosexual individual can achieve is the level of narcissistic personality development. It was not until 2002 that he updated his views to acknowledge that homosexuality also occurred in neurotics, which is (to give Dr Kernberg credit) the highest level of development any individual is able to achieve in that nosology (Kernberg, 2002).

The history of psychoanalytic writings concerning homosexuality indicates that it was not the clinical study of gay men and lesbians that led to a more nuanced psychoanalytic understanding of the nature of homosexuality, and that changes in the culture and society within which our specialty practised played a significant role.[2] Discourse about homosexuality has always been linked to the culture surrounding it. Until the nineteenth century, discourse on the practices that would subsequently come to be understood as manifestations of homosexuality qua (sexual) identity was almost exclusively the domain of religion. It was not until 1869 that a Hungarian journalist by the name of Kertbeny coined the terms homosexual and homosexuality whilst writing a treatise against the Prussian law that criminalized sodomy. He argued that homosexuality was a normal variation, inborn and unchangeable, undeserving of the moralizing attitude that characterized the sodomy laws.

Krafft-Ebing is perhaps best known for advocating a view of homosexuality as a degenerative disorder (Krafft-Ebing, 1886/1965), while the British sexologist Havelock Ellis (1905) advanced a carefully constructed normal variation theory. A German sex researcher, Magnus Hirschfeld (Hirschfeld, 1914/2000), had a similar normal variations approach and drew on Ulrichs' homosexuality as a *third sex* metaphor.

In this context Freud put together an innovative and genuinely sophisticated narrative about homosexuality (Freud, 1905). Freud was the first to put quotation marks around the '*normal*' where it concerned sexual practices (de Lautetis, 1994). By doing so, Freud placed homosexuality at the heart of sexuality at the same time as bestowing upon sexuality the role of psychic organizer. By focusing on sexual development and its vicissitudes, and placing his emphasis on the principle of *pleasure*, Freud undermined the assumption that sexuality could be conceived of as a natural attribute and rejected genderized sex as a developmentally determined given.

As we know, in his theory we are all bisexual (we are all born ambidextrous). He explicitly rejects the normal variation hypothesis and refuses to consider homosexuals as a 'third sex'. He writes in the 1915 edition: 'Psychoanalytic research is most decidedly opposed to any attempt at separating off homosexuals from the rest of mankind as a group of special character' (Freud, 1905: 144n). Freud also could not be clearer that homosexuality is not 'a degenerative condition'. With his usual extraordinary incisiveness and respect for empiricism, he states: 'it is found in people whose efficiency is unimpaired and who are indeed distinguished by a specially high intellectual development and ethical culture' [p. 139]. As we know, he spells out an intriguing theory of homosexuality as caused by arrested psychosexual development: its environmental aetiology illustrated by Leonardo da Vinci's experience of overly intense mothering in the absence of a father (Freud, 1910).

The essence of Freudian theory is that sexuality, along with other processes governing life, is the product of development. Male and female do not (pre-)exist but are structured through oedipal and pre-oedipal dynamics: the expectations, fantasies and beliefs of the human infant in relation to his or her objects that ultimately equip us for varying adult realizations of male and female. He argues that 'the sexual instinct is in the first instance independent of its object; nor is its origin likely to be due to the object's attractions' (Freud, 1905: 148).

Freud's insistence that *object choice and desire are independent* is highly pertinent to modern formulations. It reflects his wish to reject the 'normative', not out of a wish to embrace homosexuality (in his writings on femininity he is quite deprecatory at least about female homosexuality) (1931, 1933), but because of his intellectual exposure to sexual fantasies and sexual practices, which leaves him open to a historically remarkable degree of relativism and a wish for deconstruction. For example, he sees homosexuality as essential in driving positive social forces such as group identity, as well as social orientation in general (Freud, 1921), although it should be noted that he remains uncomfortable with unsublimated full erotic expression of homosexuality (Lane, 2001).

While Freud frequently conflated gender identity with homosexuality, there can be no doubt about his essential humanity in relation to homosexuality and his commitment unswervingly to explore his patients' subjective experiences. In a letter to an American mother written in 1935 he wrote:

> Homosexuality is assuredly no advantage, but is nothing to be ashamed of, no vice, no degradation; it cannot be classified as an illness; we consider it to be a variation of sexual function produced by a certain arrest of sexual development.
> (Freud, 1935/1960: 43)

Freud and Rank both believed that homosexuals could and should be trained by psychoanalytic institutes. It was Ernest Jones, someone who only narrowly avoided conviction for paedophilia, who strenuously opposed homosexuals becoming psychoanalysts, on the grounds that it might discredit the profession (Clarke and Blechner, 2011). Sandor Ferenczi (1902) and analysts of the Budapest school, along with most other Central European psychoanalysts, held libertarian views similar to Freud's.

So what happened? Perhaps the diaspora of a Jewish profession determined to adapt to the norms of an Anglo-Saxon adopted land was a contributory factor. Together with the socialist politics of classical psychoanalysis, the emergent open-minded view of homosexuality was sacrificed in exchange for social acceptability. Freud's open attitude gave way to a vindictive pathologizing theory that reflected the predominant values within the United States and Great Britain (see also Chapter 1 for a more detailed historical analysis).

An interesting example is another Hungarian, Sandor Rado (1940, 1969), the founder of the *Columbia Center for Psychoanalytic Training and Research*. He eschewed Freud's developmental ideas, dismissed the possibility of homosexuality as a biological norm, and any possibility of 'normal' homosexuality. Homosexuality, in his view, could be reduced to anxiety about heterosexuality; it was due to inadequate parenting and could be cured. This, of course, opposed

Freud's (1920) assertion that 'to undertake to convert a fully developed homosexual into a heterosexual does not offer much more prospect of success than the reverse, except that for practical reasons the latter is never attempted' (p. 151).

So what is the nature of the writings on homosexuality produced in the second half of the twentieth century? These semi-classical contributions highlight the vulnerability of psychoanalytic clinical thinking in ways that are just as relevant today. The common theme in reports of gay and lesbian individuals treated in psychoanalysis, of which there are a fair number (between 20 and 30 a year between 1955 and 1965), is that homosexuality is 'caused' by conflict over heterosexual impulses. This, in turn, drives intense unconscious anxiety that is avoided through the compromise of the homosexual act. Anxiety is seen as leading to a developmental deviation or arrest. Arrest is now viewed as malignant, rather than as Freud saw it, something relatively benign. The narrative focusing on immaturity gives way to a blaming perception where patients 'wilfully' and destructively adopt a stance that undermines or attacks the 'facts of life', the gender distinction as we know it, and must all be brought to recognize as part of reality.

These papers have a moralistic taint. The analyst is seen as a rescuer, a champion and preserver of the *truth*, no matter how painful and unpalatable. Often the narratives are presented in terms of a somewhat personified conflict between ideas, for example, the grandiose wish to feel omnipotent and in control set against the *reality* of one's infantile vulnerability. Alternatively the anxiety may concern the possession of power against a background of destructive and aggressive wishes. Or the story may involve existential anxieties generated by extreme environments or extreme behaviours of one's carers. There is little in these clinical descriptions that is unique; they 'explain' (post hoc) why homosexual orientation was chosen by an individual, but when set against other explanations or other behaviours which are seen to deserve clinical attention, there is nothing to differentiate these accounts.

The success rates for 'conversion' reported in these papers are staggering. For example, in the early 1960s Bieber and colleagues claimed to have *cured* over a quarter of patients of their 'homosexual pathology' (Bieber et al., 1962). When asked, however, Bieber was unable to produce *just one* patient from the 100 that he said he had successfully converted. *The issue here is the evident false logic of psychoanalytic clinicians who focused the subtlety of their understanding of the intra-psychic and inter-personal on a socially defined problem or more accurately the problem of an individual caused by a social definition.*

The human problem was that whilst homosexuals, for the most part, experienced their relationships as a source of joy, medicine and psychiatry defined their pleasure as an illness. Notwithstanding Kinsey's (Kinsey, Pomeroy, and Martin, 1948; Kinsey et al., 1953) likely over-estimation that the prevalence of homosexuality is up to 10 per cent, in 1952 DSM-I defined homosexuality as a *sociopathic personality disturbance*. Even when gay activists succeeded in shifting the views of the nomenclature committee of the American Psychiatric Association in the 1970s, psychiatrists from the psychoanalytic community petitioned the APA to hold a referendum of its entire membership to reverse the decision. The decision to remove was upheld by 8 per cent. The reasoning, however, is of interest. The definition of mental disorder adopted by DSM-III was 'causing subjective distress or associated with generalized impairment in social effectiveness or functioning' (Spitzer, 1981: 211). To vote for retaining homosexuality in DSM was voting for homosexuality causing distress. Definitely not pleasure!

Psychoanalytic clinicians collectively failed to think about their homosexual patients as people who were struggling with a world where secular and religious authority combined to condemn them for what gave them joy. It is galling to read some of the 1950s psychoanalytic accounts where the patients' imputed desire to deny the facts of life, reality as is, is actually manifested by the clinicians' accounts of interpersonal experiences in which the patients' experience of pleasure is systematically scotomized at best, pathologized and derogated at worst.

Yet homosexual sex is relatively less burdened by the mediation of social functions than its 'normal' straight counterpart, which carries weighty responsibilities for mediating many crucial social functions (the definition of social status, organizing procreation, creating a family life, assuring the fair transfer of property across generations). Without these complications, homosexuality can be a more straightforwardly sensual pleasure – a reality which, perhaps, rather than being envied, had to be denied and repudiated. This is of course not to say that homosexual sex is free of the complications created by the inevitable link of sexuality to representation of mental states in human beings.[3] It was also hard for psychoanalysts to become attuned to the subjective reality of homosexual experience because they ejected homosexual individuals from their own community. Those homosexuals who were accepted for training had to deny their own reality and collude with a systematic distortion of subjectivity that was imposed by social order rather than by experience.

The present

Can modern social science help us to understand the paradoxes revealed in the psychoanalytic encounter with homosexuality? Queer theory (Jagose, 1996; Sullivan, 2003) is an outgrowth of an American, politically motivated academic movement emerging about 20 years ago out of dissatisfaction with the understanding of homosexuality within the categories of identity and oppositional politics. The 1960s and 1970s witnessed powerful intellectual and social movements to establish the rights of homosexual people in relation to the heterosexual world, as we have seen in the context of the fight to remove homosexuality from the DSM. However, such movements are considered with scepticism by Queer theory because they are based on minoritizing conceptions of sexuality. Queer is a radical repositioning that reflects doubt about universalizing explanations; it asserts scepticism in relation to universal or objective truth. The term 'queer' marks something odd or strange, deliberately transposed from its derogatory use to designate homosexual men. It is inevitably a contentious term which individuals embrace to highlight their difference and thereby reveal it.

This sophisticated intellectual movement, built on late twentieth-century thought, was strongly influenced by Freud and French post-structuralists, particularly Michel Foucault. It was Foucault's (1976) analysis of sexuality, beginning with a critique of identity and identity politics, that defined itself against the normative. Following Foucault, Queer theory questions the definition and deployment of sexuality that makes minority groups not only the victims of regulatory power regimes but also their product. Foucault's fundamental insight, in some ways arguably a psychoanalytic one, lay in his recognition that resistance is not opposed to power but inseparable from it. His *History of Sexuality* challenged the commonly accepted narrative (the 'repressive hypothesis') according to which the Victorians were held responsible for a wholesale repression of sexuality that lingered on into the modern era and even now has yet to be fully dismantled to achieve sexual liberation. Foucault's retelling of the story suggests that both the agents of repression and the challengers who seek to liberate sexuality are characters in a kind of cover story produced by the workings of power mechanisms, as is the tendency to talk in terms of sexuality 'itself' (rather than a diverse range of particular practices and experiences).[4] From this perspective, the Gay Liberation movement can arguably be seen as part of a larger mechanism of control and exploitation, and is criticized for continuing to rely on a conception of sexuality that subsumes a heterogeneous and conflictual flux of experiences under a fixed and limited identity.

Queer theory opposes definition and views with suspicion those oppositional strategies that try to displace ascendant ideologies and put non-normative conceptualizations in their place (Jagose, 1996). Such strategies are considered inherently (self-)contradictory because all identity categories inevitably entail rigidity and an implicit belief in the immutability of these categories. Following Foucault, homosexuality is understood as a position rather than an identity: a position of having been marginalized as a result of sexual preference, which could befall anyone regardless of their orientation.

Foucault warned that 'we must not think that by saying yes to sex, one says no to power' and suggested that the '*counter-attack against the deployment of sexuality ought not to be sex-desire, but bodies and pleasures*' (Foucault, 1976: 157). In this sense our Freudian interest as psychoanalysts overlaps almost completely with Queer theory. It is precisely this (bodies and pleasures) aspect of homosexuality that was denied by psychoanalysis in the 1960s.

In *Gender Trouble*, a key text for Queer theory, Judith Butler (1999) argued that gender identity is culturally constructed through the reiteration of acts: gender is performative, constituted by the very actions that are said to be its results (Butler, 1999: 25). Viewing gender as an ongoing discursive practice destabilizes the traditional categories of sex, gender and sexuality. This is an inevitable consequence of the post-structuralist reconceptualization of identity as multiple and polyvalent.

Notwithstanding Foucault's suspicion of psychoanalysis, from its earliest beginnings psychoanalysis has been concerned with how unconsciously determined subjective dimensions, the fluidity of primary process, preclude the possibility of belief in a firm identity. The inherent instability of sex, gender and sexuality may be the appropriate focus for psychoanalysis in considering homosexuality, and indeed heterosexuality. Our role is to scrutinize the processes by means of which what appears to be an identity is constructed, and to do so in a manner that leaves open the potential for alternative constructions. This would open the field to the possibility of studying the context, including the influence of the therapeutic relationship and the gendered actions of the analyst on both analyst's and patient's experience of this process.

Abandoning concern with identity can free us to focus on precise ways of knowing, of being, of exploring subjectivity, of identifying relationships of a more or less complex, stable or multivalent nature. The relationships may be between ideas, between individuals or between relationships. In psychoanalysis we (ideally) attempt to liberate individuals from the sense of marginalization they feel because of implicitly held, publicly accepted forms of knowledge that deny the singular truth of the individual's experience. We (should) work to undermine these myriad expectations, distinguishing the individual's experience from the discourse of wider society, their immediate social group and their family relations.

It is striking how widely the theory and the term 'queer' has been adopted by those writing about gay and lesbian, bisexual and transgendered issues. The resistance to definition inherent in the approach strikes a familiar chord with all those who work in the field. In psychoanalysis, this resonates with the Lacanian framework where the concept of the *real* has no predetermined content but rather is the site of the traumatic cause of sex and desire, where the subject encounters an order that resists assimilation to any imaginary or symbolic universe (Bailly, 2009).

Queer seems to signify the messiness that notions of identity unsuccessfully attempt to tidy away. The nature of desire is to resist definition in terms of discrete identity categories. When we attempt such definitions, we transform something dynamic into something static, betraying rather than capturing its essence. Desire can only be misrepresented. Elsewhere we have located the radical challenge it poses to identity and coherence as characteristic of what we call the *primary unconscious* (Fonagy and Allison, 2011). We refer to the non-conscious states of fragmentation, incoherence and negativity characterized by properties of the death instinct as the primary unconscious, as distinct from the non-conscious brain activities which are not associated with awareness and which simply reflect a feature of brain function. In normal development primary unconscious content appropriately remains inaccessible to conscious experience. We call the intrusive, disturbing, disruptive mental contents that we as psychoanalytic clinicians work with *the psychoanalytic unconscious*. Since these contents have achieved a degree of phenomenological status, they can and do intrude on, disturb and disrupt consciousness. The content of the primary unconscious can only be manifest as disturbances of consciousness since it is inherently destructive of the coherence and intentionality constitutive of consciousness. However, in trying to describe it, the language of 'destructiveness' or 'negativity' is potentially confusing as these carry the echoes of intentionality and imply an attack on an object. We have in mind a more fundamental undoing of the synthetic processes by means of which objects are normally constituted as such. Without the sense of meaning conferred through projective identification, there is no intentionality in the process.

The primary unconscious manifests itself to the extent that it finds realization through social responses, and it shows itself through constant undermining of all sexual and social identities. We refer to the resultant disruptive, albeit potentially somewhat controlled, part of mind which we as psychoanalysts constantly struggle with, as the *psychoanalytic unconscious*. One way in which unconscious desire may come to be partially socially realized is as a result of trauma, where its negativity finds a distorted mirror in experiences of profound deprivation and abuse. More commonly, specific *partial failures* of mirroring occur in relation to an infant's unconscious desire because the manifestations of this desire (sexuality and aggression) generate too much unpleasure in the caregiver, making him or her reluctant to respond fully contingently. This leaves all of us with internal experiences which are phenomenal but which do not feel quite our own, because we were not helped to develop representations for them. As a result, we are driven to find partners with whom we can externalize them in order to experience them fully (evocative projective identification by another name).

Our contention is that normal sexual desire is inherently unknowable and when it becomes socialized it is part of a picture that resembles psychopathology in structure and form. Part of the essence of desire is that there is something anti-conceptual, something indefinite and unknowable about it. As Freud wrote, 'we must reckon with the possibility that something in the nature of the sexual instinct itself is unfavourable to the realization of complete satisfaction' (Freud, 1912: 188). It has as Dean put it 'a disquieting disregard for gender and persons' (Dean, 2000: 239).

These ideas attempt to integrate a somewhat Lacanian perspective on the nature of desire with developmental conceptualizations that our group has been working on for some time (Fonagy, 2008; Target, 2007). Lacan's (1964) claim that love has nothing to do with sex (which turns out to be true from an empirical point of view even for monogamous rodents) also recognizes that desire is developmentally shaped by the social system within which it is vested. For the infant these are relationships with caregivers. Desire in our view, and in that of some French psychoanalysts like Laplanche (1995), is shaped and socially constructed by the non-responsiveness of the object (or seductive responses in the case of Laplanche) to the infant's desire.

It follows from this understanding of the nature of desire that neither homosexuality nor heterosexuality are 'normal' and that neither can be an identity. Human desire is characterized by the same sense of incongruence and striving to be fully experienced that we see in borderline projective identificatory phenomena. It seeks another body through which an internal experience can find voice. In our view, desire (psychosexuality if you will) drives interpersonal experiences because the power relationships of early infancy gave the infant's desire no meaning. Knowledge (in Foucault's sense) in relation to the sexual is institutionally withheld from the infant and young child by all levels of society. We have noted and empirically demonstrated the curious predilections of the carer (the object) mostly to ignore, overlook but perhaps also to entice the infant's excitement (Fonagy, 2008; Target, 2007).

This leaves all of us with a gap, a failed definition, a rupture of the *epistemic trust* of our pedagogic stance (the social contract which obliges the adult to teach, to acculturate the child into the mysteries of social meanings). Sexuality becomes a pattern of desire shaped and constrained by the non-response of the object, to be made unreal, for ever to be experienced with trepidation and uncertainty, and imbued with what Laplanche might emphasize as the enigmatic.

How does same-gender sexual orientation come about from this matrix? We have argued that since the essence of desire is its indefiniteness, its construction into a defined identity will betray its essence. Once we have a scientific theory of homosexuality we have something that has lost its psychological roots in desire. We suggest that the role of psychoanalysis is to understand same sex experience through the deepest possible scrutiny of the individual's current and historical subjectivity.

A theory of same sex orientation based on these developmental ideas would be focused on the role of a caregiver who happened to have created momentary meaning for the infant from her or his desire. Of course, it is not the caregiver's overt behaviour but rather that which the infant's constitution elicits in her or him. And of course, it is not the actions of the other that matter to the infant but the impact of those actions on her or his subjectivity. The multiple qualifications on these statements underscore the dubious validity of any such theory.

We are certainly not saying that alternative social response (say a sexually more open reaction to an infant's psychosexuality) would result in the taming of unconscious desire. The sheer variety of social experimentation in relation to sexual acculturation over past millennia speaks volumes about the naïveté of such a proposal. Since by nature desire is resistant to representation, the discomfort of desire as made real by its social experience is here to stay. We predict that, if anything, its potential for impingement will be enhanced by the increased contingent mirroring of psychic experience made available by the panoply of electronic media, the iPhone and Android apps or the infinite set of as yet unimagined realizations of the primary unconscious. When desire is intimately experienced with another person, in all its instinctual complexity of oral, anal, phallic and goodness knows what else, the human reflection from another appears developmentally to tame our desire by gradually creating symbolic representations of the experience that help regulate rather than sensitize (Fonagy, 2008). But this takes time. A lifetime. And perhaps it was so intended.

Taking our argument to its logical conclusion, we may object to the assumption that *homosexuality* stands in particular need of explanation; it seems to belie the purpose of psychoanalysis and to embrace the implicit hetero-normativity which the term conveys. The institutions and social constraints that underpin the normative deny the possibility of an appropriately nuanced and subtle exploration of particular subjectivities. Taking a broader perspective, psychoanalysis needs to embrace de-legitimization, the wish to make strange, to frustrate, to counteract

(Sullivan, 2003). It is only through de-legitimization that a genuinely mentalizing approach to subjectivity will be generated, that is, an approach that eschews assumptions about both other people's and one's own thoughts and feelings in favour of an inquisitive stance that leaves room for discovery. It is attention to the discontinuities, the breaks in the surface, that will reveal what is driving and significant, both by causing anxiety and by the positive perturbation of intense desire. Understanding this brings us closer to creating a genuine psychologically informed narrative of personal experience.

In brief, starting from a developmental perspective, we believe that the sexual has to be regarded as a developmentally constructed, sometimes misshapen, derivative of desire that by seeking an object denies its essence. None of us have found a way of retaining desire without an object. This is the paradox of all our lives. Condoning some forms of object choice while rejecting others simply serves to deny the subtlety and complexity but perhaps also the vulnerability of our own position in relation to the (mis)shaping of our own desires.

This uncertainty about our own position, and its roots in the developmental taboo of bringing the child in contact with her or his desire prematurely, may account for the social rigidity and wish for certainty that the subject of sex continues to provoke in all of us. Whilst we can and should try to understand such deep-seated if misplaced wishes for definition in our patients, it behooves us to be suspicious of ourselves when our wish for simplicity begins to override our respect for the complexity of subjective experience that our patients engender and bring with them in relation to their experience of their sexuality.

Notes

1 Earlier versions of this paper were presented at the *Psychoanalytic Psychotherapy NOW Conference*, London, 24 January 2012, and at Scientific Meetings of the British Psychoanalytic Society and of the Tavistock Clinic, London, 17 October 2012 and 13 May 2013. Prof. Mary Target's ideas and writings contributed significantly to the writing of this paper, and we gratefully acknowledge Rose Palmer MA who made invaluable comments on earlier drafts of this paper.
2 There has been a striking discontinuity between the public and private theories of psychoanalysts in this domain (Sandler, 1983), the former perhaps showing greater awareness of the multi-layered nature of issues concerning homosexuality while the latter may have been more open to influence from prevailing culture. Private theories may have been more influential in determining educational curricula, admission policies to institutes and evaluations of candidates and colleagues where much was done which now seems regrettable.
3 To anticipate our later argument, the resistance of desire to representation means that no object choice can be completely satisfying. However, there is no ground for assuming that it is any more problematic than its heterosexual counterpart other than the social stigmatization which homosexuality has to contend with.
4 'Briefly, my aim is to examine the case of a society which has been loudly castigating itself for its hypocrisy for more than a century, which speaks verbosely of its own silence, takes great pains to relate in detail the things it does not say, denounces the powers it exercises and promises to liberate itself from the very laws that have made it function' (Foucault, 1976: 8).

References

Bailly, L. (2009). *Lacan: A beginner's guide*. London: Oneworld.

Bergler, E. (1956). *Homosexuality: Disease or way of life?* New York: Hill & Wang.

Bieber, I., Dain, H. J., Dince, P. R., Drellich, M. G., Grand, H. G., & Gundlach, R. H. (1962). *Homosexuality: A psychoanalytic study*. New York: Basic Books.

Butler, J. (1999). *Gender Trouble*. New York: Routledge.

Clarke, J., & Blechner, M. (2011). Interview with Dr Mark Blechner. *Psychoanalytic Psychotherapy, 25*, 361–379.

de Lautetis, T. (1994). *The Practice of Love: Lesbian sexuality and perverse desire*. Bloomingdale, IN: Indiana University Press.

Dean, T. (2000). *Beyond Sexuality*. Chicago, IL: University of Chicago Press.

Drescher, J. (2002). Causes and becauses: On etiological theories of homosexuality. *Annual of Psychoanalysis, 30*, 57–68.

Drescher, J. (2007). From bisexuality to intersexuality: Rethinking gender categories. *Contemporary Psychoanalysis, 43*, 204–228.

Ellis, H. (1905). *Psychology of Sex*. New York: Harcourt Brace Jovanovich.

Ferenczi, S. (1902). Homosexualitas feminina. *Gyogyaszat, 11*, 167–168.

Fonagy, P. (2008). A genuinely developmental theory of sexual enjoyment and its implications for psychoanalytic technique. *Journal of the American Psychoanalytic Association, 56*(1), 11–36.

Fonagy, P., & Allison, E. (2011). *A Theme in the Work on the Nature of Psychic Reality: The nature of consciousness*. Paper presented at Ron Britton Today, A Conference in Honour of Dr Ronald Britton London, December.

Fonagy, P., & Higgitt, A. (2007). The development of prejudice: An attachment theory hypothesis explaining its ubiquity. In H. Parens, A. Mahfouz, S. W. Twemlow & D. E. Scharff (Eds.), *The Future of Prejudice*. Plymouth: Jason Aronson.

Foucault, M. (1976). *The History of Sexuality 1: The will to knowledge*. London: Penguin Books.

Freud, S. (1905). Three essays on the theory of sexuality. In J. Strachey (Ed.), *The Standard Edition of the Complete Psychological Works of Sigmund Freud* (Vol. VI, pp. 123–230). London: Hogarth Press.

Freud, S. (1910). Leonardo da Vinci and a memory of his childhood. In J. Strachey (Ed.), *The Standard Edition of the Complete Psychological Works of Sigmund Freud* (Vol. XI). London: Hogarth Press.

Freud, S. (1912). On the universal tendency to debasement in the sphere of love (Contributions to the psychology of love II). In J. Strachey (Ed.), *The Standard Edition of the Complete Psychological Works of Sigmund Freud* (Vol. XI, pp. 177–190). London: Hogarth Press.

Freud, S. (1920). Beyond the pleasure principle. In J. Strachey (Ed.), *The Standard Edition of the Complete Psychological Works of Sigmund Freud* (Vol. XVIII, pp. 1–64). London: Hogarth Press.

Freud, S. (1921). Group psychology and the analysis of the ego. In J. Strachey (Ed.), *The Standard Edition of the Complete Psychological Works of Sigmund Freud* (Vol. XVIII, pp. 69–143). London: Hogarth Press.

Freud, S. (1931). Female sexuality. In J. Strachey (Ed.), *The Standard Edition of the Complete Psychological Works of Sigmund Freud* (Vol. XXI, pp. 221–246). London: Hogarth Press.

Freud, S. (1933). Femininity. In J. Strachey (Ed.), *The Standard Edition of the Complete Psychological Works of Sigmund Freud* (Vol. XXII). London: Hogarth Press.

Freud, S. (1935 /1960). Anonymous (Letter to an American mother). In E. Freud (Ed.), *The Letters of Sigmund Freud* (pp. 423–424). New York: Basic Books.

Hirschfeld, M. (1914/2000). *The Homosexuality of Men and Women* (M. Lombardi-Nash, Trans.). Buffalo, NY: Prometheus Books.

Jagose, A. (1996). *Queer Theory: An introduction*. New York: New York University Press.

Kernberg, O. F. (1975). *Borderline Conditions and Pathological Narcissism*. New York: Jason Aronson.

Kernberg, O. F. (2002). Unresolved issues in the psychoanalytic theory of homosexuality and bisexuality. *Journal of Gay and Lesbian Psychotherapy, 6*(1), 9–27.

Kinsey, A. C., Pomeroy, W. B., & Martin, C. E. (1948). *Sexual Behaviour in the Human Male*. Philadelphia, PA: W. B. Saunders.

Kinsey, A. C., Pomeroy, W. B., Martin, C. E., & Gebhard, P. H. (1953). *Sexual Behavior in the Human Female*. Philadelphia: W. B. Saunders.

Krafft-Ebing, R. (1886/1965). *Psychopathia Sexualis* (H. Wedeck, Trans.). New York: Putnam.

Lacan, J. (1964). *The Four Fundamental Concepts of Psychoanalysis*. New York: Norton, 1978.

Lane, C. (2001). Freud on group psychology. In T. Dean & C. Lane (Eds.), *Homosexuality and Psychoanalysis*. Chicago, IL: University of Chicago Press.

Laplanche, J. (1995). Seduction, persecution, revelation. *International Journal of Psycho-Analysis, 76*, 663–682.

Rado, S. (1940). A critical examination of the concept of bisexuality. *Psychosomatic Medicine, 2*, 459–467.

Rado, S. (1969). *Adaptational Psychodynamics: Motivation and control*. New York: Science House.

Sandler, J. (1983). Reflections on some relations between psychoanalytic concepts and psychoanalytic practice. *International Journal of Psycho-Analysis, 64*, 35–45.

Spitzer, R. L. (1981). The diagnostic status of homosexuality in DSM-III: A reformulation of the issues. *American Journal of Psychiatry, 138*, 210–215.

Sullivan, N. (2003). *A Critical Introduction to Queer Theory*. New York: New York University Press.

Target, M. (2007). Is our sexuality our own? A developmental model of sexuality based on early affect mirroring. *British Journal of Psychotherapy, 23*(4), 517–530.

Ulrichs, K. ([1864] 2001). *The Riddle of 'Man-Manly' Love*. In J. Drescher, *Psychoanalytic Therapy and The Gay Man*. Hillsdale, NJ: The Analytic Press.

Chapter 7

Intimacy, desire and shame in gay male sexuality

Paul E. Lynch

> . . .'Sweet youth,
> Tell me why, sad and sighing, thou dost rove
> These pleasant realms? I pray thee speak me sooth
> What is thy name?' He said, 'My name is Love.'
> Then straight the first did turn himself to me
> And cried, 'He lieth, for his name is Shame,
> But I am Love, and I was wont to be
> Alone in this fair garden, till he came
> Unasked by night; I am true Love, I fill
> The hearts of boy and girl with mutual flame.'
> Then sighing, said the other, 'Have thy will,
> I am the Love that dare not speak its name.'
>   From 'Two Loves', Lord Alfred Douglas 1894

Men are from Mars, and women are from Venus (Gray, 1992), but where in the universe will we find elucidating accounts of gay men and lesbians? With wishful bids to differentiate between broad categories, we sidestep the complexity of actual people, who are similar and different in such varying ways that they are often hard to explain. We want to break down complexities to components that are simple and easy to understand, although we lose a great deal in the process. Psychoanalysis offers a more thorough method for the exploration of enormous quantities of sameness and difference, yet it has often failed to see the overlapping of the two, settling instead for distinct categories of people that no real person has ever actually fit into. As Sedgwick observed,

> Psychoanalytic theory, if only through the almost astrologically lush plurality of its overlapping taxonomies of physical zones, developmental stages, representational mechanisms, and levels of consciousness, seemed to promise to introduce a certain becoming amplitude into discussions of what different people are like – only to turn, in its streamlined trajectory across so many institutional boundaries, into the sveltest of metatheoretical disciplines, sleeked down to such elegant operational entities as *the* mother, *the* father, *the* pre-oedipal, *the* oedipal, *the* other or Other.

(1990: 23–4)

Psychoanalysis in America has moved beyond speaking of *the* homosexual, more so than psychoanalysis in many other parts of the world. American psychoanalysis has also moved away from the supposition of universal norms in development, and toward configurations of gender and sexuality that are more individualized (Chodorow, 1992, 2002, 2012). Yet, it remains a challenge to speak about desires and sexualities of gay men, without reduction to *the* desires and *the* sexualities of gay men.

In this chapter, I explore gay male psychosexual development and adult sexuality as it is influenced by proscriptions of the real world. As 'the love that dare not speak its name,' such constrained desires can be burdened with shame.

(Homo)sexuality in early childhood

Sigmund Freud (1905) shocked the world with ideas about sexuality in infants and children, but as psychoanalysis evolved its central focus on sexuality declined, even for adults. After Green (1995) asked, 'Has sexuality anything to do with psychoanalysis?' many attempted to answer the questions of what causes sexual excitement, and where sexuality fits in contemporary psychoanalysis, with its emphasis on object relations, attachment, and relationality. A developmental model of sexuality based on early affect mirroring was proposed collaboratively by Fonagy (2008) and Target (2007), heavily influenced by LaPlanche's (1995) theories of early mother–child interactions and unconscious (enigmatic) communication. In this model, overt sexual excitement is un-mirrored, uncontained, ignored, or mirrored incongruently, disrupting the child's sense of self-coherence. Building on the work of Stein (1998a, 1998b), Fonagy and Target emphasize that the enigmatic excitement, urgency, and pleasure of sexuality is experienced only when it is elaborated, found, or placed in the other. To the extent that sexual stimulation may begin as urges or drives coming from within, interpersonal interaction is needed for the excitement of sexuality to be elaborated or experienced. 'Because sexual excitement is by its nature incongruent with the self, excitement has to be experienced in the other and only therefore with the other' (Target, 2007: 524).

Lichtenberg (2008) proposed that sensuality is distinguished from sexuality by the parents' approval or disapproval of the child's enjoyment of bodily sensations and fantasies. He proposed that bodily sensations and accompanying fantasies that are shared in and encouraged by the parent constitute sensuality, whereas the disapproved of, shamed, and prohibited forms of bodily sensations and fantasies constitute sexuality. He states, 'sexuality takes a path toward excitement that builds from both a hedonic quest and a response to transgressing the shaming and prohibiting.' This echoes Stoller's theory of sexual excitement (1976), in which the goal of any individual sexual fantasy or scenario is to take previously painful or humiliating experiences 'and convert to them to pleasure – triumph.' Frustration of an infant's wish to derive pleasure from his own body parts, and the body parts of caretakers, is central to the development of sexuality. Frustrations provide fuel for the promise of pleasure, in the triumph of overcoming limitations. Desire to enact bodily pleasures coupled with the pain and humiliation of prohibition are then the substrates on which are built triumphant sexual pleasures.

The infant's pleasure seeking with its own body or the body of its caretaker is not consciously sexual, and society is structured to keep young children from knowledge of overt sexuality. Yet, interactions with parents are essential in the development of sexuality, and include parental messages that are unconscious to both parent and child. In LaPlanche's (1997) theory of the transmission of 'enigmatic signifiers,' the enigma in parental unconscious messages is itself an unconscious seduction that contributes to the development of the child's unconscious, and to the development of sexuality. LaPlanche sought to displace theories of a self-centered ego from the heart of our theories on sexual development, in favor of an other-centered theory of the ego's enigmatic experience of 'alien-ness' in relation to the unconscious of the Other (the parent). In the mélange of unconscious messages, it is possible that any variety of notions may be transmitted. While the value of transgression and eccentricity, for their excitement and rebelliousness, may have a place in the unconscious of many parents, most will veer toward the safety of conformity. Attached to a particularly anxious parent's messages about sexuality might be fears about a particular child; for example, fear that the child will be aberrant – possibly the embodiment of disavowed aspects of the parent's sexual desires or fantasies. In any case, as the child develops and comes to know something of his or her own subjectivities and desires, even before they are fully conscious, the child learns that some subjectivities and desires are more welcome than others.

Central to what follows in this chapter is the possibility that the child learns very early that some of his or her urges and wishes are unsanctioned by others, and that he or she learns therefore to be ashamed, and to anxiously hide or disavow prohibited desires to avoid abandonment and loss of love.

Oedipal rejection

Among the most frequent concerns of young gay men are worries about whether they are or will be accepted by their families. Isay (1987) drew our attention to the *erotic* relationship between gay boys and their fathers, and postulated that the rejection gay boys felt was actually due to the withdrawal of their fathers' attention and affection, when they sensed, consciously or not, their sons' erotically charged attraction. Goldsmith (2001) focused not only on the attraction of the little boy for his father in the Oedipal period, but also on the unexpected competition with his mother, and the resultant tensions in that relationship.

In our current culture, families generally do not expect, welcome, or celebrate a little boy's libidinal desires for his father in the same way that they generally do endorse a little girl's libidinal desires for her father, in the form of imaginative romance. While many families are amused when daddy's little girl wants to marry daddy, they don't enjoy it when their little boy wants to marry daddy. Longing for and ultimately being turned down by a parent in the Oedipal period can be seen as an expectable trauma of childhood. If the family and the outside world can entertain such longing it is safer for the child to give expression to romantic feelings and playfully, creatively negotiate the disappointment, usually with the empathic participation of the family. Oedipal rejection with scorn for the child's same-sex romantic desires, or with withdrawal of the parent who is desired, is an empathic failure that can add to feelings of shame, condemnation, and isolation. This empathic failure is but one of many disappointments for same-sex libidinal strivings, and the world presents more overt dangers as well.

A gay or proto-gay boy's developing ego must navigate the world's attacks on his subjectivities and desires. Freud (1923) told us that the ego serves three masters, and is

> consequently menaced by three dangers: from the external world, from the libido of the id, and from the severity of the superego. Three kinds of anxiety correspond to these three dangers, since anxiety is the expression of a retreat from danger.
>
> (p. 56)

A boy's psychosexual development, and his understanding of himself and his desires, must be affected by explicit and implicit knowledge of the desires and behaviors that his environment acclaims, authorizes, recognizes, permits, or scorns. Rose (2007) studied the adult relationships of gay men, and found detrimental 'echoes' of Oedipal rejection, including poor self-image and tendencies toward relationships that recreated the Oedipal rejection, either by rejecting or getting rejected in ways that echoed the painful relationships that his subjects had with their fathers.

Recent emphasis on the father as Oedipal object for boys should be considered a corrective emphasis to remedy a long-standing blind spot, and not a total explanation of gay male development. Mother remains in the picture, and both parents perhaps take on various symbolic roles and meanings during different phases of development. Also, boys who become gay are not the only ones who are affected by their world's inhibition of same-sex erotic fantasy and romantic play. Anton Kris (2012) noted that some freedom to express love for men, particularly one's father, assists in the development of heterosexual intimacy as well. Along these lines, some amount of hedonistic desire (aim) and intimacy with an other (object) might only secondarily, and perhaps often incorrectly, be labeled as hetero or homo. This might be more easily noticed if we were not as anxious and vigilant about constantly distinguishing between the sexes (e.g. Chasseguet-Smirgel, 1983), whether in any given moment it matters or not. Perhaps a child's desire for mommy or daddy may at times arise from any number of needs or desires, without always being subsumed rigidly by a singular or fractional sex or gender categorization.

Adolescence and adult (homo)sexuality

Reactions to infantile sexuality in the form of incongruent mirroring and unconscious messages are among the earliest communication of the caregivers' feelings about sexuality. As the child develops and begins to learn in new ways, he detects his caregivers' feelings, judgments, and reactions to his subjectivities and aspirations. Admonitions about (Oedipal) desires for the same-sex parent are just one example of the ongoing disciplinary education of the child's sexuality. The subtle messages gradually become more specific, even concrete.

'De-legitimized' desires (Sullivan, 2003) may become dangerous to express, and risk censure. The more strident the prohibiting reaction, the more danger the child will register, and the more likely that the child will learn to conceal, feel alien, and feel shamed. Seeking to elaborate desires that are proscribed runs the risk of rejection and further alienation, so such desires are best kept away from loved ones. The sequestration of desires becomes more fraught and more conscious with the onset of puberty and adolescent sexual development. Freud (1912) showed that sequestration of sexual potency from love in adult heterosexual men resulted from excessive opposition to their sexual object choices in adolescence, and his schema is particularly apt for the problems of love, sex, and shame that some gay men struggle with.

In Freud's view, the dramatic turn that sexuality takes at puberty, and a point of potential difficulty, is the coming together of the two 'currents' of the libido. Freud's is a mechanistic drive model, yet it has an inter-subjective aspect that meshes well with the developmental and shame models described earlier. What Freud calls the affectionate current is attached to the caretaker objects from the time of infancy, and while sexual in nature, it is not conscious of its sexual aims. At puberty, the sensual current joins the affectionate current, and the libido is no longer innocent of its sexual aims. The barrier against incest must then force the libido away from forbidden incestuous objects, toward socially sanctioned objects outside the family, objects 'with which a real sexual life may be carried on' (p. 181). Freud adds that in the course of time the new sexual objects will attract to themselves the affection that was tied to the earlier ones, 'affection and sensuality are then united' (p. 181). However, if the family or the environment too strongly opposes the youth's choice of new objects, it decreases the value of the objects for the person concerned and impedes unification of the affectionate and the sensual/sexual. In this case, the sensual and the affectionate remain split, rather than united.

Where there is no possibility of acceptable new objects, the sensual current seeks partial satisfaction as an outlaw, with objects that do not evoke the affectionate current or recall the forbidden, incestuous objects. We might think of the extra frustration in reality as effectively expanding the barrier against incest to include all forbidden objects. The affectionate current is constrained also, such that any object that is embraced with the affectionate current will be off limits to sexual excitement – taboo.

Freud emphasized that it is *extra* opposition to the youth's choice of objects that leads to the splitting of the libido into the two realms of the sacred (familial, affectionate, highly valued) and the profane (debased, animal, sexual). He used this splitting of the libido to understand his patients who were impotent with valued others – their wives, but could perform sexually with debased others – prostitutes and mistresses. Freud showed that 'extra frustrations in reality' were implicated in the Madonna/whore split of love/sex, and it was this 'extra' opposition that I see as relevant to the love/sex splits of many gay men.

I (2002) followed this model of Freud's to connect the family's opposition to same-sex sexuality in adolescence with the problems I saw that some adult gay men were having performing sexually with familiar others (partners), as compared with unfamiliar, anonymous others. For gay men who have trouble integrating intimacy with sex, I locate the problem in shame and anxiety that results from the failure of the family or the social environment to sanction a homosexual boy's erotic desires. Following the schema of Freud, for prohibited same-sex sexual desires to get partial satisfaction, they must function as outlaw desires and seek objects that do not recall familial relations. On the other hand, same-sex objects that attract affectionate, familial feelings will recall incestuous objects and therefore will be insulated from sexual feelings. Excessive anxiety and shame over the danger of unacceptable desires leads to sequestration of sexual desires from intimate relations, and relegates the sexual to fantastic expression with unfamiliar or denigrated others (e.g. in anonymity, with strangers, etc.).

Said another way, excessive shame impairs the ability to elaborate sexual drives or integrate sexual desires with an other in the intimacy of a real world relationship. The difficulty some gay men have elaborating sexuality in intimacy has its beginnings in the hostile or insufficiently receptive environment (or inter-subjective play field) for a boy's homoerotic fantasy and play in childhood. Coupled with Oedipal rejection, stronger familial interdictions in adolescence, and exceptional societal admonitions, the resulting anxiety and shame over outlawed and de-legitimated desire burdens attempts at expanding enigmatic pleasures with a known, loved or needed other in adulthood. The *extra* opposition to homosexual object choices is relevant to the love/sex splits of many gay men, as the resultant anxiety and shame is an impediment to the friskiness and adventurous risk-taking needed for the elaboration and linking of sexuality and intimacy. When no tolerance for particular desires exist, those desires are best kept from those one loves. One learns to behave as Freud described,

> Where they love they do not desire and where they desire they cannot love. They seek objects which they do not need to love, in order to keep their sensuality away from the objects they love.
>
> (1912: 183)

I will discuss my work with a patient for whom same-sex interdictions and the lack of early liveliness and mirroring resulted in a split between yearnings for love and cruising for sex, and led to the experience of ample shame and anxiety. But first, a brief consideration follows of a topic that could serve as focal point, or lightning rod, for bodily sensations and fantasies that are not sanctioned by mothers, fathers, or society – anal sexuality.

Anal sexuality: another dark continent

In childhood and adolescence, the paucity of parents' mirroring or mentalization of benign or loving homosexual possibilities is complemented by our culture's blindness to commonplace homosexual longings, and by the use of homosexuals as 'other.' Until recent decades, the homosexual in our cultural awareness was relegated to the role of outsider, often lumped with pedophiles and predators, and with the cannibals, murderers, and villains in Hollywood movies, such as Dr. Hannibal Lecter in *Silence of the Lambs* (Tally, 2001). Anal sexuality can represent the extremes of helpless passivity or of forceful, violent penetration, or the worst of both as in rapacious engulfment. In any case, it fits the Hollywood bill as a monstrous threat to scare us.

Anal sex is among the unconceivable sexual behaviors that are also prominently associated with mundane, run-of-the-mill homosexuals, who were inadvertently thrust into the general public's consciousness with the HIV/AIDS epidemic. The association with anal sex added to the stigma of the disease, and it simultaneously broke down barriers to public consciousness about anal sex. Still, in my clinical experience, gay male patients talk about anal sexuality far less than might be expected, given anal sexuality's evocative, titillating, shameful, and repulsive possibilities, and its cultural association with homosexuality.

While anal sex is often associated with gay men, it is not uncomplicated for gay men. When two cowboys in the movie *Brokeback Mountain* (Lee, 2005) gave way to their desire for one another with quick and wordless anal penetration, many of my gay patients were perplexed and curious about how that happened. For many gay men, a passionate kiss between closeted cowboys would have been equally momentous and more natural, perhaps leading to fondling and fellatio. Anal sex is less generally expected among the uninitiated, at least not without some amount of verbal negotiation and mechanical cooperation to navigate the fine lines of pain and pleasure. For gay men who never do venture there, anal penetration can remain mysterious and scary. For some who come to enjoy anal penetration by a penis, the thought or feeling of a tongue on an anus might seem like ecstasy, while others still shudder in disgust at the thought of it. Psychoanalytic understanding of these feelings and behaviors requires exploration in individual analyses, which would likely return a myriad of explanations for a wide variety of experiences. Thus far, the psychoanalytic literature has generally kept its distance from overt anal sex acts, and contented itself with more general references to homosexual passivity. Even in the traditional, impossibly simple version of sex, where penetrating means active and receiving means passive, this reduction of all anal sexuality to a locus of passivity ignores at least one half of most copulating couples, and most certainly ignores much more.

Botticelli (2010) considered the relationship between bodily and psychic penetrability, and the feeling among some gay men that it was important to have their fathers 'mentalize' their anal sexual desires. Botticelli tells us of a patient whose father had previously made graphic comments that showed pride in his son's sexual prowess with a girlfriend. The patient said, 'What kills me is I could never imagine him feeling the same way about me shooting a load up my boyfriend's ass.' We could say that a component of this patient's 'father hunger' (Herzog, 2001) is a wish for his father to recognize (now) what he failed to mentalize (earlier) of his son's sexuality. Botticelli elaborates similar longings of his patients for their fathers to imagine their pleasurable, passive, anally receptive physical sensations as well.

Another patient that Botticelli tells us more about had a father who showed no pride in his son at all: only impatience and contempt. 'Ted is a man who prides himself on his ability to 'ruin' (his word) other men by fucking them so expertly that they thereafter despair of ever having a comparable sexual experience with another man' (2010: 119). Ted perhaps defends against the castrating glare of his father, and certain aspects of emotional and relational experience with his partner, by his functioning sexually as an aggressive 'top' exclusively. Whether defensive or expressive, anal sexuality has the potential for a myriad of psychic meanings beyond the traditional associations with passivity, failed masculinity, effeminacy, and perversion.

Corbett (1993) considered the construct of masculinity with regard to men's physical receptivity, and potential psychic correlates. He contended that male homosexuality 'is a differently structured masculinity, not a simulated femininity or nonmasculinity' (p. 347). He suggested that masculinity should be able to expand to encompass passivity and longing in relation to another man. Corbett counters the idea that anal sexuality is an enactment of female identification or castration, pointing out that the experience of being penetrated usually causes gay men to become aroused and erect (p. 352). Invariably some of my students find this detail surprising and confusing, naturally desiring to keep the active and the passive both physically and mentally distinct. Conversely, I had a patient who loved to be anally penetrated, and he had a boyfriend who could not understand why he did not have an erection while he was being penetrated. My patient, who did get erections and ejaculate when his penis was stimulated, struggled to convince his boyfriend that he didn't notice or care if he was erect during anal intercourse because the anal sensations he experienced were intense and enjoyable. His boyfriend was versatile, meaning he liked both to penetrate and to be penetrated. He got erections when he was being penetrated, and he found his partner's lack of an erection disconcerting. Perhaps the flaccid penis registered for my patient's boyfriend as too passive for his comfort – that is, as not demonstrating enough physical (phallic, masculine, exterior) evidence of his excitement and pleasure.

Botticelli's patient Ted attached particular meanings to aggressive anal penetration, and his analysis appears to have opened new possibilities for Ted regarding his relating to men (including his analyst), new 'openings' for psychic penetration (Elise, 2001), and new openness to fantasy about physical receptivity. Interestingly, even the rigid meanings of being a 'top' avowed by Ted at the start of his analysis are not quite opposite the meanings of being a 'bottom' avowed by some of the anally receptive patients described by Guss (2010a, 2010b). At the very least, the exclusive tops and exclusive bottoms shared a sense of agency, of actively choosing self-gratification. In Guss' words, 'the wish to be filled, although seemingly passive, can be subjectively experienced as highly active, demanding, and even voracious. The conflation of psychological passivity with receptive desire considerably underestimates the complex nature of both.' Similarly, assumptions that receptive and penetrating physical positions correlate only with the positions of mother and father are too simplistic for psychoanalytic inquiry, and undermine comprehension of more nuanced identifications and desires. The blindness that psychoanalysis had for penetrating anal sexuality as an *active* sexual construct, and for receptive anal sexuality as a possibly vigorous, muscular, and *active* option, was surely multiply determined, and without doubt related to a similar undervaluation of the *active* workings and possibilities that can be a part of vaginal receptivity.

Battles have been waged for and against particular meanings of anal sexuality in theoretical, philosophical, and cultural arenas (e.g., Hocquenghem, 1972; Bersani, 1987). The beauty of working with patients instead of theories is that they are not so determinedly insistent on conclusions about their own sexuality, and are more often trying to find some way to make sense of themselves, their bodies, their pains and pleasures, and their relationships. Anal sexuality can play an endless number of complex roles in endeavors such as affirming or transgressing gender identities, or negotiating risk and danger, interior and exterior, mine and yours, and any other give-and-take of self-knowledge or of relationships. For analysts as well as the general public, the association between anal sexuality and passivity, violence, danger, disgust, transgression, shame, and strangeness or otherness, makes it more difficult for us to broaden our thinking (or mentalizing) about its roles without some effort. For example, how often would the words 'adolescent boy masturbating' evoke the image of a boy with a cucumber, broomstick, or dildo in his anus? We are predisposed to a particular view of masturbation, as we are to other aspects of sexuality, and in order to expand our thoughts we will have to work against our interdictions and blind spots.

Yearning for love and cruising for sex: a clinical example

> 'Profoundly committed to the better life, the promiscuous, like the monogamous, are idealists. Both are deranged by hope, in awe of reassurance, impressed by their pleasures.'
>
> (Adam Phillips, 1996: 3)

Dave did not want a relationship – adamantly so. He told me that he was complete without one, and that he was a liberated gay man who was free to meet his sexual needs without the dreaded constrictions of a relationship. Traveling frequently for work provided ample opportunity to visit bathhouses and sex clubs, and Dave felt proud of his clandestine accomplishments with the men he found there. However, Dave only had sex when out of town, and discussed it with nobody but me. He acknowledged that his pride in his liberated sexuality would give way to tremendous shame if anyone found out about his anonymous excursions.

When Dave first consulted me, he admitted to some concern about the amount of time he was spending in bathhouses – it was becoming excessive. Dave claimed the bathhouse was a place where he could get what he wanted – sexual gratification from guys with hot bodies. In analysis, his ambivalence was readily apparent, as Dave also suffered unbearable envy for any couple that appeared to be happy together. He consoled himself with faith that their apparent nirvana would eventually bring inconsolable pain, when one inevitably disappointed the other. Dave said that he could not bear disappointment, and relationships were loaded with risk, so better to be happy alone.

Dave treated his own desire as 'a catastrophe that must be averted' (Moss, Chapter 3, p. 71). Because he could not bear disappointment, he therefore would not want anything from anyone. In the bathhouse he could get what he needed, without risk. But Dave questioned his own behavior at times, when the thrill and honor of being chosen by a fit, attractive man to suck on his penis was followed by the thought, 'Why am I doing this? This is boring!' At those times, the magnificence of being chosen by the superior man wore off as it became evident that the man was more focused on his own penis than he was on Dave, and the liberated ability to suck freely did not give Dave the pleasure he had imagined and craved.

Consider the contrast, however, when in a bookstore stall Dave was able to suck the penis of a handsome, athletic young black man who cooed and hugged Dave with appreciation, and also sucked Dave. In that case, believing that the black man may feel inferior to a white man, and therefore could be attracted to Dave, Dave ejaculated all over the man's chest, 'like a porn star!' When he left the bookstore, he saw a BMW in the parking lot, and wondered if perhaps it belonged to the man he'd had sex with. Dave's thoughts wandered; maybe the man was a successful professional, and maybe he'd see him at the bookstore again someday, and maybe he'd like to have dinner . . . In this way, Dave's refusal to avow his desires gave way momentarily to the realization that he had enjoyed the excitement of feeling seen and wanted by another, and that he would like to have more of that with a successful man in the real world. Sadly, Dave had little hope that he could bring that to fruition in real life, and every pleasant anonymous encounter led back to the hopelessness that he associated with his father's passivity and unavailability.

Dave's childhood completely lacked passion or liveliness with either parent. He said of life at home, 'it was just like being numb.' His father came home from work each day and quietly drank until he fell asleep on the couch while the family watched TV, without speaking or disturbing him. His mother's main concern for the children seemed to be that they not disturb their father, whose behavior she excused because he worked hard all day, and that they not draw attention to themselves outside the house. His childhood of emotional deprivation with two impassive parents provided no childhood romance of any kind, and left him with severe narcissistic vulnerabilities and mild paranoia.

Dave began treatment with me at age 33. Early in treatment, he saw a posting on an internet sex site from someone advertising a 'big dick,' and he imagined that I had posted it. Our first month was filled with furtive curiosity about me and my sex life; wondering if I was like him engaging in belligerent sexual forays, or if I had a partner. Sexualizations soon evaporated into a (self-object) transference in which my sexuality was non-existent. Dave required my silent approval of his every wish and deed, and if I spoke, my separateness overwhelmed and over-stimulated him, regardless of what I said.

For years Dave kept me at an impersonal distance. His fantasy life was full of lively battles and grandiosities that kept me awake, but I felt left out, excluded, and deadened by the lack of interaction between us. Sometimes I would ask only a clarification of what he'd said, and he would become anxious and flustered, and complain that he felt criticized, shut down, angry, and confused. When this happened, he could not say what had upset him. In time, Dave was able to hear that I had often simply repeated his words, and yet he still had the same reaction. After several years of this, Dave responded to one of my innocuous comments, 'I want to say, 'NO! NO! NO!' – and fight you on that! – But, I don't even remember what you just said.'

In time, we saw that Dave felt abandoned in the moments when he heard my voice. When I was quiet, or only grunted my acknowledgement of his words, he could feel purely heard and appreciated. When I spoke, I shocked him with my presence as a separate person, and he always took that as a rejection. Several years into analysis Dave saw a very large BMW parked in front of my office, and he was very angry because he was sure that it was mine and that I had parked it there to humiliate him. I commented that his painful belief might be oddly comforting, in comparison with any idea of me parking in front of my office for my own convenience, without a thought about him. The night after we discussed the BMW, Dave had a very vivid dream.

> *I came here for an appointment and you had a couch in the waiting room and I fell asleep . . . it was 6:20 AM and I was trying to remember how long I had been there . . . You weren't in the dream . . . and I was wondering who put the blanket over me and let me sleep? Who watched over me and took care of me? Who had put the light on in the hallway to sort of light the room without disturbing me?*
>
> *Somebody put a blanket over me, checked up on me, and took care of me!*
>
> *That somehow relates to you. Nobody else had come in while I was sleeping. I was your sole project. All of your attention was devoted to me . . . It was you taking care of me, putting a blanket over me. Me being asleep, and you taking care of me.* (Dave went on to say) *You're absent, but present.*

In this absent presence I recognized Dave's father (and mother), and found an opening to re-examine the question of why Dave persisted in keeping me emotionally distant. I had felt restricted to the two transference roles Dave allowed me; I could sit back and remain in a deadened silence, like the sleeping, incompetent, drunk father in the living room, or I could say something and overwhelm him like the father of his passionate imaginary fights. I could see that much was excluded between the poles of these two positions, but the place of sexuality took more work to elaborate.

I came to see that both transference positions defended against longings for parental tenderness, and that 'caring' easily evoked sexual longings and confusion (overstimulation) for Dave. This confusion about affectionate caring and sexual desire was evident, for example, in his response to a television show in which a young man lost his father, and was befriended and mentored by the father of the television family. 'They seemed to hit it off right away . . . but it didn't seem to be sexual. That was confusing to me – it was just that he wanted to help him.' I found it enormously difficult to get traction with the transference implications of this confusion, due to the rigidity of Dave's defenses.

As Dave and I understood more about his longing to be taken care of, and his disconcerting confusion about caring, intimacy, and sex, it became easier for me to call attention to the ways in which he sheltered himself from me in a childlike position, innocent of sexuality. For example, during a storm he left his snow boots in the center of the hallway, where someone could trip on them, and proudly stated that he had figured out the correct place for his boots. The boot tray to the side was surely there for my boots, not his. Along with gently taking up the aggression of blocking the path, I said that he seemed very careful that his boots should never touch my boots (too sexual), and that they could not possibly even belong in the same place – that is, that he could never see himself wearing adult boots like mine. Dave said, 'It's strange, but true, and it feels scary to hear you say that.'

It still took great intention and energy to remain alive with Dave in some hours, and in the seventh year of analysis, a monologue about an upcoming trip to a glass-blowing factory seemed designed to keep me deadly silent – as if behind a glass watching. Once again I commented on his shutting me out, but uncharacteristically I added that I happened to know that the glass factory had a very good restaurant – an interest of Dave's – so an advance reservation might be helpful. I immediately recognized that I had departed from my usual analytic technique by blurting out this bit about the restaurant, and I was very surprised by what we learned from this enactment about Dave's need to keep me out. He said that he could see what I meant about the intensity with which he kept me out of the conversation, and it was confusing to him, not least because he very much appreciated knowing about the restaurant. Yet, he said something felt very wrong with me telling him about a restaurant. In a very emotional upheaval, Dave scolded, 'that was inappropriate – it felt like something sexual.' In the week that followed Dave's very enjoyable visit to the factory and the restaurant he was extremely critical, and said he couldn't trust me because I'd given him 'wrong information' – the restaurant did not take advance reservations. I remarked that he could not acknowledge that I had given him something. Dave agreed and added, 'The neediness that comes out is so strong, and it interferes with common sense. I'm reacting to wanting something, wanting to enjoy something . . . and being too afraid to.'

I believe that Dave's difficulty integrating sexuality and intimacy began much earlier than the trouble point in adolescence that Freud called our attention to. It seems to me that his inability to play – to take risks and engage with another, was the result of impoverished emotional interactions in his very early childhood. In my view, this left Dave without the skills to engage with another, to negotiate boundaries, and to elaborate pleasures, which became overwhelming when sexuality was added to the mix. Dave was therefore doubly burdened, not having skills to engage creatively and negotiate intimacy and dependency, plus having particular desires that were outlawed and de-legitimated. Excitement and pleasure were possible in the anonymity of the bathhouse, while respectability was maintained by not needing anything from anyone.

When I crossed the line on Dave's wish for and defense against dependency, by giving him information about a restaurant, Dave was overwhelmed by emotion and he couldn't think clearly; the circuits were crossed between his longings for dependency/intimacy and for taboo sexuality. The separation for Dave was as fragile as it was rigidly and anxiously guarded. His long analysis helped him to distinguish between wishes to be cared for, wishes for sexual pleasure, and amalgamations of the two. His analysis also helped him to develop a capacity to do the work of desire – to avow his wishes and take risks for their fulfillment. Dave came to tolerate the knowledge that he desired something more personal and caring, in addition to hot sex. With years of analysis, he came to see me as a separate person who had both helped and disappointed him, and he began to take more social risks with hope for friendship and romance.

Further considerations of love, sex, and shame

The rising number of gay men and women happily marrying and raising families is proof enough that all of Dave's problems do not inevitably come with the territory of being gay. Yet, some gay men with ego skills that allow for richer and more flexible interpersonal relations also seek out sexual excitement in venues devoid of affectionate involvement or emotional risk at times. Phillips (2001) pointed out the pervasiveness of potentially over-stimulating experiences for gay youths in the same-sex segregation of our culture – in school locker rooms, for example. In this milieu, adolescents disavow their outlaw desires in order to avoid stimulation, and to remain safe from scorn and retribution. For all gay men, interdiction against same-sex desire functioned as a danger to the developing ego and libido. For Dave, I believe that the dearth of early childhood interpersonal interaction left him with few of the basic skills necessary for transformative play and transgression – the skills needed to elaborate previous humiliations with another for the sake of pleasure. Gay men who have more dynamic early relations in childhood will likely have better ego skills going into puberty, and can more creatively negotiate the conflict caused by extra opposition to their sexual desires in adolescence – and therefore have a better chance of finding creative ways to navigate around shame to integrate intimacy and sexuality.

However, as they likely experienced their sexuality as an outlaw in their youth, gay men may still sometimes find partial satisfaction in the expression of their sexuality as an outlaw in adulthood. As I described previously (2002), a certain amount of anonymous sexual play may function in different ways at different times. For example, it may be a choice and occur with regularity, e.g. whenever on vacation – a binge of hedonistic pleasure when temporarily freed from mundane accountabilities, or possibly as a defensive compensation at times of instability, anxiety or loss – when in need of an 'ego boost.' Modern technology has dramatically increased the availability of 'potential space' for anonymous play (Corbett, 2013), making bathhouses seem outmoded. For restorative experimentation, compulsive repetition, or any other enactment of fantasies and desires, the internet and mobile device applications have made it easier for homosexuals and heterosexuals alike to arrange sexual encounters in any location, at any time.

In obscurity, gay men's outlaw desires can be avowed and hedonistically performed, as Freud's straight men performed with prostitutes. Enacted fantasies of recognition, appreciation, and phallic grandiosity can briefly mollify the hurts, humiliations. and shame for proscribed erotic desires. Saketopoulou (Chapter 11) takes this idea further, proposing that transgressive sexual behaviors may be an enactment or embodiment of un-represented, un-symbolized, or unformulated early experience. The degree to which a man's sexual desires are played out in the relative safety of detachment and anonymity, or in the very different safety of an intimate relationship, is surely dependent on skills developed in his earlier experience of relative safety or danger with others – while transgressing and experimenting at the borders of prohibition with caretakers and with society.

Quite consciously, our culture is changing, and gay men's sexual desires are now allowed more explicit cultural visibility. President Obama and hosts of other famous people have posted videos on YouTube assuring young gay people, 'It gets better.' The need for such videos confirms that, for them, it can be pretty bad. In the age of fast media, young people know plenty about the torture and death of Matthew Sheppard in Wyoming, the exposure of sexual behavior that shamed Tyler Clementi prior to his jump from New York City's George Washington Bridge, and the repressive anti-homosexual laws enacted in Russia prior to the Sochi Olympics. Vehement protests erupted in 'liberal' France to oppose equality in marriage laws, and religious leaders from America to Africa regularly accuse same-sex desires of being destructive to the family, marriage, and civilization. In Uganda, and several other nations, avowing same-sex desire can risk death. Despite persistent and reactionary shaming and threats, gay men and women are publicly acting on their desire to avow loving and sexual relationships by marrying in any place that will allow it.

Drive versus attachment: question terminable and interminable

As barriers to same-sex relationships are undeniably retreating in much of the world, at least one psychoanalyst sees this as having a detrimental effect on the sexual satisfaction of gay men. Regarding some of the young gay men he works with, Cole (in McNamara, 2013) stated, 'it is as if the intensity of excitement decreases as the boundary of taboo recedes.'

Kenneth Lewes (2005) takes psychoanalysis to task for domesticating homo-sexuality and failing to embrace the full sexual possibilities of a gay liberationist movement. He laments the loss to psychoanalysis of the ideas that a generation of men who died of AIDS might have contributed. Might those 'liberationist' voices have emphasized phallic drives when psychoanalysis shifted to a more empathic, relational orientation, which favors attachment over phallic drive. Lewes states, 'By replacing the central notion of phallic sexual and aggressive drives with yearnings for attachment and affiliation, the new, gay-friendly psychoanalysis favors — or, as we now say, 'privileges' — the latter.'

In a chapter titled 'Fantastic Phallicism,' Corbett (2009) argues less dichoto-mously, in his distinctive prose, that in our current theorizing, 'the burlap of desire too quickly becomes the pashmina of mutual recognition' (p. 216). Corbett dem-onstrates beautifully that phallic drives can be relational, too, and argues for a play space that allows for fantastic mutual recognition, in which bigness, aggression, competition, and a wish to grow are all welcomed in inter-subjective play, as a respite from 'the tedium of phallic reality' (p. 213).

I find these ideas compelling, as I ponder the juncture of gay male sexuality and intimacy. It seems to me that Lewes's positing a liberated, unashamed gay sexu-ality against a sexuality moored in intimacy and attachment mirrors the frequent (universal? unavoidable?) conflict seen in individuals of autonomy/aggression versus mutual dependence. Among my patients, some want more exciting sex, some want more love and comfort, but rare is the patient who doesn't to some degree want it all. So perhaps we can settle the question of drive versus attach-ment with an answer of both/and, rather than either/or. In fact, this brings us back to Fonagy and Target's developmental model of sexuality, where both drive (the infant's excitement) and attachment factors (mother's incongruent mirroring) are involved. Following that model throughout the lifecycle, the interpersonal (attachment) interaction is the arena for the elaboration of what (drive) comes from within.

Dave was not able at first to know that he wanted it all – in keeping with his character, he saw it as strictly either/or, a divergent conflict (Kris, 1977) – and he had few ego skills for elaboration with a known Other. Analysis can contrib-ute to the expansion of psychic capacities or ego skills – and this can free the patient's ability to choose, rather than be restricted. For gay men this can mean capacities to creatively negotiate the interdictions against their subjectivities and sexual desires, and to assemble lives with intimacy and sexuality more freely lived, rather than constricted or foreclosed. For some it might mean a capacity to choose risks in intimacy with another, which was deficient in Dave, and for others it could mean greater capacity to choose risks in independence. In keeping with the general goals of psychoanalysis, the choice would be the patient's – whether sexual acts should take place in intimate attachment or in liberated abandon – in lace or in leather. The goal is for the patient to develop greater psychic flexibility and freedom to choose, and make more informed and more conscious decisions as a willing agent in his own life – including decisions about physical and emotional risk-taking and safety.

Summary

Sexuality is elaborated, and therefore educated, inter-subjectively from earliest childhood. All individuals face general interdictions against childhood and adolescent sexuality, and this chapter focused on the fate of the libido in the face of interdictions particularly against same-sex desire. Throughout development, and particularly in the Oedipal period and at the onset of adolescent sexuality, strong injunctions against same-sex desire pose an extra danger to the developing ego, and cause prohibited desires to be hidden in shame and anxiously kept away from intimate relations with loved ones. Such outlaw sexual desires may then be expressed in obscurity and detachment, and intimate relationships may suffer a dearth of sexual pleasure.

The degree of separation between intimacy and sexuality will be influenced by the vulnerability of the individual to shame and anxiety, and by the strength of the prohibitions. While many constraints on sexuality exist in the world, same-sex taboos are generally pervasive in families and in society. Anal sexuality is a desire or pleasure that carries an extra burden of outlaw status, and has generally been relegated to the simple position of abject passivity, grossly misunderstanding and underestimating its untold meanings in gay male sexuality.

In the clinical example of Dave, the patient was particularly vulnerable to shame and anxiety, due to a childhood that lacked emotional interaction or mirroring, and therefore lived a life where shame and anxiety maintained a vigilant and fragile separation between his deep longings for care and for taboo sexual excitement. Individuals who develop capacities to creatively transgress against and engage with caretakers will likely be better equipped with ego strengths and psychic capacities to work through conflicts between desires and prohibitions, although all those with same-sex desires may be more vulnerable to some degree of anxiety and shame as a result of extra prohibition and a sometimes derisive environment.

Although familial and public proscriptions of same-sex desires have eased in some places, they remain a significant danger to the developing libido, and present a barrier to integration of intimacy and sexuality. In clinical work, attention to shame and anxiety inherent in conflicts over desires for intimacy and outlawed sexuality will help with working through such conflicts, particularly in shame-based transferences. Such awareness will undoubtedly assist the analyst in mirroring aspects of experience and desire that are split off by shame.

References

Aisenstein, M., & Moss, D. (2015) Desire and its discontents. In *Sexualities: Contemporary Psychoanalytic Perspectives*, ed. A. Lemma and P.E. Lynch. London and New York: Routledge, 63–80.

Bersani, L. (1987) Is the Rectum a Grave? In *AIDS: Cultural Analysis, Cultural Activism*, ed. D. Crimp. Cambridge, MA: MIT Press, 197–222.

Botticelli, S. (2010) Thinking the Unthinkable: Anal Sex in Theory and Practice. *Studies in Gender and Sexuality*, 11: 112–123.

Chasseguet-Smirgel, J. (1983) Perversion and the Universal Law. *Int. R. Psycho-Anal.*, 10: 293–301.

Chodorow, N.J. (1992) Heterosexuality as a Compromise Formation: Reflections on the Psychoanalytic Theory of Sexual Development. *Psychoanal. Contemp. Thought*, 15: 267–304.

Chodorow, N.J. (2002) Gender as a Personal and Cultural Construction. In *Gender in Psychoanalytic Space: Between Clinic and Culture*, ed. Muriel Dimen and Virginia Goldner. New York: Other Press, 238–261. Reprinted from Chodorow, *The Power of Feelings*, Yale University Press, 69–91.

Chodorow, N.J. (2012) *Individualizing Gender and Sexuality: Theory and Practice*. New York: Routledge.

Corbett, K. (1993) The Mystery of Homosexuality. *Psychoanalytic Psychology*, 10: 345–357.

Corbett, K. (2009) *Boyhoods: Rethinking Masculinities*. New Haven, CT: Yale University Press.

Corbett, K. (2013) Shifting Sexual Cultures, the Potential Space of Online Relations, and the Promise of Psychoanalytic Listening. *J. Am. Psychoanal. Assoc.*, 61(2): 25–44.

Douglas, A. (1894) Two Loves. *The Chameleon*, 1: 28.

Elise, D. (2001) Unlawful Entry: Male Fears of Psychic Penetration. *Psychoanalytic Dialogues*, 11(4): 499–531.

Fonagy, P. (2008) A Genuinely Developmental Theory of Sexual Enjoyment and Its Implications for Psychoanalytic Technique. *J. Am. Psychoanal. Assoc.*, 56(1): 11–36.

Freud, S. (1905) Three Essays on the Theory of Sexuality. *The Standard Edition of the Complete Psychological Works of Sigmund Freud*, Vol. 7, pp. 125–244. London: Hogarth Press, 1953.

Freud, S. (1912) On the Universal Tendency to Debasement in the Sphere of Love (Contributions to the Psychology of Love: II). *The Standard Edition of the Complete Psychological Works of Sigmund Freud*, Vol. 11, pp. 177–190. London: Hogarth Press, 1957.

Freud, S. (1923) The Ego and the Id, Chapter V, The Dependent Relationships of the Ego. *The Standard Edition of the Complete Psychological Works of Sigmund Freud*, Vol. 19, pp. 48–59. London: Hogarth Press, 1957.

Goldsmith, S. (2001) Oedipus or Orestes? Homosexual Men, their Mothers and Other Women Revisited. *J. Am. Psychoanal. Assoc.*, 49(4): 1269–1288.

Gray, J. (1992) *Men Are from Mars, Women Are from Venus*. New York: HarperCollins.

Green, A. (1995) Has Sexuality Anything to Do with Psychoanalysis? *Int. J. Psycho-Anal.*, 76: 871–883.

Guss, J.R. (2010a) The Danger of Desire: Anal Sex and the Homo/Masculine Subject. *Studies in Gender and Sexuality,* 11: 124–140.

Guss, J.R. (2010b) (Pre)occupied Locations: Subverting Marginality: Reply to Commentaries. *Studies in Gender and Sexuality*, 11: 168–172.

Herzog, J. (2001) *Father Hunger: Explorations with Adults and Children.* Hillsdale, NJ: The Analytic Press.

Hocquenghem, G. (1972 [1993]) *Homosexual Desire.* Durham, NC: Duke University Press.

Isay, R. (1987) Fathers and Their Homosexually Inclined Sons in Childhood. *Psychoanal. St. Child*, 42, 275–294.

Kris, A.O. (1977) Either-or Dilemmas. *Psychoanal. St. Child*, 32: 91–117.

Kris, A.O. (2012) Personal communication.

Laplanche, J. (1995) Seduction, Persecution, Revelation. *Int. J. Psycho-Anal.*, 76: 663–682.

Laplanche, J. (1997) The Theory of Seduction and the Problem of the Other. *Int. J. Psycho-Anal.*, 78: 653–666.

Lee, A., & Proulx, E.A. (2005) Brokeback Mountain. [S.l.], Entertainment in Video.

Lewes, K. (2005) Homosexuality, Homophobia, and Gay-friendly Psychoanalysis. *Fort Da*, 11: 13–34.

Lichtenberg, J.D. (2008) *Sensuality and Sexuality across the Divide of Shame.* New York: The Analytic Press.

Lynch, P.E. (2002) Yearning for Love and Cruising for Sex: Returning to Freud to Understand Some Gay Men. *Ann. Psychoanal.*, 30: 175–189.

McNamara, S. (2013) Gay Male Desires and Sexuality in the Twenty-first Century: How I Listen. *J. Am. Psychoanal. Assoc.*, 61(2): 341–361.

Phillips, A. (1996) *Monogamy.* New York: Vintage Books.

Phillips, S.H. (2001) The Overstimulation of Everyday Life I: New Aspects of Male Homosexuality. *J. Am. Psychoanal. Assoc.*, 49: 1235–1267.

Rose, S.H. (2007) *Oedipal Rejection: Echoes in the Relationships of Gay Men.* Youngstown, NY: Cambria Press.

Saketopoulou, A. (2015) On Sexual Perversions' Capacity to Act as Portal to Psychic States that Have Evaded Representation. In *Sexualities: Contemporary Psychoanalytic Perspectives*, ed. A. Lemma and P.E. Lynch. London and New York: Routledge, 205–218.

Sedgwick, E.K. (1990) *Epistemology of the Closet.* Berkeley, CA: University of California Press.

Stein, R. (1998a) The Poignant, the Excessive and the Enigmatic in Sexuality. *Int. J. Psycho-Anal.*, 79: 253–268.

Stein, R. (1998b) The Enigmatic Dimension of Sexual Experience: The 'Otherness' of Sexuality and Primal Seduction. *Psychoanal. Q.*, 67: 594–625.

Stoller, R.J. (1976) Sexual Excitement, *Arch. Gen. Psychiatry*, 33: 899–909.

Sullivan, N. (2003) *A Critical Introduction to Queer Theory.* New York: New York University Press.

Tally, T. et al. (2001) The Silence of the Lambs. Santa Monica, CA, MGM Home Entertainment.

Target, M. (2007) Is Our Sexuality Our Own? A Developmental Model of Sexuality Based on Early Affect Mirroring. *British Journal of Psychotherapy*, 23(4): 517–530.

Chapter 8

Objecting to the object

Encountering the internal parental couple relationship for lesbian and gay couples

Leezah Hertzmann

Introduction

Intimate adult couple relationships offer possibilities for growth and development as an integral and hoped-for part of being a couple, but will for many involve difficulties and challenges at some point. After all, what so often brings people to therapy are the problems they experience within their relationships, or the difficulties attendant with not being in a relationship. Lesbian and gay couples present for therapy with difficulties that may look little different from those brought by heterosexual couples. However, in my experience of psychoanalytic psychotherapy with individuals and couples, both gay and straight, there are specific factors particular to the psychic conflicts of some lesbian and gay couples that have a considerably different phenomenology and trajectory to those of heterosexual couples.

Psychoanalysis, and specifically psychoanalytic couple theory, views our encounter with the internal parental couple relationship as a fundamental psychic event in the course of our development (Ruszczynski, 1993) but it is important to note that traditionally this has been an heteronormatively constructed concept. For some lesbian and gay couples, and particularly those who have grown up with a heterosexual parental couple, the representation and intrapsychic experience of an intimate heterosexual couple union, internalized as a dynamic object, is objected to because it does not belong to their conscious desired experience and self identity. Both partners desire to be in a couple relationship but not like the one they grew up with. I am proposing that some lesbian and gay couples may in fact '*object*' to the intrapsychic presence of the internal heterosexual parent couple as a dynamic object residing within their shared unconscious world (Bannister et al., 1955). The consequences of this can be rigidity and sense of rejection between the partners which I suggest is related to the psychic objection. I have named this predicament 'objecting to the internal heterosexual parental couple object', for brevity shortened to 'objecting to the object'.

In this chapter, I begin with a description of how psychoanalysis has traditionally viewed same-gender desire. Then I consider early object relationships, psychosexual development, the importance of identifications and innate bisexuality including a description of some contemporary psychoanalytic reformulations of same-gender desire. Using a fictional composite case example I illustrate the clinical manifestation of 'objecting to the object', including some thoughts on why this may be a problem for lesbian and gay couples. I reflect on how being part of an intimate adult same-gender couple relationship brings to life early object relationships and embodied experiences. Throughout, I draw on theoretical concepts which inform my ideas about the encounter with the parental couple relationship (Bannister et al, 1955; Ruszczynski, 1993; Ruszczynski and Fisher, 1995; Morgan 2001, 2005, 2009; Grier, 2005; Ludlam and Nyberg, 2007).

The ideas presented here are based on my experience with lesbian and gay couples and individuals in psychoanalytic psychotherapy who have grown up with heterosexual parents, though not necessarily parents who were always together as a couple. These ideas may also be relevant to heterosexual as well as homosexual couples, and to those who have grown up in other family formations who become troubled and seek psychoanalytic therapy.

Psychoanalysis and lesbian and gay couple relationships

Historically, psychoanalysis has energetically focused its understanding of homosexuality as evidence of perversity and pathology, proceeding on the basis, largely unquestioned, that the only 'healthy' outcome of the Oedipus situation is full heterosexuality. The application of the Oedipus complex within psychoanalysis to explore homosexuality was especially damaging, in part because of the conviction that there has to be a resolution in psychosexual development where the eventual outcome was heterosexuality and where the desire for the same-gender parent was relinquished. Sexual desire was only considered healthy when directed towards someone of the opposite gender to oneself. Homosexuality was then understood to indicate that psychosexual development had gone awry and was indicative of problems in resolving desire for the 'forbidden' same-gender object.

This construction of gender and sexuality has meant that a deeper exploration of the psychic conflicts faced by many lesbian and gay couples has been split off and shut down from the main body of psychoanalytic theory and practice, and with it the possibility of understanding more about lesbian and gay people's struggle to find and maintain an intimate couple relationship. However, psychoanalytic theories of the couple relationship, previously based almost entirely on heterosexual partnerships, have been changing. More recently, the development of psychoanalytic thinking and technique which could be of benefit to lesbian and gay couples whose relationships get in to difficulty has been gathering pace. For instance Lynch (2002) returns to Freud to understand the search for integration of love and sex for gay men, and D'Ercole and Drescher (2004) in their landmark volume deal specifically with psychoanalytic approaches to same sex couples and families. This paper aims to explore the problems for lesbian and gay couples of encountering the internal parental couple relationship and the impact of this internal object in the couple's shared unconscious world.

Early object relationships and psychosexual development

The urge to pair is understood to be a powerful human drive begun in infancy, continued in development and, for many, culminating in the formation of adult couple relationships (Grier, 2005; Ludlam and Nyberg, 2007). Psychoanalysis brings to the fore an understanding of this drive and the complexity of that which is deeply desired, emphasizing the connection between adulthood and infancy, between past and present. Subsequently, adult couple relationships are a place where these earliest object relationships and embodied experiences will be evoked and brought to life between partners. Early infantile experiences with parents may not be consciously recalled, but may be present in dreams, daydreams, and sexual phantasies including those of the primal scene.

Both partners bring to their couple relationship unconscious sexual phantasies in relation to their parents, and these will be prompted and awakened by the sexual intimacy and accompanying regression and vulnerability which comes from being part of a couple. Intimate adult sexual relationships recall not only these early aspects of genital sexuality and phantasy, but also experiences with parents during infancy and childhood – the priming of sexuality through the attention to and tending of bodily functions. As Freud (1912) put so clearly, sexual instincts and 'components of erotic interest' (p. 180) are discernible and correspond to the child's primary objects:

> ... sexual instincts find their first objects by attaching themselves to the valuations made by the ego-instincts, precisely in the way in which the first sexual satisfactions are experienced in attachment to the bodily functions necessary for the preservation of life ...
>
> (pp. 180–181)

Boys and girls use their mothers and fathers – their primary objects – differently in the process of identification, and parents play a central role in structuring children's gender and influencing psychosexual development. Laplanche and Pontalis (1973) define identification as:

> the psychological process whereby the subject assimilates an aspect, property, or attribute of the other and is transformed, wholly or partially, after the model the other provides. It is by means of a series of identifications that the personality is constituted and specified.

From the time a child is born and anatomically assigned a sex, parents respond to the child's gender and encourage development in ways they find appropriate to the child's sex. This priming of the child's gender and sexuality will be informed by parents' phantasies about the child and their gender, and also by the parents' own gender and sexual identity. In the course of development the child seeks out aspects of both parents that feel congruent to the self, including features they admire and want to model themselves on. They may also construct a sense of self which aims to feel in certain ways, unlike their primary objects. Children's primary identifications with their parents both male and female provide the basis for their innate bisexuality which Freud noticed and described (Freud, 1905). Stoller (1972) highlighted how important this observation was throughout Freud's writing, using as an example:

> Since I have become acquainted with the notion of bisexuality I regarded it as the decisive factor, and without taking bisexuality into account, I think it would scarcely be possible to arrive at an understanding of the sexual mani-festations that are actually to be observed in men and women.
>
> (Freud, 1905: 220)

Fast (1984, 1990) emphasizes the centrality of a child's need to identify with both parents and use identifications across both genders to formulate important parts of their self-representations, imaginatively elaborating their phantasies about erotic relations between the sexes. Freud (1905) considered that an inherent constitu-tional mix of female and male traits not only influenced the degree of a person's femininity or masculinity but also influenced object choice. Freud commented that in terms of constitutional bisexuality: 'all human beings are capable of making a homosexual object choice and have in fact made one in their unconscious' (1905: 145 footnote 1915). The unconscious homosexual object choice in development that Freud referred to is particularly pertinent for the lesbian and gay couples I am considering here, as is the unconscious heterosexual object choice as exemplified by the internal parental couple which is objected to.

Childhood sexuality and parental responses

A further important aspect of psychosexual development is the parental response to a child's early expressions of sexuality, which may significantly influence the trajectory of psychosexual development for lesbian and gay people. Target (2007) and (Fonagy (2008) both describe how aspects of early psychosexual development and particularly sexual excitement are necessarily poorly mirrored by parental figures. The infant in a state of sexual tension 'is generally not offered a congruent metabolized representation of his or her psychosexual feelings, even when other feelings are sensitively responded to' (Target, 2007: 522). Both authors highlight how whilst it is possible for parents to contingently mirror a range of feelings such as sadness or anger for instance, there would appear to be no conscious way to mirror sexual arousal. Because there is no contingent representation of the infant's experience, there can be no real containment of these sexual feelings and experiences. This means that 'sexual arousal can never truly be experienced as owned' (Target, 2007: 523) and therefore, there will always be a need to have one's sexuality elaborated by another. 'Because sexual excitement is by its nature incongruent with the self, excitement has to be experienced in the other and only therefore with the other' (Target, 2007: 524). Furthermore, where a parent's response to their child's state is unmarked or inaccurate, the child is unable to find themselves in the mind of the other and is forced instead to internalize the representation of the object's state of mind as if it were their own.

Parents' experience of not mirroring sexual arousal may be necessary and protective in many ways, but for lesbian and gay people, this unmarked, unelaborated response may have an adverse effect on aspects of psychosexual development. For fathers and mothers with a child of either gender it would seem important that they possess a healthy integration of their innate bisexuality that can be comfortably acknowledged within themselves, something which indeed may occur out of conscious awareness. If things proceed fairly well, the child's sexuality, desire, and expressions of gender identity can then be responded to by parents without discomfort, rejection, or alarm. However, where the parental response to a child's expression of same-gender desire and emerging sexuality in childhood is unwelcoming, then the trajectory and eventual fate of identifications with both parents, as well as the capacity to experience and inhabit one's innate bisexuality, will be significantly affected. In terms of innate bisexuality, I am describing an intrapsychic process whereby it is possible to identify with and feel desire for both genders as distinct from the bisexual object choice where there is a desire to enact one's sexuality with both genders.

I am suggesting that where a child's emergent sexual orientation is different to that of their parents, the parents' responses to sexual arousal in a child of the same-gender as themselves may be to react with an even greater degree of alarm, disapproval, or disgust which in turn the child then internalizes. This may come to exacerbate the difficulties for the child or young person in coming to accept their same-gender desires and sexual phantasies, and then cause immense internal conflict. It is not difficult to surmise that where the parental response to a young person's emerging sexuality and desire for someone of the same gender is ignored, invalidated, disputed, or overridden, the result may be that the path of psycho-sexual development is profoundly impacted upon. Crucially, in development as a child interacts with their parents, they may encounter two specific aspects of experience: firstly, their desire for the parent of the same gender and secondly, the reaction of the other parent to this expression of desire. In my experience of psychoanalytic therapy with both individuals and couples, I have often listened to descriptions of experiences from lesbian and gay patients where as children they were either told directly – or it was indicated to them less directly by both parents – that it was more acceptable to express desire towards the parent of the opposite rather than the same gender. This was frequently accompanied by a commentary on whether their behaviour was either not sufficiently masculine or feminine enough for their gender, or too much so in the parents' view. Frequently gender identity and gender roles are conflated with sexual object choice. It is most often taken as a given that opposite gender attraction is what makes a couple rela-tionship, or where couples are the same gender, a binary gender divide between masculinity and femininity is constructed. As a patient of mine once said 'people always say that when you're gay or lesbian in a couple, one is the man and the other the woman'. The idea that same-gender desire is acceptable not only to others but also within one's own mind, and need not reflect a heterosexual union, may be especially difficult to consider particularly if in the first instance it is one's parents who are clearly disapproving.

Same-gender desire: reformulating theory

In an attempt to reformulate psychoanalytic ideas about the homoerotic desire for the same-gender parent, several contemporary writers have contributed to a more in-depth understanding of the trajectory of this desire in the psychosexual development of lesbians and gay men, including the eventual manifestation in adult couple relationships. In relation to gay men, Roughton (2002), Goldsmith (1995, 2001), Frommer (1994, 2000), Corbett (1993) and Isay (1987, 1989, 1991) all put forward new constructions of the Oedipus complex, importantly not dominated by heteronormative bias, but rather attempting an understanding of sexuality with more fluidity. They recalibrate traditional disparagement and pathologizing of same sex desire, most specifically by revising Freudian ideas about boys' attraction to their fathers. They make the case convincingly that this may occupy an equally important and crucially benign role in male development. Furthermore they emphasize that it is not indicative of disturbance as previously had been widely proffered. Goldsmith (1995, 2001) and Isay (1987, 1989, 1991) particularly elucidate aspects of desire in childhood and consider the way in which this may impact on later development for men in their adult relationships.

Describing female experience, Elise (2000) elucidates how women use their bodies unconsciously as a protection against fully experiencing female desire. Elise describes how a mother's heterosexuality, which does not incorporate a healthy integration of her own psychic bisexuality, and is not comfortably acknowledged and expressed in relating to her daughter, can inadvertently cause her to reject the little girl's sexual desire. This desire for her mother then is 'typically erased, negated, made invisible, nonexistent' (p. 219). In a later article Elise (2002) describes how in development the heterosexual gaze a boy has for his mother and the girl's desire for her father can be validated and seen, but the mother tends to be blind to the girl's sexual impulses and desires for her, something noted by several other authors (Butler, 1990, 1995; Kernberg, 1991; O'Connor and Ryan, 1993). The meaning of this rejection in childhood can influence the fate of identifications formed with both parents as well as the capacity to inhabit one's innate bisexuality flexibly.

The points made by Elise (2002) in relation to women, and Goldsmith (1995, 2001) and Isay (1987, 1989, 1991) in relation to men, are especially helpful in understanding the consequences of rejection of homoerotic interest in a parent of the same gender and I think is particularly relevant here in terms of elucidating how these experiences of rejection can be brought to life in an adult couple relationship between partners. When parents insist that the child's emerging sexual desires should be directed elsewhere, or that the expression of their gender identity should be manifested in a stereotypically accepted way, it may be harder for the child to identify with the parent who has been rejecting, or with the other parent who has allowed or encouraged the rejection to occur. Where identifications *are* made, they may then have to be disavowed or split off because they carry with them difficult or aggressive feelings relating to important attachment relationships. The need to identify closely with one parent or the other in order to be like them and as a way to gain parental approval may be particularly acute if homoerotic desires are disapproved of by either parent. These aspects of identification might have to be held on to tightly for fear they may be attacked or undermined. Identifications with parents of both genders can then become rigid, uni-dimensional, or distorted and it may become more difficult to allow greater integration of male and female identifications. Such integration is necessary in order to acknowledge one's innate bisexuality, the identification with and desire for both genders, to inhabit this, allow it to be known and understood in oneself. In this way there is the possibility for a range of identifications that can be flexibly available in the mind. In the midst of the ensuing confusion about desire, whom one desires, whom one should and should not desire, what can be expressed or kept secret, it can be difficult to make a sexual object choice, enact one's desires with freedom and flexibility of mind, and, subsequently, to maintain an adult sexual relationship.

Such early psychosexual developmental experiences as described here may for some individuals shape the unconscious beliefs about being a couple which each partner brings to the relationship. Morgan (2009) describes how unconscious beliefs form a central part of the unconscious life of the couple. Although they are 'beliefs', they reside in the unconscious like facts, unless they become conscious and can be thought about (ibid.: 3). These unconscious facts then become certainties that can drive many aspects of our conscious life. For some lesbian and gay couples whose parents were hostile or rejecting of same-gender desire, their early psychosexual experiences are not modified by development and become fixed in the unconscious as a belief about all subsequent relationships, residing as an interdiction prohibiting same-gender desire.

Objecting to the object

I want to describe how the presence of the internal heterosexual parental couple relationship can lead to particular difficulties for some lesbian and gay couples. The internal parental couple relationship-as-object is not just the mere addition of mother plus father. In development, the parental couple relationship is externally perceived and emotionally experienced by the child both consciously and unconsciously, and experienced in the caretaker's physical handling of the infant or child. It is a complex blend of the parents' relationship with each other, as well as both parents' gendered identities and sexuality expressed towards each other, and towards the child in their interactions with her/him. The presence of the internal parental couple as a dynamic object is thought to shape both an individual's relationships with couples generally, and specifically, the formation and maintenance of couple relationships in adulthood, including the shared unconscious world of the couple (Ruszczynski and Fisher, 1995; Grier, 2005). Each partner's relationship to the internal parental couple relationship as a dynamic object will influence the hopes, anxieties, expectations, and beliefs about choice of partner as well as the way the relationship develops and grows. By dynamic object I mean the complex system formed by the interaction between two human beings and the interplay between their two subjective worlds. Put simply, it is the continual flow of reciprocal mutual influence, both interpersonal and intrapsychic, between partners, one which contributes to creating the couple's shared unconscious world. Something of a shared unconscious image of the internal couple relationship as object will bring partners together and structure their attachment to each other. Kernberg (1995: 48–63) states that the longing to become a couple is a wish to fulfill deep unconscious needs for a loving identification with the parental couple. For many, such a loving identification with the internal parental couple will play an important part in sustaining their adult couple relationship. However for the lesbian and gay couples I am considering here, this presents a problem because some of the ideas, phantasies, and experiences about being a couple that are internalized in development feel incongruent. The heterosexual imprint is dissonant from the desires and phantasies in being part of a same-gender couple. I am proposing that the internalized heterosexual parental couple relationship is experienced as an incongruent and unwanted object in the couple's shared unconscious world and is fundamentally contrary to what they desire.

In trying to further understand this phenomenon I return to the ideas of Fonagy and colleagues (Fonagy et al., 1995; Fonagy and Target, 2000; Fonagy et al., 2003). They describe the centrality of mirroring, where parental responses resonate and reflect the internal state the infant displays. The parent simultaneously distorts the infant's state through the use of exaggeration, 'motherese', irony, thereby conveying to the infant that they understand but, crucially, are not overwhelmed by or necessarily experiencing the same affective state. There is concurrently both contact with and distance from the infant's internal state. Where feelings are left unacknowledged, or are poorly mirrored and are therefore non-contingent reflections of internal self states, this can lead to internal representations which are incongruent to the self. This creates an alien experience within the self, brought about because 'ideas or feelings are experienced as part of the self which do not seem to belong to the self' (Fonagy et al., 2003: 439). In turn, this creates an instability within the self. I am proposing that the internalized heterosexual couple relationship as a dynamic object, incongruent for some lesbian and gay couples, is felt to be alien. This feeling of something alien within the self then meets a hostile external environment privileging heterosexual relationships which can, for some lesbian and gay couples, lead to further difficulties (for a more detailed discussion see Hertzmann, 2011).

In my experience lesbian and gay couples objecting to this incongruent and alien object can present with difficulties in several ways. Frequently there is a quality of rigidity in the relationship and this can be in relation to various issues such as: questioning what kind of a relationship the couple are in together or want to form despite often having been together for many years; difficulty negotiating flexibly what roles are taken up in the relationship and the meaning of these roles for both partners; or a constant low level mutual rejection creating a feeling of uncertainty about whether the relationship will survive or not. One might say that many couples, both gay and straight, struggle with these kinds of problems. I am suggesting that the rigidity and sense of rejection for some lesbian and gay couples may well be related to a psychic objection to the internal heterosexual parental couple. Where there is adverse parental response to same-gender desire, a same-gender coupling can not be securely introjected and neither can one's innate bisexuality then be flexibly anchored. Consequently, rigidity is employed in the service of keeping things stable, giving a semblance of security between partners, and for some couples, they may simultaneously try to emphasize their *lesbian* or *gay* coupledom as legitimate.

In the following clinical example, I focus on a couple who, in struggling with this psychic objection, went to considerable lengths to ensure they did not feel or know about the presence of the internalized heterosexual parental couple in their shared unconscious world. This example highlights each partner's identifications with parents of both genders, where rigidity and splitting were employed in order to disavow themselves of the knowledge of the range of identifications and accompanying feelings. It also illustrates the difficulties they experienced in relation to the range of identifications and desires for both genders and the problems they faced in coming to know and understand these aspect of themselves, both individually and as a couple.

Clinical example

Morris and Jim had been together for about 10 years when they sought help for their relationship difficulties. The presenting problem was a recent waning of their sexual relationship. They described how Jim had always been the 'passive' partner, Morris the 'active' partner and that they had previously been satisfied with these roles which felt to each of them an established part of their identity as gay men. More recently, Jim had expressed a wish to be the active penetrating partner in their sexual relationship, something which Morris was not prepared to consider as he wanted to maintain his current role. Morris could not understand why Jim now wanted to do something differently and Jim became increasingly dissatisfied and angry that Morris would not allow him to take up an active position, accusing him of being overly rigid. Morris said he found the idea of becoming passive 'unbearable' and Jim responded by insisting that if something did not change, he would seek sex outside of the relationship. Jim appeared to be pressurizing Morris and also seemed to be under some internal pressure within himself to make these changes to their roles immediately. Consequently they had reached an impasse: resentments had built up between them and they were thinking of splitting up.

In the early stages of the therapy, it seemed to the therapist that Morris and Jim had very rigid ideas about their respective roles, both in the relationship generally and sexually. However, it was unclear why at this point they were having issues with the roles they took up in the relationship which formerly had worked well. The therapist continued for some time to experience the couple as both inflexible and impenetrable and was struck by how this reflected closely the couple's presenting complaint about each other. In terms of their histories, although Morris had to some extent spoken about his parents and experiences growing up, Jim had generally been more closed. The therapist noted their reluctance to describe their histories more openly, especially anything about their own parents' couple relationship.

Initially, the therapist tried to pick up on Morris's strong feeling about how being passive would be 'unbearable'. The therapist did not get very far with exploring this feeling but sensed it might be important for them both. The meaning of Jim's need for change and why it had occurred at this point in their relationship was also very difficult to elaborate. The therapy began to feel restricted and stuck. The therapist was perplexed by how problematic it was to explore the material they brought to the sessions. The couple went to great lengths to ensure the therapist 'completely got' what they were saying. A significant amount of time could be spent pursuing precisely the correct word or phrase. They often corrected the therapist if there was anything less than an exact reflection of what they had said. In addition, they noted to the second the exact start and end of each session and commented when the therapist was not in lock step with them. They frequently refuted interventions and interpretations that seemed reasonably congruent with their thoughts and the material they communicated. The therapist's countertransference was of feeling straightjacketed, exhausted by their continual need for entirely congruent, precise responses. It felt to the therapist as if almost every intervention was rejected.

A few months in to the therapy, something unexpected occurred which punctured the therapeutic paralysis. In the middle of a session, Jim's phone rang, he grimaced, muttered something inaudible and switched off the phone. There was a long pause before Jim said he was sorry for the interruption, it was his mother calling but that it was not important. The therapist, having noted his facial expression and the subsequent long pause, commented that Jim had not said very much about his current relationship with his mother although he had briefly described that his parents divorced when he was 11. Jim said:

(continued)

(continued)

> Oh, didn't I explain? It's not really very important. But when I was 11
> and just about to go to secondary school, I found out my mother had
> been having an affair with my class teacher. She left the family to live
> with him and that's how my parents got divorced.

Jim went on to describe how his father had brought them up on his own
and managed quite effectively. Jim found this change in the family difficult and for years he was very angry with his mother, refusing to speak
to her. However, in the past few months there had been the beginnings of
a tentative rapprochement between him and his mother, initiated by her.
Jim remarked that for years he had not thought about her and was only now
becoming aware of the extent of his anger towards her. The therapist put
to the couple the link between the intrusion of the phone call in the session
and the 'intrusion' of Jim's mother in to his life at this point, bringing Jim's
mother unexpectedly in to the therapy and in to their relationship. This time,
rather than the couple rejecting the therapist's intervention, Jim and Morris
were more thoughtful and considered what the therapist had said for several
minutes. Eventually Jim said that he was relieved to talk about what had
happened in his childhood and although pleased at the possibility of things
changing with his mother, the tentative rapprochement had also brought to
the surface many complex and contradictory feelings about her.

This event in the therapy made it possible for the therapist to begin
to interpret more of their material in terms of its unconscious content.
Although there was a deepening in the work, it was notable to the therapist
that the couple still rejected interventions that did not entirely mirror their
feelings. They particularly disliked more saturated interpretations including
those focusing on the analytic situation, although they communicated their
dissatisfaction less immediately than before. The therapist remained curious
about the way in which this couple required such therapeutic 'accuracy' and
was not sure of its meaning, but continued to note its presence, deciding that
it was necessary for the time being to adjust technique accordingly so that
the couple felt safe enough to explore the contents of their minds.

Despite this progress, the couple continued to argue about their respective sexual roles. The therapist felt it was important to try to return to each
partner's feelings about these roles, Morris's feeling of it being unbearable
to be passive and Jim's sense of urgency for change. When the therapist
tried to explore this internal pressure Jim's association to it was that he
had felt something similar with his father. It occurred to him that he had
always had a need to be close to his father but that this had become much
more marked after his mother left. As Jim began to talk about his childhood, what emerged was that not only did he admire the way his father had
remained 'internally strong' after finding out about his mother's affair, but
he also remembered a holiday to the seaside where he had found his father's

muscular body attractive. As he described this scene he was shocked by his own observation and memory of his father as an 'Oedipal' object of desire. The therapist commented that these thoughts and feelings felt as though they were taboo and that, previously unavailable to him, they had now been brought to conscious awareness. Jim could now permit thoughts and feelings to emerge more flexibly from his mind and correspondingly, rather than rejecting the therapist's thoughts, allow them in.

Jim's exploration of these feelings seemed to help Morris think about the unbearable feeling with which he was struggling. Morris said that being masculine was very important to him and that he associated being passive with a woman's sexual position. Morris's father had been very judgmental about Morris's emerging sexuality in childhood. He had constantly criticized his mannerisms, telling him they should be '*MANnerisms*' not '*WOMANnerisms*'. Morris's mother had joined in with these criticisms and pointed out the ways in which he was 'effeminate'. Morris's father took him to many different sporting activities in the hope that this would 'toughen him up'. Morris enjoyed these times with his father though he remained, as he put it, 'woeful at sport'. His mother objected to the amount of time Morris's father spent with him and, in hindsight, Morris thought she probably felt very excluded. For the first time in the therapy, he became very upset as he recounted how hard he had tried to be more masculine in order to gain his parents' approval. Morris remembered thinking that if he was more like his father, then he might love him more and be less critical. He also had a memory from the age of about 9, where he thought that because his mother loved his father, being more manly like his father would be a way to gain his mother's love and approval. In the therapy, Morris came to understand that he too had homoerotic desires towards his father, which his mother may have discerned at some level. He was left with a sense that to do anything which for him was sexually associated with being feminine, to take up the passive position, was unbearable as it brought to mind painful and humiliating feelings from the past.

The therapist's countertransference at this point was of feeling less rejected by the couple. There was a feeling both of greater flexibility, being under less pressure to get things exactly right and the couple allowed interpretations to land and take effect. For instance the therapist was able to put to the couple that perhaps their active-passive roles might be connected to their early experiences with both parents in different ways and what then emerged was a greater understanding and exploration of their identifications with them.

First, Jim said that it had occurred to him recently that being the passive sexual partner brought his own parents' relationship 'right in to our bed'. Specifically, being passive made him feel very uncomfortable, as he equated it with his mother's experience of sex with his father, a thought which was

(continued)

(continued)

now abhorrent to him. The therapist suggested that perhaps in order to counter these disturbing thoughts and feelings, the solution for Jim was to enact something different, to be the active partner, thereby ensuring he was now in his father's position. This also accorded with the desire he had felt for his father in childhood which had until now been disavowed. The therapist added that this might also explain the urgent feeling gripping Jim at this time.

Morris, in turn, came to understand more about the meaning for him of being active. His way of feeling properly masculine had several aims – to gain his mother's approval and most particularly to find a way to be both close to his father and resemble him. To be a passive partner was in his mind closely linked to being feminine and to the constant criticism by both his parents. The thought of taking up what he saw as a sexually passive position brought alive Morris's anger towards his mother, something previously he had managed to keep at bay. Morris had a very strong belief that being penetrated was akin to being in a heterosexual relationship and being feminine. To be active made Morris feel more like his father, a potent male, which was for him a feature central of his identity as a gay man.

Jim and Morris described how they had both believed that by being a gay couple they did not have to think about anything female, and that to do so was akin to a betrayal of their hard-won sexual identity. Both of them had previously equated a change in their active-passive roles as recalling a heterosexual couple, something they objected to in different ways. Gradually, the rigidity about their roles as a couple loosened and a greater flexibility was allowed between them. With this came a new idea – that they could remain active and passive as before but that they could freely move in their minds between active and passive sexual phantasies and aims. They also discovered that they did not necessarily have to change the manner in which they enjoyed their sexual relationship because they felt there was a more mutual and flexible psychic penetration of each other. There was now room to explore where their desires and phantasies led them together. This less oppressive relationship to aspects of masculinity and the disavowal of anything to do with what they thought of as femininity meant that they could enact their sexual phantasies safely and not feel they were a threat to the relationship. What was striking was that their relationship to their internal heterosexual parental couple relationship both as a couple and individually, felt less persecutory. They no longer used a heterosexual template to reference the way in which they enjoyed their sexual life together and define their couple relationship. This in turn loosened the unconscious tie to their parents' expression of gender identity and sexual orientation integral to their internal parental couple relationship object. Not only was the unconscious tie to the internal heterosexual parental couple now more flexible, so too was the bond between gender identity and sexual orientation, which had previously been binary and somewhat unidimensional.

Discussion

Jim and Morris seemed to want to create something qualitatively and distinctly different from the parental couples they had grown up with and internalized in development. To try to counter the incongruent internal object residing in their shared unconscious worlds, aspects of their sexual relationship which recalled the parental couple had to be kept out of mind and their respective roles inflexibly held on to. The experience of the incongruent internal object was also present in the transference to the therapist, where there seemed to be a very distinct need for the therapist's interventions to be highly congruent with the material Jim and Morris brought to the sessions. Their psychic objection to the object and to the authority of the object, the influence it exerted, was brought to life in their frequent rebuttals of the therapist's interventions.

It is a feature of couple relationships that aspects of both partners can be split off and projected into the other, and where the couple's projective system (Ruszczynski, 1993) is operating benignly it can make those conflicted parts of the personality more tolerable and understood within oneself. Relationships can work well for many years in this way, as was the case for Jim and Morris. However, the couple's projective system can also produce the need to control or attack this less agreeable, conflicted part of oneself which, now located in the other, can be seen more clearly. With some projections and split-off aspects of the self, there inevitably comes a time when these can no longer lie dormant. In terms of identifications with aspects of a parent, where these have been split off and projected in to one's partner, they can then be brought to life in the couple relationship in troublesome and alarming ways. Eventually projections have to be reclaimed because the maintenance of a split makes an unsustainable demand on the psychic economy of the self as well as on the couple. Not to reclaim these parts of the self could even threaten the survival of the relationship. In order for the potential developmental capacities of a couple relationship to presage growth, these previously dormant issues can then emerge between partners and be reworked. In development, the fate of identifications and innate bisexuality can be profoundly impacted upon particularly, as previously described, where there has been parental rejection of homoerotic desires. This may lead to rather rigid, one-dimensional identifications and a rejection of aspects of masculinity and femininity. Some lesbian and gay couples may manage such a predicament by splitting off identifications and therefore their desire, projecting it in to their partner and in this way disavowing themselves of the knowledge of both the desire for and rejection by their parents. These identifications and experiences may then inform the unconscious beliefs (Morgan, 2009) about same-gender desire and relationships which each partner brings to the relationship.

Jim and Morris had somewhat binary gender identifications. They considered physical receptivity as passive, female in construct, and an enactment of feminine identification. Being the penetrating active partner was in their minds male in construct and a central way to express masculinity. They struggled together with the previously unconscious contract to keep active and passive sexual positions distinct both mentally and physically. Corbett reminds us (1993: 347) of the possibility that masculinity should be able to incorporate aspects of desire, passivity and activity in sexual relationships between men. Lynch (Chapter 7) highlights that far from being castrating, receptivity can in fact be highly active and demanding. He also emphasizes the need for psychoanalysis and society more widely (p. 144) to broaden attitudes particularly to anal sexuality, to adopt a more flexible and, one might say, 'versatile' position to exploring the myriad of meanings it holds, not just for gay men.

For Jim and Morris their sexual roles had important meaning and were part of their couple fit. For Jim, by being the passive partner he was, in phantasy, able to be close to his father by taking up his mother's role in the primal scene. He could then in his mind undo or rework the rejection by his father of the erotic desires he felt towards him in childhood. However it was striking that any identification with his mother's sexual experience, or indeed any desire Jim may have felt towards her in development, was not something he was consciously aware of. In addition his identification with his father's desire to be the penetrating active partner to his mother had been split off from conscious awareness and projected in to Morris in whom there was a valency. By being the active penetrating partner with another man Jim would be able to recalibrate the recent disturbance to his identifications brought about by the reemergence of his mother. For Morris the idea of being the passive penetrated partner brought him close to his mother's experience in the primal scene, something which had been split off from conscious awareness and projected in to Jim in whom there was a desire to be penetrated. Morris found Jim's request for him to be passive very disturbing not only because of his split-off identification with his mother, but also because he associated it with being feminine. Being masculine was a way to maintain his original tie to his father. Anything other than being entirely masculine was objectionable to Morris who rigidly needed to hang on to his active role.

Both men had felt homoerotic desire for their fathers and identified with them in different ways. The rejection by their fathers and mothers to the expression of same-gender desire had a significant impact on the eventual fate of Morris's and Jim's identifications with both genders. It became more difficult then to identify with aspects of both genders, and also with a loving parental couple where aspects of masculine and feminine can be freely expressed. Rigidly holding on to their respective roles and identifications meant that they could not flexibly live out a range of phantasies and desires which evoked other identifications, nor inhabit aspects of both masculine and feminine positions in their relationship. The rapprochement between Jim and his mother had destabilized this couple's shared unconscious world by bringing to life their identifications with parents of both genders including those feminine identifications which had been split off. Neither wished to recall the internal parental couple object and objected to its very presence in their shared internal world. They could not allow themselves in phantasy to think about, identify, play with in their minds, the sexual experience of both genders and to fully own their innate bisexuality. Furthermore, to change their active-passive roles meant challenging some of the identifications they had formed in childhood and fortifying others. These carefully laid structures in both their minds had previously been essential to the development of their sexual identity and their unconscious beliefs about same-gender relationships.

The therapist's countertransference feelings of rejection and dismissal were palpable. The couple gave the therapist a powerful experience of rigidity and they demonstrated a significant need to keep particular thoughts out of mind. In the transference the therapist, amongst other things, stood for their feminine identifications that they had had to keep split off and they related to the therapist in the same manner as they related to female identifications. It was striking how their rejection of the therapist's interventions gradually lessened around the same time as Jim's mother came in to the therapy. The rapprochement between Jim and his mother was mirrored in the therapy in the couple's rapprochement to the therapist and also to their female identifications. It became possible to allow interpretations to reach them and to take in the experience of the therapy and the therapist. They could now know consciously about their homoerotic desires towards their fathers in childhood. Split-off aspects of themselves could then be brought to conscious awareness and reintegrated. Their innate bisexuality could be inhabited with greater flexibility and identifications with both genders used to more securely anchor a same-gender union.

Conclusion

This paper has drawn attention to the psychic objection felt by some lesbian and gay couples to the presence of the heterosexual nature of the internal parental couple relationship, including the masculine and feminine gender binary. The objection by one or both parents to their child's expression of homoerotic desire in development is an integral part of the psychic objection to the internal parental couple. I have described how identifications, innate bisexuality, and homoerotic desires in early development can be brought to life in the intimacy of an adult couple, and can present rigidly and inflexibly in both sexuality and gender identifications. Although this example illustrates a gay male couple relationship, in my experience many similar issues arise for lesbian couples. The presentation of their difficulties may be somewhat differently portrayed, but common to both is an inflexibility in relation to innate bisexuality. In psychoanalytic therapy with lesbian and gay couples, it is important to explore their relationship to their innate bisexuality, the availability of a range of identifications, and the meaning of their identifications with both genders. If these aspects can be considered it may be especially helpful in understanding a couple's interactions, particularly in relation to gender roles and unconscious beliefs they bring to the relationship and which drive the way the partners relate to each other. Both lesbian and gay couples and heterosexual couples can have difficulties with identifications and desire for both parents, but for same-gender couples there may be an added hostility and objection to the heterosexuality of their internal parental couple perhaps due to implicit masculine and feminine binary constructs of gender identity and object choice. *I would suggest that there is an even greater need to explore and anchor securely a range of identifications in same-gender relationships because of this.* The therapist's flexible stance in relation to gender and sexuality communicates that these matters can be safely explored without either value judgment or being seen through a heteronormative lens. This can provide the couple with a therapeutic experience where the pain of early rejection and split-off aspects of the self can be worked on, identifications with both genders made available and eventually, innate bisexuality integrated and more flexibly inhabited. This may require clinicians to acknowledge and revisit the relationship to their own innate bisexuality, cross gender identifications and the potential to desire someone of the same gender.

References

Bannister, K., Lyons, A., Pincus, L., Robb, J., Shooter, A., and Stephens, J. (1955). *Social Casework in Marital Problems.* London: Tavistock Publications.

Butler, J. (1990). *Gender Trouble: Feminism and the Subversion of Identity.* New York: Routledge.

Butler, J. (1995). Melancholy Gender: Refused Identification. *Psychoanalytic Dialogues,* 5: 165–180.

Corbett, K. (1993). The Mystery of Homosexuality. *Psychoanalytic Psychology*, 10: 345–357.

D'Ercole, A., and Drescher, J. (Eds.) (2004). *Uncoupling Convention: Psychoanalytic Approaches to Same-Sex Couples and Families.* Hillsdale, NJ: The Analytic Press.

Elise, D. (2000). Women and Desire: Why Women May Not Want to Want. *Studies in Gender and Sexuality*, 1 (2): 125–146

Elise, D. (2002). The Primary Maternal Oedipal Situation and Female Homoerotic Desire. *Psychoanalytic Inquiry,* 22 (2): 209–228.

Fast, I. (1984). *Gender Identity.* Hillsdale, NJ: The Analytic Press.

Fast, I. (1990). Aspects of Early Gender Development: Toward a Reformulation. *Psychoanalytic Psychology,* 7: 105–118.

Fonagy, P. (2008). A Genuinely Developmental Theory of Sexual Enjoyment and Its Implications for Psychoanalytic Technique. *Journal of the American Psychoanalytic Association*, 56 (1): 11–36.

Fonagy, P., and Target, M. (2000). Playing with Reality III: The Persistence of Dual Psychic Reality in Borderline Patients, *International Journal of Psychoanalysis*, 81: 853–874.

Fonagy, P., Leigh, T., Kennedy, R., Mattoon, G., Steele, H., Target, M., Steele, M., and Higgitt, A. (1995). Attachment, Borderline States and the Representation of Emotions and Cognitions in Self and Other. In D. Cicchetti and S.S. Toth (Eds.) *Rochester Symposium on Development Psychopathology, Vol. 6: Cognition and Emotion.* Rochester, NY: University of Rochester Press, pp. 371–414.

Fonagy, P., Target, M., Gergey, G., Allen, J.G., and Bateman, A.W. (2003). The Development Roots of Borderline Personality Disorder in Early Attachment Relationships: A Theory and Some Evidence. *Psychoanalytic Inquiry*, 23 (3): 412–459.

Freud, S. (1905). Three Essays on the Theory of Sexuality. *Standard Edition,* 7: 130–243. London: Hogarth Press.

Freud, S. (1912). On the Universal Tendency to Debasement in the Sphere of Love. Contributions to the Psychology of Love II. *Standard Edition,* 11: 177–190. London: Hogarth Press.

Frommer, M.S. (1994) Homosexuality and Psychoanalysis: Technical Considerations Revisited. *Psychoanalytic Dialogues,* 4 (2): 215–233.

Frommer, M.S. (2000). Offending Gender: Being and Wanting in Male Same-sex Desire. *Studies in Gender and Sexuality,* 1: 191–206.

Goldsmith, S.J. (1995). Oedipus or Orestes? Aspects of Gender Identity Development in Homosexual Men. *Psychoanalytic Inquiry,* 15 (1): 112–124.

Goldsmith, S.J. (2001). Oedipus or Orestes? Homosexual Men, Their Mothers, and Other Women Revisited. *Journal of the American Psychoanalytic Association,* 49: 1269–1287.

Grier, F. (Ed.) (2005). *Oedipus and the Couple.* London: Karnac.

Hertzmann, L. (2011). Lesbian and Gay Couple Relationships: When Internalized Homophobia Gets in the Way of Couple Creativity. *Psychoanalytic Psychotherapy,* 25: 4, 346–360.

Isay, R.A. (1987). Fathers and Their Homosexually Inclined Sons in Childhood. *Psychoanalytic Study of the Child,* 42, 275–294.

Isay, R.A. (1989). *Being Homosexual.* New York: Farrar Strauss Giroux.

Isay, R.A. (1991). The Homosexual Analyst. *Psychoanalytic Study of the Child,* 46: 199–216.

Kernberg, O.F. (1991). Sadomasochism, Sexual Excitement, and Perversion. *Journal of the American Psychoanalytic Association,* 39: 333–362.

Kernberg, O.F. (1995). Superego Functions. In O. Kernberg, *Love Relations: Normality and Pathology.* New Haven, CT: Yale University Press.

Laplanche, J., and Pontalis, J-B. (1973). *The Language of Psychoanalysis.* London: Hogarth.

Ludlam, M., and Nyberg, V. (Eds.) (2007). *Couple Attachments: Theoretical and Clinical Studies.* London: Karnac.

Lynch, P.E. (2002). Yearning for Love and Cruising for Sex: Returning to Freud to Understand Some Gay Men. *Annals of Psychoanalysis,* 30: 175–189.

Morgan, M. (2001). First Contacts: The Therapist's 'Couple State of Mind' as a Factor in the Containment of Couples Seen for Consultation. In F. Grier (Ed.) *Brief Encounters with Couples.* London: Karnac Books.

Morgan, M. (2005). On Being Able to Be a Couple: The Importance of a 'Creative Couple' in Psychic Life. In F. Grier (Ed.) *Oedipus and the Couple.* London: Karnac Books.

Morgan, M. (2009). *Beliefs about a Relationship and Beliefs about the Other: Working with Both Paradigms to Bring about Change: A Day with Mary Morgan.* Paper presentation to the Northern California Society for Psychoanalytic Psychology (NCSPP) and the Bay Area Psychoanalytic Couple Psychotherapy Group (BAPCPG), in San Francisco, CA, on October 24, 2009.

O'Connor, N., and Ryan, J. (1993). *Wild Desires and Mistaken Identities: Lesbianism and Psychoanalysis.* New York: Columbia University Press.

Roughton, R. (2002). Rethinking Homosexuality: What It Teaches Us about Psychoanalysis. *Journal of the American Psychoanalytic Association,* 50: 733–763.

Ruszczynski, S. (1993, reprinted in 2005). *Psychotherapy with Couples: Theory and Practice at the Tavistock Institute of Marital Studies*. London: Karnac Books.

Ruszczynski, S., and Fisher, J. (Eds.) (1995). *Intrusiveness and Intimacy in the Couple*. London: Karnac Books.

Stoller, R. (1972). The 'Bedrock' of Masculinity and Femininity: Bisexuality. *Archives of General Psychiatry*, 26: 207–212.

Target, M. (2007). Is Our Sexuality Our Own? A Developmental Model of Sexuality Based on Early Affect Mirroring. *British Journal of Psychotherapy*, 23 (4), 517–530.

Part IV

Perversion revisited

Chapter 9

Sexual aberrations

Do we still need the concept? If so, when and why? If not, why not?

Donald Moss

A 35-year-old woman in analysis feels possessed by the increasingly urgent decision of whether to provide her 13-year-old child with 'top' surgery (radical mastectomy) on the child's way to 'transition' from 'female' to 'male'. Since age 3, the child had expressed her conviction that, in spite of her anatomy, she was, in fact, a boy. The parents had uncomfortably supported this notion, but now, with the impending surgery, the stakes for the mother were rising to an unbearable level. The father thought that surgery was the only option. The child expressed anguish and dismay at anything else. A surgeon, experienced with doing the surgery on transitioning pubescent girls, was ready to go. The child had received psychiatric and medical clearance.

The mother gives voice to her irresolvable quandary:

> I have to do something but what I want is to do nothing until I can figure out what all of this means. But it can't be figured out. There's no place where I can start to begin figuring. A long time ago we tried that. We wanted to know why. What's causing this? But now that's over. We never got anywhere with questions like that. It's just 'This is what I am'. And what she is won't go away. Nothing to figure. Nothing to think. I have to do something. I can't say no and I can't say yes. I can't do what I have to do.

Neither taking nor delaying action was an option.

The analyst treating the child has supported 'transition' and hormone therapy has begun. This analyst's opinion was now receiving unanimous support – from the patient's husband, her family of origin and her friends. The patient described herself as 'the last holdout'. She wept as she spoke about her daughter's impending loss of her breasts but, while weeping, she dismissed her own tears as 'retro and selfish'.

My reaction to the patient's steadily heightening tension was to sense, along with her, that mutilating surgery was about to be performed on her child. I felt that this surgery was receiving reflexive sanction by way of a widespread – nearly commonsensical – embrace of a seemingly radical advance in the culture's ways of thinking about and theorizing transsexuality. I had long been aware of the press of this commonsensical current but here was the first time I had felt its direct force in the context of an urgent clinical situation. Soon, I noticed that this force was having an unexpected and disturbing impact on me. In trying to think about my patient's 'daughter', I found myself wondering whether, in fact, she ought to be called 'daughter' at all.

I had been, in effect, knocked off my pins by a force not only verbal and atmospheric – a general cultural moment – but also legal and administrative. During the time of this emerging crisis, I was paying particularly close attention to the public media. Here are four pertinent stories:

1   A Colorado state court was presented with a case of a 6-year-old child born with male genitalia who, nonetheless, was certain that she was really a 'girl'. Her public school had refused her parents' request that 'he' be allowed to use the Girls' restroom.

The court ruled against the school, saying: 'Depriving Coy of the acceptance that students need to succeed in school creates a barrier where none should exist, and entirely disregards the charging party's gender identity'.

2   At Yale and other Ivy League universities, 'Transgender employees who are managerial & professional staff, faculty, postdoctoral associates, postdoctoral fellows, clerical and technical, service and maintenance and security are eligible to receive sex reassignment surgery. Both Yale HEALTH and Aetna will follow the standard of care for transgender health and sex reassignment surgery as defined by the World Professional Association for Transgender Health (WPATH: www.wpath.org)'.

3   A third-year candidate at a major IPA Psychoanalytic Institute in New York is transitioning from female to male. He has had top surgery and is currently receiving hormone treatments. His first training analysis collapsed when, in its fifth year, he came to his transitioning decision. He then found a second training analyst with whom he is now continuing. The candidate has written about and given many presentations in analytic venues about his experience, which includes working with some patients who have been with him throughout his transition. A recent audience of about 100 – mostly analysts – was clearly and unambiguously supportive of this candidate's efforts to have us all reconsider our fundamental orientation toward anatomical 'bedrock'. The tone of the applause was instructive. It seemed a response to this analytic candidate's courage and bravery in the face of a suddenly dawning sense of anatomy-as-bedrock's oppressive force.

4   'One of the highest-ranking transgender military officers in the world – if not the highest – is Lt. Col. Cate McGregor of the Australian Defense Force. Most "alpha Aussie blokes", she says, were content that she was "still into chicks" and could still hit a cricket ball, which amused her: "There is a groping towards a paradigm of blokeyness they can accept". "Every day now", she says, living as a woman, "it feels amazing to be alive".

General Morrison said that watching Colonel McGregor's struggles has deepened his understanding of what it means to be transgender: "My hat goes off to everyone who does it because they are trying to be true to themselves. It takes an enormous amount of courage. And if an army can't respect courage, then there's something wrong'" (NY Times, Sunday Review, Julia Baird, Feb. 23, 2014).

'Facts on the ground', like these and many others, cannot be reasonably ignored. Nor can they be reasonably dismissed as the triumph of psychotic thought. Coupled with what I was hearing about my patient's daughter, these facts, though coming from the outside, hit me with the force of a drive: disturbing, exigent, and inescapable. My mind was as attached to these cultural 'facts' as it might be to comparable internal 'facts' emanating from my own body. Each set of 'facts', whether coming from my interior or from the external world, made, as Freud puts it, 'a demand on my mind for work'. These ongoing cultural facts – and their cumulative demands – will not disappear. Nor can they reasonably be fled. As such, they contradict Freud's canonical assertion that the possibility of flight marks the definitional distinction between inside and out. These ostensibly 'external' facts are, in effect, permanent, which makes the necessity of working psychoanalytically with them also permanent. Facts like these mean that I can no longer rest on what had, prior to their arrival, been an absolute certainty regarding anatomy's privileged power to determine gender. And once absolute certainty is shaken – no matter how slightly – nothing will restore it.

The patient melancholically resigned herself to complying with her daughter's demand, saying to me:

I think you're right in here – we don't know what's going on – but you're not right in the real world. In the real world, the surgery is what I have to do. That's what's going on. I can't not do it. No one is with me in that. I have to.

Neither my patient nor I could find a platform from which to think effectively. We each had very strong, very negative, reactions to the prospect of the impending surgery. But also, we each could sense strong forces pushing us to scrutinize not only the impending surgery but also our hesitation to go ahead with it. My patient's anguish and mine might be the expression of retrograde emotions – anachronistic and authoritarian – signs of allegiance to a bygone, and essentialist, notion of anatomical/psychic reality.

'They're your daughter's breasts, not yours', the pediatrician of my patient's daughter told her: 'She can do as she wants with them. It's her body. It's her mind. It's her life'.

My patient, telling me this, added:

But that's not how I feel. I feel they're our breasts, mine and hers. We belong to each other. If she loses her breasts then I lose something too. I know it makes no sense. How can I say yes to losing my daughter? I don't gain anything. My daughter's not something I can exchange. I'm the mother of a daughter. That's how we're attached. I get that. That's owed to me. I have to let it go, though. It's 2012. What does that make me? What does it make her?

Whose breasts, then, are they? And who has the right to determine whether they will be removed? These urgent clinical questions derive from a more elemental conceptual one: is the daughter's sexual identity 'aberrant'? While feeling the wobble of our once-reliable clinical platform, how do we effectively explore that question? Where can we find firm ground when the 'bedrock' we stand on quakes?

The mother and I both speak in what feels like our own voices – voices legitimated by the voices of ancient predecessors – for her, say, an endless chain of mothers; and for me, an entire Judeo-Christian canon plus Freud and a century of psychoanalysis. And yet each of us also feels that our voices, like those of our predecessors, might have now lost their legitimacy. What we thought of as ancient and legitimate might have become old-fashioned and illegitimate.

It is here, then, at the point where our certainties are disrupted, where 'ancient legitimacy' collides with 'old-fashioned rigidity', that my patient and I meet, and where the question of 'sexual aberrations' springs forth.

From its beginnings, psychoanalysis has had, and still has, a vexed and unstable relationship to the permanently contested category of sexual aberrations. On one hand, we have provided, and continue to provide, both clinical and theoretical support to a conservative, prescriptive vision of the properly sexual. While consistently 'tinkering with the mechanism', we have never abandoned the principle that lines can, and must, be drawn between the normal and the aberrant.

On the other hand, we have provided – and continue to provide – clinical and theoretical support to renegade sexualities that, then and now, have insisted, against propriety, that such lines violate their intrinsic integrities and therefore warrant erasure. Here too, we 'tinker with the mechanism' – but now the lines turn contingent and scare quotes appear around the term 'normal'.

These two apparently incompatible vectors – one grounding us in the conservative work of regulation, the other grounding us in the radical work of setting free – infiltrate all that we do and think about sexuality. Their fundamental incompatibility can easily disturb us, implying as it does a potentially profound fault in our conceptual and clinical foundations.

In pursuit of rational consistency and a steadier foundation we can try our best to choose between the two vectors – to use one of them as a guide, and therefore perhaps provide ourselves with a default position, a starting point, what Otto Fenichel called a 'dry spot' (1946/1995).

Fundamentally oriented by the regulatory vector, an analyst can lean on apparently fixed notions of, say, 'nature', 'law', 'anatomy', and 'fact' by which to begin thinking about normal and aberrant sexuality. Precisely because they seem fixed, these notions supply an analyst with a stable grid by which to map sexuality. However, this analyst may now find him/herself sharing the grid with an unwelcomed cluster of biased zealots while reasonable and liberal colleagues renounce the grid and accuse him of an unthinking and rigid orthodoxy.

Fundamentally oriented by the libratory vector, another analyst – leaning on treasured notions like freedom, possibility, and individual and human rights in order to begin thinking about normal and aberrant sexuality: excitedly confident now – loosed from inhibiting convention – this analyst might also find himself in unwelcome company, though, company that Ted Hughes has called 'the underground heretical life, leagued with everything occult, spiritualistic, devilish, over-emotional, bestial, mystical, feminine, crazy, revolutionary and poetic' (Hughes, 1994: 132) while trusted colleagues accuse him of abandoning first principles and denying the facts of life.

Each strategy begins in bedrock: the conservative one in the fixed elements of nature, the libratory one in the plastic elements of history.

If we want to avoid the monochromatic – finally brittle, and finally thin – outcome befalling either orienting strategy, we must take on the never-ending labor of thinking and working within a zone infiltrated by both of these irreconcilable vectors – being alert to, but never actually choosing between, the two of them. In this zone, scare quotes appear around the notion of 'bedrock'. Originally the basis of interpretation, bedrock in this zone becomes an object of interpretation.

That zone is elusive. We look for it in theory; we look for it in clinical practice.

But when it comes to issues of normal and aberrant sexuality, clinical experience proves as vexing and destabilizing as the problems it promises to clarify. Clinical experience can always affirm us in our efforts to preserve yesterday's sexual order against today's 'perverse' pressures. And it can also always affirm us in working against the restrictive/inhibiting pressures exerted by that same sexual order. Theory too, finally lets us down, presenting us with only vexation and instability. Like clinical experience, theory affirms us both when our interpretation supports today's commonsensical sexual frame and when it exposes that frame as gratuitously restrictive.

At a clinical conference recently, a senior woman analyst, married to a woman, presented material from the first year of her analysis of a man who had become particularly fascinated and involved with adult illiteracy – its determinants and treatment. The visiting consultant linked this fascination to the patient's choice of a homosexual analyst, inferring that the patient in both cases was drawn to, and puzzled by, deficiency and aberration. The inference was greeted with silence, and discussion about the patient simply continued. At the end of the presentation, the consultant reiterated the interpretation. Afterwards, however, during a break in the work, two groups formed. One found the consultant's inference strong and useful, likely to be borne out as the treatment progressed. The other found the inference retrograde and even insulting. I moved from group to group. Each group grounded its confidence in what seemed self-evident 'clinical material', on one side, and venerated theory on the other. Each felt the other group gave voice to a prejudiced view – 'reactionary' there, 'politically correct' here. Neither credited the other's appeal either to the material or to theory. Each group thought itself neutral and thought the other to be employing 'experience' and 'theory' to cover a deforming bias, harmful to psychoanalysis. The issue that divided them was clear: what is the proper place of female homosexuality on a grid dividing the sexually normal, and therefore unremarkable, from the sexually aberrant, and therefore interpretable?

In relation to normal and aberrant sexuality, then, the clinical psychoanalyst can find protective support from both theory and experience for almost whatever he/she thinks. This kind of support utterly lacks utility. Its net result does nothing to affirm that the analyst is, in fact, making *psychoanalytic* judgments. Instead, it can feel like conceptual and practical padding, taking the potential pain out of whatever one thinks or does. One cannot 'learn from experience' when every experience, like every thought, has the power to simultaneously affirm and disconfirm its own premises. In each of its many parts, this theoretical/clinical padding promises to facilitate clarity and definition; in the aggregate, though, it can easily impede, leaving the analyst where he/she started – alone. Here, perhaps, we expose the conceptual weak spot associated with any effort to neutrally frame a category of 'sexual aberrations'. The first step in such framing, the tilt toward or the tilt against, must be made alone. And nothing in our theory or practice can reliably provide us with confidence that such a step – the first one, the alone one – is being made neutrally.

Although much may have changed over the past century in our approach to the lines dividing the 'sexually aberrant' from the 'sexually normal', the basic – and irreconcilable – tension between conservative and libratory impulses has remained constant. Of course, this tension simply gives local expression to a more basic, more fundamental tension that attaches to all appetitive desires; i.e. the tension between their 'civilized' and 'uncivilized' expression. Freud illuminates that fundamental tension beautifully:

> What makes itself felt in a human community as a desire for freedom may be their revolt against some existing injustice, and so may prove favourable to a further development of civilization; it may remain compatible with civilization. But it may also spring from the remains of their original personality, which is still untamed by civilization and may thus become the basis in them of hostility to civilization. The urge for freedom, therefore, is directed against particular forms and demands of civilization or against civilization altogether. It does not seem as though any influence could induce a man to change his nature into a termite's. No doubt he will always defend his claim to individual liberty against the will of the group. A good part of the struggles of mankind centre round the single task of finding an expedient accommodation – one, that is, that will bring happiness – between this claim of the individual and the cultural claims of the group; and one of the problems that touches the fate of humanity is whether such an accommodation can be reached by means of some particular form of civilization or whether this conflict is irreconcilable.
>
> (Freud, 1930)

The category of the 'sexually normal', then, delineates, in the sexual sphere, an effort at 'accommodation', an effort that means to work for now and to indefinitely defer the question of whether 'this [elemental] conflict is irreconcilable'.

I think this ongoing tension between normality's aspiration to accommodate and individuals' aspirations against accommodation and toward unrestrained liberty finds both its first and its clearest expression in Freud's foundational essay, 'The Sexual Aberrations'.

Try as he might, Freud could find no clear structural line dividing the aberrant from the normal. The search for that line proved futile. The line Freud did draw, then, was much more his than his theory's. By 'his' here, of course I do not mean idiosyncratically his. Like both my patient and me, Freud proceeded with a feeling of confidence regarding what could be assumed – a confidence grounded, in large part, I think, by his attachment to convention. He was part of a community certain of the validity of its conventional assumptions. And yet also, like my patient and me, Freud's confidence, and his attachment to that community, was steadily shaken by 'facts on the ground' – clinical, cultural, and historical facts – and the demands they placed on his mind for work.

Working with and against conventional line-drawing was, and is, a necessary and temporary precondition for Freud's psychoanalytic theorizing about 'The Sexual Aberrations'. Theory alone could not and cannot generate the line that divides the normal from the aberrant. For this, theory must borrow from common sense, from pre-existing reason, from convention. The difficult task, then, for the analyst is to first use and then immediately liberate himself from this original, and necessary, debt to convention, so as to then be able to return to relatively debt-free theorizing.

Freud models this task for us in 'The Sexual Aberrations'. The essay sports a regular rhythm. On its first beat, Freud bows to thought's necessity and constructs orienting lines – procreation, nature, biology, anatomy. On its second beat, Freud immediately exposes these lines as arbitrary and contingent; all sexuality, he demonstrates, always polymorphic, always perverse, violates each of these lines all the time. This rhetorical rhythm infuses the essay. This rhythm conveys the sustained tension that bound Freud's need for order to his intellectual program of critiquing that very order. This tension – the tension, I think, that founds psychoanalysis – persists throughout the essay; one-two, one-two; assertion, counter-assertion; no resolution, no synthesis.

Without directly confessing to the necessarily arbitrary nature of constructing such lines, Freud nonetheless communicates it. Like him, in order to both think about and do clinical work we must have lines. No matter how apparently logical their origins, the lines distinguishing the sexually normal from the sexually aberrant necessarily include an arbitrary element, a personal contribution that undermines their apparently logical rigor.

Freud's essay 'The Sexual Aberrations' is line-drawing, regulatory, and conservative while also line-breaking, libratory, and radical. The essay gives voice to an ongoing collision between two unreasonable and excessive currents. One grounds 'normal' sexuality in a fixed idea of proper aim, proper object and, as it pertains to my patient's daughter, proper gender. The other undermines that ground: no fixed aim, object, or gender.

Reason does not possess the power to either reconcile or synthesize these two currents. Yet something like reason is necessary to separate and clarify the two. For this, 'reason' needs an imaginary zero point, a dry spot that functions to divide negative from positive, the properly fixed from the fundamentally unmoored.

Freud places an 'exquisitely gifted' (Group Psychology and the Analysis of the Ego) heterosexual male at his zero point (1921). The 'exquisite gift' of this figure is to have arrived at his heterosexuality by way of a direct identification with its father. This direct identification saves the figure from a detour through passive yearning, a detour that would have marked its origin in 'feminine' insufficiency. In effect, the direct identification with the father generates a figure whose sexuality has no history. It arrives fully formed, both phallic and heterosexual. As such, it occupies a place beyond the reach of psychic determination.

Self-contented, it needs no regulation. Always heterosexual, it has escaped the burdens of having to aspire, and, along with that, any susceptibility to accusations of masquerade. The figure functions as a sexual hero, authenticity itself, a simultaneously real and imaginary object.

Freud, of course, 'knows' that this placeholder is a fiction. But he also 'knows' that this fiction is a conceptual necessity. Just as Freud's placeholder is both real and imaginary, then, his categorization of sexual aberrations is also both real and imaginary.

An imaginary icon filling an intolerable gap, the exquisitely gifted male heterosexual functions here as the theory's fetish object. Anchoring the grid, deviating neither as to aim nor to object, the figure promises, and seems to deliver, a conceptual order: promises, and seems to deliver, protection against conceptual disorder.

The destabilizing, and brilliant, force of Freud's essay 'The Sexual Aberrations' derives from its simultaneously demonstrating the fetishistic function of this icon and asserting a belief in that same fetishistic function. This impossible pairing remains our legacy, which, to this day, has not been settled. Like Freud, we are constantly exposing the fetishistic premises underlying any fixed notion of the normal. And simultaneously we are constantly affirming the necessity to treat such fetishistic 'bedrock' premises as both fundamental and real. 'Bedrock' itself might productively be thought of as functioning like a fetish – a conceptual necessity, both imagined and real, protecting us against the awareness of the disorder associated with an abyssal lack.

Deftly manipulating the fetish-like icon in and out of his argument – now you see it, now you don't – Freud was able to fabricate a coherent sexual map while simultaneously disrupting the ostensibly solid ground on which any such map would have to rest.

Much of contemporary American psychoanalysis seems determined to reshape, or even to collapse, Freud's radically unstable sexual map. The aim seems to be to expose the map's fetishistic premises so as to finally be unburdened of the necessity of employing them – in effect, to cure itself of conceptual fetishism.

The strategy is clear. Once apparently oriented to protect and defend its male heterosexual icon, American theory now, in effect, tends to leave that icon to fend for itself. The theory's new aim is to incorporate and to pull into the center – to 'normalize', and therefore to protect and defend – a variety of sexual practices it once matter-of-factly mapped onto the grid's sexually aberrant periphery. 50 years ago, the LGBT Committee of the American Psychoanalytic Association would have been the incarnation of a conceptual oxymoron.

The icon and its derived sexual grid can now certainly be made to seem anachronistic, the product of a now-surpassed, and therefore now aberrant, form of sexualized repudiation: a sexuality too anxious, too regulated, too ordered; too, well, obsessional and fetishistic – a map-making, imperious sexuality.

Armed with the notion that a sexual map necessarily depends upon a fetish-like icon holding the map together, this new strand of theory can confidently proceed by treating the map as both a way of organizing unruly and disruptive sexual desires and a way of obscuring the anxieties that such disorganizing desires can provoke.

Of course, we often hear our patients putting sexual maps together: I do this, but not that, they say; I do it with her, but not with him. And whenever our patients map their own sexualities we are keen to spot the anxious impulses their over-determined maps obscure.

We might assume that the same anxious impulses animate our own discipline's work of sexual mapping/sexual theorizing. That is, we might assume that anxiety infiltrates all sexual map-making: an individual's or a discipline's. This premise, in turn, will diminish our confidence in being able to distinguish between our efforts to masterfully map sexualities and our efforts to anxiously tame them. Since we cannot be confident of this difference, we cannot be confident of the possibility of a neutral sexual map. Mapping sexuality, like taming it, might well, then, be treated as a marker of the mapmaker's – any mapmaker's – abandonment of neutrality – a wish-driven effort to map, and organize, otherwise threatening wishes, a way of folding them in. But the conundrum persists no matter what we do. The triumphant non-map is no less a map than the one it replaces. The icon that held the original grid together is now replaced by its negative. This new non-icon performs the same fetishistic function as its predecessor: it provides relief and order. Recall for a moment my patient and her daughter. With no manifest grid and no manifest map everyone but my patient knew exactly what to do; the non-map was perfect in its capacity to provide precise direction.

A fundamental difficulty arises: perhaps we cannot actually think of sexualities without thereby mapping/taming them. We have little reason to suppose that we can validly and reliably separate thinking from mapping from taming. Looking back on the history of our sexual theorizing, we cannot fail to notice that yesterday's assertively neutral map has consistently been de-neutralized by today's critical consciousness. Our maps inadvertently create something akin to sexual zoos – increasingly naturalized zoos, to be sure, but nonetheless, like all zoos, inevitably deforming its captured inhabitants. And over time, the zoo's captured inhabitants work to shake off the map's deforming influences. Caught, tagged and mapped – theorized – some have been able to wiggle free – women, gay men, and lesbians. Others – like transgendered people now, say – remain caught, though, and, perhaps inspired by their liberated predecessors, are working to wiggle free. On and on this goes, apparently indefinitely. And there we psychoanalysts stand, I think, participant bystanders, excited by the drama – applauding our theory each time it seems to catch and map these otherwise wild sexualities, and also applauding those very sexualities each time they manage to escape. Our excitement at both the moments of capture and the moments of liberation reveals, I think, something other than a baseline neutrality. Elemental, and perhaps irreducible, our baseline deviation from neutrality bears particular scrutiny. The excitement at capture and the excitement at liberation do not cancel out each other. It is not a zero-sum conflict. If anything, the sum doubles – potential excitement no matter which way we turn – toward mapping or away from it, toward organization or toward dispersal.

The central problem, of course, with the category 'Sexual Aberrations' is that, no matter how neutral and universal its aspirations might be, the category seems to always lean on local specificities: time, place, subculture, person. Your aberration is my desire; my aberration is yours. And yet, the moment we might change the category's name to, say, 'Local Sexual Aberrations', or 'My Idea of Sexual Aberrations', the term would immediately become an object of conceptual farce. The term has force only when it transcends the local and lacks credibility if it claims grounding in the universal.

Neither local nor universal, the category nonetheless maintains its sensuous and theoretical vitality. The persistence of the category is grounded in a fundamental/ universal agreement – derived, I think, from the equally fundamental/universal incest taboo – that both the aims and the objects of sexuality must be regulated. Both repression and externally grounded norms and punishments aim to regulate, to efficiently maintain order. The persistence of the category of sexual aberrations is grounded, then, in the persistence of the necessity for sexual regulation.

We might of course disagree regarding any particular regulation, but we will not disagree, I think, as to the necessity of regulation, *per se*. This is so even when we – I certainly include myself here – might profess no confidence in the reli-ability of existing regulatory forces, internal and external. As analysts, we have both personal and theoretical ground from which to believe that many of those regulations are themselves the work of rogue forces – forces apparently operating beyond the reach of regulation. As Adorno wrote of authoritarianism – regulation run amok –'the superego services, rather than regulates, the id' (1951/1993).

These rogue forces – often disguised as neutral, reasonable, and natural – are bracketed on one end by the salacious permissiveness of participation by proxy and on the other by the punitive excesses of participatory disidentification. When regulation itself is infiltrated with the very sexuality it aims to control – when it becomes exciting to regulate – the line between an appetite for regulation and an appetite for sex vanishes. We have successfully spotted exactly this form of infiltration, repressed and warded off sexual wishes, in the nominally regulatory structures that constitute homophobia and misogyny. To the extent that we might have participated in enforcing those structures, this discovery should lead us to be skeptical, in principle, of our capacities to clearly distinguish the regulation from the appetite.

Of course, we no more want unregulated regulations than we do unregulated appetites. We therefore find ourselves in an unsteady and unpleasant situation.

We must be receptive to sensuous appetites – our own and our patients' – and also to our need to regulate them. We need regulation, and also need to know that the regulation we need may, in fact, soon be exposed as arbitrary and excessive. We need order, but also need to be forever skeptical of any order's claim to 'neutrality'. We need sublimated thought and theory even though, no matter how sublimated, thought and theory will inevitably prove themselves, as Freud said, 'roundabout ways towards wish-fulfillment'. Any wished-for order we achieve likely will soon be subject to potentially destabilizing interpretation. Our orienting distinction between appetite and regulation, then, faces the constant threat of collapsing in on itself. Our elaborate system of checks and balances may well include the sending out of hungry foxes to guard unruly chickens, or, just as likely, hungry chickens to guard unruly foxes. There is no clear way to tell in advance.

The category of patient I'm thinking is the one to whom we feel inhibited from saying 'Stop' – the patients whose behaviors seem just beyond the appropriate – some combination of hostile and erotic, bearable but disturbing – slightly aberrant, that is – patients with whom we cannot relax. These patients force us to envision what exactly we need in order to relax, what we require in order to feel we are in a 'normal' set-up. Alongside wishing such appetites away, though, we likely find ourselves interpreting them – trying to discover what they mean and what they disguise, and how, therefore, they might be transformed. In other words, our work of interpreting these appetites handily functions as a controlled, thoughtful form of wishing them away. How can we trust an interpretation whose aim is to fulfill a wish? This, I think, is the basic conundrum that tempts us to map 'the sexual aberrations'. A map fosters the belief that we have transformed a disciplinary 'judgment' into a neutral 'reading'.

A patient of mine movingly captures some of the terrible burden we carry when we straddle the map on one side, our private loves on the other. My patient is anguished by his erotic appetites. After a series of unhappy relationships with women, he is involved, for the first time, with a man. My patient said, 'I have never been as calm and settled as I am now. For the first time in my life I feel happy'. He added, though,

> It breaks my heart, though, to be with a man. I wish it were not true, but it is. I can't help it. I love him but I don't want to be happy like this. This is not what I was really meant to be.

And with that, this patient gives voice to his unbidden regulatory appetite, the boundary beyond which he cannot think, an appetite monitored by a force he names 'what I was meant to be'.

References

Adorno, T. et al. (first published 1951, republished 1993) *The Authoritarian Personality*, New York: Norton.

Fenichel, O. (first published 1946, republished 1995) *The Psychoanalytic Theory of Neurosis*, New York: Norton.

Freud, S. (1900) The Interpretation of Dreams, Chapter 7, *S.E.*, Vol. 5. London: Hogarth.
Freud, S. (1905) The Sexual Aberrations, in *Three Essays in the Theory of Sexuality*, *S.E.*, Vol. 7. London: Hogarth.
Freud, S. (1921) Group Psychology and the Analysis of the Ego, *S.E.*, Vol. 18. London: Hogarth.
Freud, S. (1930) Civilization and Its Discontents, *S.E.*, Vol. 21. London: Hogarth.
Hughes, T. (1994) *Winter Pollen: Occasional Prose*, ed. W. Scammell. London: Faber & Faber.

Chapter 10

The prostitute as mirror

Distinguishing perverse and non-perverse use of prostitutes

Alessandra Lemma

Ambivalence about prostitution and its function in society has a long history, not least within Christianity. In the Middle Ages and during the Renaissance prostitution was tolerated because brothels were seen as disposal units for sexual sin. Saint Augustine, who condemned all sexual desire as unclean, nevertheless recognized that were it not for prostitutes[1], men's lust would seep everywhere and pollute the world. As such prostitutes were damned, but their souls were to be sacrificed for the betterment of society.

Nearly 800 years later Thomas Aquinas propounded a similar outlook: 'Prostitution in towns is like the cesspool in the palace: take away the cesspool and the palace will become an unclean, evil-smelling place'. Thus was born the licensed brothel, 'a factory of evil serving the common good'[2] (Berkowitz, 2013: 161). Indeed by 1358 the Grand Council of Venice would declare that prostitution was 'absolutely indispensable to the world'. In other words, despite the denigration and distaste aroused by the function performed by the prostitute, sexually restless men could at least deposit their shameful desires into the prostitute, safely out of sight.

The Grand Council of Venice took a rather bold position if one compares it to the fate of prostitution and brothels over history when they were subsequently largely made illegal. Some European countries are now legalizing prostitution, with the most liberal laws in Germany. In the UK, at the time of writing this chapter, however, current proposals operate in the direction of criminalizing the buying of sex.

No discussion of the use of prostitution can ignore the external social context within which the sexual transaction occurs and the fact that sex workers generally often come from emotionally and socio-economically deprived backgrounds and are at the risk of abuse and exploitation. However in this chapter I will not be focusing on these important social realities or on the psychic functions of prostitution from the perspective of the prostitute. There is already (a sparse and largely dated) analytic literature on women who engage in prostitution or fantasies of prostitution (e.g. Hollender, 1961; Hutto and Faulk, 2000; Agoston, 1945). The analytic literature is also not short of contributions focusing on patients who use prostitutes to enact perverse fantasies or those who might be regarded as being 'addicted' to sex and for whom the use of prostitutes, as of pornography, can acquire a compulsive quality rendering the seeking out of sex indispensable to psychic equilibrium (Wood, 2013). This focus has also led to a good number of generic psychological studies on sex addiction and the compulsive use of prostitutes (Gordon-Lamoureux, 2007; Hall, 2011; Vanwesenbeeck, 2013; Zapf and Carroll, 2008). However I could not identify analytic literature that explores in any detail the use of prostitutes by men outside of the theoretical framework of perversion and addiction.

In this chapter I want to argue another psychic function of the prostitute in the minds of *some* men seeking her/his services, that is, the way the prostitute may provide an opportunity for working towards an integration of psychosexuality. One of the strengths of an analytic approach is that, at its best, it aims to understand behavior and the unconscious states of mind that give rise to the behavior without categorizing it and making generalizations. This is especially important when we try to engage with a sub-culture – that of the workers and users of the sex trade – which can arouse our voyeurism and defensive moralizing. In approaching this subject I hope to steer clear of such pitfalls and I am informed by my work with young prostitutes and latterly by my work as an analyst with male patients who have used prostitutes.

Perverse and non-perverse use of prostitutes

Many years ago I worked with young women who, for a variety of reasons, had become prostitutes. One unusually articulate girl stands out in my memory not only because of her own moving story, but also because of the insights she shared with me about the men who paid her for sex. In one of our encounters she spoke candidly about how she viewed these men and she outlined her homespun typology: 'There are the weirdoes, the saddoes and the losers'.

When I invited her to elaborate on this categorization, she explained that some of the men – the so-called 'weirdoes' – used her to enact perverse and typically degrading sexual acts either towards her and/or towards themselves (the typical sado-masochistic spectrum of enactment psychoanalysis has traditionally focused on in relation to prostitution). Other men – the so-called 'saddoes' – seemed to need her to make them feel they were 'ok'. She did not mean that these men were feeling inadequate in their bodies or in themselves more generally: those men she labeled the 'losers'. Rather the 'saddoes', she added, 'seem to feel that what they enjoy sexually is dirty, bad, and they want me to make them feel it's not. And they're not weirdoes: enjoying blowjobs is not weird!' Importantly she went on to describe how she felt the 'saddoes' *looked* at her in a way that was different to how the 'weirdoes' looked at her: 'they [the weirdoes] shit on you with their eyes; the saddoes . . . they're searching for something in my eyes'. She did not comment further on the 'losers'.

Of course, transferentially, this young girl was searching my eyes/face to find herself, for me to see the whole of her who felt weird, sad and a loser to different degrees. But her description of the men stayed with me and was later elaborated in my experience of working with men who declared their use of prostitutes during their analyses.

In approaching this chapter I have found it useful to reflect on this young girl's focus on the particular quality of how she felt these men were looking at her. Drawing on her experience we might say that one group of men (the perverse group) use the prostitute to evacuate into, to project into her what is felt to be intolerable within the self – in the viscerally evocative language of the young girl, 'they shit on you with their eyes'.

In the other, non-perverse, group (that I think comprises both the 'saddoes' and 'losers' because they are not as clearly distinguished in my clinical experience), by contrast, the man is literally *looking to* the prostitute in order to see something in her eyes. I want to suggest that these men are looking for themselves in the prostitute's eyes/mind to have a hitherto un-integrated aspect of their sexual, embodied experience reflected back to them so that it can be recognized, accepted and eventually reintegrated into their representation of themselves as sexual in their own minds.

Here the etymology of the word prostitute is of note. The online Etymology Dictionary states that the notion of 'sex for hire' is not inherent in the etymology. One explanation is that *prostituta* is a composition of *pro* and *statuere* (to cause to stand, to place forward). The notion of 'placing forward' aptly ties in with the psychic function I am proposing here because I am suggesting, and as I hope to illustrate through my work with two male patients (one heterosexual and one homosexual), that for some men the prostitute provides a *psychic* service mediated by her explicit sexual role outside of an attachment relationship. This role is to 'place forward' sexuality, that is to represent sexuality unequivocally and to mirror back to the man his sexual desire unambiguously in a shame-free context. In this specific context, for some men, what the prostitute provides is an experience of their sexuality as contingently mirrored and validated as acceptable. In putting forward such a possibility I am not advocating the use of prostitutes – a practice that was not uncommon amongst sex therapists in the 1970s – but simply trying to understand their psychic function whilst distinguishing the use of prostitutes to enact perverse scenarios from the non-perverse use.

More specifically I want to suggest that such men use the prostitute to mirror their sexual self as a way of regulating the overwhelming feelings associated with it, as a way that is of organizing their sexuality and the representation of the sexual body in the mind. Such men can then potentially use this experience to approach in a less anxious manner their sexual partner in the context of an attachment relationship.

I am mindful here that my formulations about the impact of the encounter with the prostitute cannot be considered separately from these men's involvement contemporaneously with an analytic process where they were able to elaborate the experience with the prostitute, not least through the transference, and be helped to integrate the meaning of this into their representation of themselves as sexual. In other words I am not suggesting that the experience with the prostitute 'cured' these men. I am, however, interested to explore how this experience, for these men, appeared to represent a development. Even if this entailed a concrete seeking out of the literal gaze and touch of the other – and it could thus be argued that it represents an enactment – this appeared to be nevertheless a necessary and helpful step for them towards the representation of their sexual self and its integration into their overall experience of themselves.

The prostitute's implicit function of 'placing forward' sexual feelings is important: as Fonagy (2008) has argued, emotion regulation arises out of the mirroring of affect by a primary caregiver, but sexual feelings are different in this respect because they are systematically ignored and left unmirrored or are only partially so. At the core of this view thus lies the specific difficulty the mother has in mirroring the infant's sexuality – an adaptive failure that structures psychosexuality, indelibly inscribing in the mind the need for an other who makes it possible to experience our sexuality through their elaboration of it (see also Target, Chapter 2).

Approaching sexuality from the standpoint of attachment and mentalization Fonagy underlines that 'a key facet of psychosexuality is a sense of incongruence with the infant's actual experience [that] disrupts the actual coherence of the self' (Fonagy, 2006: 17). He proposes that sexual feelings remain fundamentally dysregulated in all of us, that is there is a specific deficit in the mentalization of sexual feelings be they heterosexual or homosexual, though the latter, admittedly, may prove to be even harder for many caregivers to empathetically recognize in their child (see Lynch, Chapter 7, p. 140).

As a result of this specific early deficit in mentalizing sexual feelings, we are driven to find partners with whom we can externalize our sexual feelings and fantasies in order to experience them fully. In the healthiest scenario shame about one's own excited, craven lusts is modulated by the presence of an other who validates this through their own transgressions against the shame they also feel (Stein, 2008). However where shame is excessive and/or where the sexual partner is unable to validate one's sexual self because of his or her own conflicts this can impair the ability to integrate sexual desire within an attachment relationship specifically. In turn this precludes the organization of one's own pleasure and desire in an optimal secondary level way. This may present in a range of symptoms (e.g. somatic symptoms) that are not specific to this type of conflict, but that analysis reveals to be connected to the anxiety aroused by one's own desirous self. In such cases it may be helpful to consider whether sex with a prostitute is best understood as a way of *evacuating* unwanted feelings or denigrated parts of the self or, as I am speculating here, of working towards *integrating* the sexual self whereby the prostitute acts as a mirror.

Mr A

Mr A was an attractive, professionally successful heterosexual man in his late twenties. He was popular with his peers and reported two significant intimate relationships with women at the start of his analysis prior to the current relationship he was in. Although he could have sex with his partner he was very anxious about being impotent and therefore relied on Viagra to manage this. It was this sexual anxiety, along with other somatic anxieties, that led him to seek help.

He had been sent away to boarding school quite young. He felt his parents were very wrapped up with their own lives. His mother was depicted as emotionally detached, physically unaffectionate but supportive in a functional sense. He recalled that she was often critical of his physical appearance. His father emerged as a more benign figure but largely physically absent. His experience of them as a couple was one of sexless 'convenience', marked by a sense that his mother could be forbidding and at time belittling.

At school Mr A recalled being teased for being 'sensitive'. He had been a small, 'spindly' child and a late developer. It was apparent that during adolescence this had mobilized considerable anxiety about his body and his masculinity. He recalled masturbating but trying to curb this as he worried that this would somehow impede his development further, as if he would be punished and imprisoned/castrated in a little boy's body if he derived pleasure from his body.

He reported a recurrent dream from his adolescence in which he tried to build a sculpture out of wire, under timed conditions, and told me that he would wake in anxiety before the task was completed. We came to understand this dream as reflecting his early anxiety about his spindly, wiry body that would never grow into a potent man. This resonated deeply with his anxiety about lagging behind his peers in his delayed physical development and a feeling that time was running out for him. In the transference I took up how the dream alerted us early on to a core anxiety that analysis could never repair what felt damaged within him, that our time together would run out and he would walk away still feeling wiry, with no internal structure that could help him to sustain himself as a potent man. I understood this to be connected to the internal sexless couple in his mind where he was largely identified with his father at the hands of a cold, and at times humiliating, woman/mother.

Despite Mr A's adolescent anxieties, by the time he went to university he managed to establish a sexual relationship with a young woman. Nevertheless he felt uncomfortable sexually and sex became something he 'did', but preferred to 'get it over with quickly' in so far as his own sexual pleasure was concerned. He did not like to discuss sex with his partner; he said he felt embarrassed and could not imagine even looking at his girlfriend straight in the eyes during sex. He acknowledged that he was plagued both by an anxiety that he could not 'perform' and also that his sexuality would be seen by his partner to be shameful. Yet he was clear that there were no 'weird' sexual fantasies that he was concealing from me, that is was all 'vanilla', and that he just felt that 'being sexual' was overwhelming for him: 'It's like I'm in a storm when I'm having sex – I am fighting to get cover, to be safe, and there's no space for fun or relaxation'. However he was clear that he felt close to his partner in many ways and it pained him that he could not feel at ease with her. It was clear too, however, that his partner could be experienced by him as cold and forbidding (as was I too at times in the transference), and that this was especially so when they became sexually intimate. There were many ways in which he needed to 'get cover' to avoid the felt-to-be censorious gaze of the other. I often felt that the couch provided such 'cover' as he painfully avoided my gaze on arrival and departure from the sessions.

Over the course of his four-times weekly analysis on the couch, he revealed that he occasionally paid for the services of a prostitute. He was not in any sense addicted to this nor did he enact perverse fantasy scenarios with the prostitutes. On the contrary he paid for very straight sex on an occasional basis. Although he regarded the exchange with the prostitute as a transaction devoid of emotional involvement there was no sense that she functioned as a repository for denigrated aspects of himself or that he needed to humiliate or shame her. Rather I gained the impression that sex with this emotional stranger eased his anxiety, that he was no longer prey to the emotional 'storm' that he was caught in when being sexual with his partner.

One of the things that intrigued me at first about Mr A was that this was not a man who was emotionally cut off or who could not bear any kind of emotional intimacy; rather he appeared to have a specific difficulty in sharing the affects associated with 'being sexual' – a core aspect of himself that could not yet be comfortably accommodated into his relationship with his partner to whom he was attached. With his partner he felt that she 'seemed to' respond to him sexually, but he was always left in doubt at best and at worst he experienced as belittling of him sexually, feeling that she did not like to touch him or kiss him once he became aroused.

Over the course of the analysis we focused a great deal on understanding what made a difference in his encounters with the prostitutes. After one of these encounters he said:

> *Paying her for sex helps me because it is clear what I am there for and what she is there for. There is no ambiguity: it is about sex and only sex. I can be just . . . well . . . sexual. She encourages me, makes me feel potent, like I am alright . . . that me wanting sex, wanting pleasure, is normal.*

On one occasion, after seeing the prostitute, he observed that he felt much calmer and that he had looked at his body in the mirror at home and it looked 'bigger, stronger'. He then reported the dream he had after seeing this particular prostitute:

> *I am abroad with work colleagues for a team-building event. We are on an adventure course. I am dreading getting changed into my sports clothes in front of them. I start to take my trousers down and all I see are these sticks, my legs have turned into sticks and I am sure that I am going to wet myself. And then out of nowhere this woman appears: she is dressed in a very provocative manner and she whistles. All my colleagues turn towards her. I feel relieved because they are now distracted. I immediately start to pull up my trousers and then they all turn round again and look at me and one of them says, 'Get a move on, you're holding us up!' So I start to pull my trousers off again but this time my legs are muscly and I feel so relieved. We go out on the pitch and start to play football and I score two goals.*

After he shared the dream he laughed and said: 'I have never scored two goals in my life!'

Mr A went on to say that he woke from the dream feeling a mixture of relief and satisfaction. He then associated that he had sex with his partner that morning (before our session) and that he had felt less pressure to rush things and that she had remarked he seemed different. They had both, unusually, managed to climax.

I said that in a way he had managed to 'score two goals' perhaps thanks to the presence in his mind of a 'provocative' woman – like the prostitute he visited – who rescued him from the brink of humiliation, enabling him to recover his manly legs and have good sex with his partner.

Mr A laughed and said that the woman in the dream looked a bit like the prostitute but was in fact 'even more tarty'. He said he was most drawn to the 'tarty' looking ones because they were more 'truthful'. When I asked him what he meant by this he explained to me again that the appeal for him of prostitution was that it was so unambiguous: that it was purely about sex. So the more 'tarty', the more the message was clear: 'It's like she's saying 'I'm up for it, come and join me''. He was at pains to acknowledge the implicit degradation of women at the heart of prostitution and went on to talk in a very anxious manner about how aware he was of the danger prostitutes were exposed to and how many of them came from very deprived backgrounds.

I took up how he now feared that I would cut off his newly recovered manly legs with my harsh disapproval of his shameless desire for sex. Mr A replied that he could not imagine that I could approve of him having sex with a prostitute.

I said he could not imagine that I could see him as a sexual man who enjoys sex without the trimmings of love and intimacy as if sex in its rawest expression was inherently a bad thing.

Mr A became tearful. He said he felt very moved by what I had said, that he recognized that he had a good relationship with his partner and that he was going to spoil it if he did not relax a bit, but that he feared she would not accept that he liked sex.

I said that perhaps the provocative woman in his mind, like the prostitute, and me now, helped him to feel that it was legitimate to feel sexual but that there was still a painful gulf between this experience with a prostitute and in the context of the relationship with his partner. Mr A agreed and said that was why he generally avoided looking into his partner's eyes when they were making love, that he feared her disapproval of him enjoying sex. He knew this was a 'preposterous' idea because she was not like that at all, and yet this is how he felt in the moment.

Mr B

I now want to turn to Mr B, a professionally very successful man in his forties who came into a three-times weekly analytic psychotherapy (face-to-face for the first two years) because of marital difficulties. He felt he was not really heterosexual but homosexual, although he had not yet had any sexual relationships with men at that point and he said his wife was unaware of his 'true' sexuality.

Mr B had been married for five years at the time he started therapy and had one child. He had very much wanted to be a father and considered his 'heterosexual phase', as he called it, to have been his way of becoming a father. He reported that sex with his wife did not disgust him but it left him feeling 'empty'. He managed to sustain an erection by relying in his mind on homosexual fantasies. He said he could not look at his wife, not only because he felt so ashamed about the contents of his mind, but also because if he looked at her he was reminded she was a woman and he would lose his erection. Once intercourse was over he then felt repugnant because he felt he was lying to his wife through his undeclared fantasies, which he was sure she would find repellent, and also because his homosexual longings created a lot of conflict for him. Despite his difficulty in also looking at me during our sessions he nevertheless opted for the chair at first because, as we eventually understood it in the transference, he needed to monitor how I was looking at him.

As a child Mr B had grown up in a religious, conservative family of high achievers. Sex outside marriage was frowned upon and he felt that his parents had kept both his sister and him on a tight leash throughout their adolescence. There had been few opportunities for experimenting sexually. Homosexuality was explicitly relegated to the category of 'perversions' and he recalled his father being especially denigratory of a male friend of the family who was reputedly gay. His mother was experienced as physically distant and brusque in her physical handling of both children.

Mr B recalled being tormented at secondary school by his attraction to an older boy. He masturbated to the fantasy of this boy and said that he invariably felt anxious once he had climaxed. He never had any sexual experiences with others until he went to university away from home. His first sexual experiences appeared to have comprised rather desultory encounters with women during which he often felt impotent. Again, as had happened at secondary school, he became fixated on a male university acquaintance, but never dared to actualize his strong homosexual desire. He then spent many years living alone, having short-lived relationships with women until his late thirties when, at a friend's instigation, he started online dating and eventually met his wife.

He said that he hated his appearance. He thought his legs were too short and that his skin was too fair, 'like I blend into the background at best and at worst I look like a cadaver', he said. He had contemplated an eyebrow transplant because his eyebrows were so fair that it looked like he had shaved them off. I had taken up over time various dimensions of his experience of his body: how inhospitable his body felt to him, his deep-seated anxiety that his body betrayed how he felt: that he had nothing alive in him, that his skin and his hair were so light that it made him invisible to the other, and that he desperately wanted me to resuscitate something dead inside him.

Shortly after his honeymoon, which he recalled as a strained experience, Mr B decided to visit a male prostitute. He told me that this had been one of the most important experiences of his life but he had been anxious and in the event he could not allow himself to be touched or to masturbate in front of the man.

Mr B had not sought out prostitutes again since that time but had relied on homosexual pornography to masturbate. He said that when he thought about his wife possibly finding out he panicked and could only imagine her revulsion, that she could not 'stomach' that he could be aroused by a man. When he started therapy he eventually told me that he was feeling a strong urge to seek out the 'services', as he put it, of a male prostitute again. He told me this with detachment, which I nevertheless felt belied considerable anxiety about my reaction. I did not experience it as provocative or rejecting of my 'services', but as a decision taken by a man who had no expectation that I could 'stomach' his sexual self. I felt that therapy, at this stage, was however at risk of being no more than another pretence, like his marriage.

I took up in the transference how his decision to go to a prostitute was a communication about how hopeless he felt that I could accept him as he was. Therapy, I added, was perhaps another version of being seen to do the right thing, and he could not yet trust that I could tolerate his homosexual desire, that this could only be revealed in the safer context of being with a prostitute where he could stop the pretence.

Mr B was quiet at first and then replied that after he had put his son to bed the night before his wife had told him she was worried about their marriage. Mr B said that he had been shocked and relieved at the same time as he felt he was suffocating and at least he now felt his wife was aware that they had a sexual problem. He added that he felt pain at the thought of his son being confronted with all the complications of a broken marriage. That night in fact they had never got round to talking in any depth, but it was then that he had resolved in his mind to see a prostitute. He said that he needed to feel real, to know who he was, before he could approach his wife and what to do about their situation. The session ended on this note.

When we met the next day Mr B told me that he had sex with a male prostitute the night before. He said that he had not been able to relax at first but the man was 'kind' and had started to look at him with 'very sexed up eyes', told him how attractive he was and invited Mr B to tell him what he wanted to have done to him or to do to the prostitute:

It's like he was holding my hand as I crossed the road, a bit like you do here when I cannot go somewhere difficult in my mind, like yesterday's session . . . egging me on to do what I am afraid of doing. And I guess that in the end he was so insistent that I let myself go and I had the most amazing orgasm. I felt so alive for the first time in my life. I looked at him in the end, after I had come, and I felt like I was just born. I know intellectually that I am just another punter for him and I am not obsessed with him like I was with the other men when I was younger, but in that moment, just then, I felt something so profound happened . . . strange to think I've had this experience with a total stranger that I am paying . . . I know, I know . . . then I pay you for my confessional . . .

He was temporarily silent and then said that he wished he could live as a gay man, that he was tired of the pretence, that he hated cheating on his wife and depriving her of sexual satisfaction. He recognized that she was a kind woman but that he could not stay with her. He then reported a fragment of a dream in which a balloon he had inflated for his son for his birthday party had burst and his son cried inconsolably. He had desperately wanted to comfort him, but he could not stop him crying.

Through his associations we came to understand this dream as reflecting his anxiety that his homosexual desire would 'burst' the safe bubble of family life for his son and expose him as not a 'real' man, something that mobilized tremendous guilt in him towards his son and shame. I also took up how he feared that now that he had 'confessed' to me how alive he had felt after sex with the male prostitute that I would burst his excited bubble with my analysis of his 'confession'.

I will not report more of this session. Suffice to say that during the following months in his therapy Mr B was very preoccupied with 'coming out' and the consequences of this. During this time he visited prostitutes regularly. Mr B described in some detail his experience with the male prostitutes and I noted the words he used: for example, he said that he felt 'accepted', he felt 'seen for who I am and who I am is a gay man', he now felt his 'penis is alive, not some meat with no life in it', 'when he looks at me I feel I know who I am', 'he is not disgusted by what I want sexually'.

After one of the encounters with a prostitute he had sex with a few times and whose manner he liked, Mr B brought a very vivid dream:

> *he was a child and he was cooking but had no idea what ingredients he needed. He was looking for the cookery book his grandmother used but he could not find it. He decided to throw in the ingredients he had to hand and he started mixing a dough-like texture that looks golden and gradually thickens. His mother was shouting at him in the background calling him an idiot, that he should not even try to cook, that this was something only grown ups did.*

In his associations Mr B said that his mother was not at all like that in reality: she was 'mousy', a quiet woman. His grandmother by contrast was an 'imperious' character who had never remarried after the untimely death of her husband. Instead she had devoted herself to her work as a teacher at a girls' school and became a surrogate mother to several of the girls who still wrote to her in gratitude.

I said he was very grateful to the male prostitute for helping him to learn about himself sexually, that it was as if he had given him a book that contained the recipe for his sexuality, but that as soon as he knew what he needed, who he was, this then gave rise to a disapproving voice in his head that cut him down to size, telling him he is only a child who does not know what he's doing. I wondered whether this humiliating other was how he experienced me just then, after he told me how much he had enjoyed sex.

Mr B paused and then remarked that he resented the way his parents had always treated sex as something dirty, something that had to be kept under wraps. He knew he could really only blame himself for not having confronted his demons sooner, but he could not help but be angry about lost time, about marrying a woman when he knew he was gay and about inflicting all this mess on his son. He said he knew that I did not criticize him 'as such', but he was aware all the same that psychoanalysis pathologized homosexuality and so he could not be entirely sure of my position on this.

I said that maybe a part of him feared that the mousy me who did not admonish him 'as such' might suddenly turn into a shouty me who would impose my own analytic recipe for his 'right' sexuality. Mr B said he knew I would have to be neutral about it but he also thought that no-one can be that objective, that my training will have left its mark, somehow.

I said that he had no confidence that I could take up a position other than the one he believed to be handed down to me by my training family, not unlike how he struggled to stand up to his own family in his head whom he felt looked down on him for being gay. Mr B. agreed and said he was perhaps projecting his own fears about telling his parents that he was so very different to what they expected.

Discussion: the difficulty with 'being sexual'

Mr A and Mr B are men who, notwithstanding their differences at the level of the sex of the object of their desire, nevertheless share a great deal in common superficially and at a deeper level. They are both attractive men who function at a high level in their professional and social lives. But beneath the successful veneer and the appearance that their personal lives are as 'they should be' (Mr A has a steady girlfriend and Mr B is married with a child) they both carry inside themselves a feeling that their sexuality is unacceptable, that 'being sexual', as Mr A put it, is something that mobilizes significant anxiety and shame resulting in symptoms of actual and feared impotence or, in the case of Mr B, in a pretend life that conceals his homosexual longings.

Both men found an important source of solace through their contact with prostitutes. However what they were seeking was more than simply solace or an outlet for their frustrated sexual desire – the more popular assumptions of why people seek out prostitutes. Neither were they seeking to enact perverse scenarios – the more common psychoanalytic assumption. Neither man manifested any paraphilias and hence there was nothing obviously disturbing about the content of their sexual fantasies or practices. Rather they both appeared to struggle with the fact of 'being sexual', with the 'burlap of desire', to play on Corbett's (2009: 216) apt turn of phrase.

I want to suggest that what they were unconsciously looking for and found in the prostitute was someone who 'unambiguously' (as Mr A emphasized) and contingently mirrored back their sexual desire and made them feel they were acceptable. The toxicity of the anxiety and shame associated with 'being sexual' that infused their relationship with their sexual partners was thus bypassed, providing an opportunity for experiencing themselves as sexual and gradually representing in a secondary order level their bodies as sexual.

The changes in their representation of their bodies are moving and striking: after his contact with the prostitute Mr A saw himself in the mirror as stronger and he discovered 'manly' legs in his dream and then in his actual relationship with his partner. Mr B felt 'real' after his encounters and in his dream he cooks a 'dough-like texture that looks golden and gradually thickens', which reflected his emergent representation of a sexual body that had colour/life and substance.

Mr A and Mr B were not in denial about the shame they felt – they both felt it acutely and could reflect on it with me. However, at first, the subjective experience of shame was not affected by my interpretations of it. It appeared to be partly transformed, however, through the *unambiguous* physical sanction of their sexuality by the prostitute who was felt to be there explicitly for sex, which was why for Mr A the more 'tarty' the look the less ambiguous the situation and the easier it was for him to enjoy it.

For Mr A, the intimate relationship he was in had the potential to accommodate his greater integration of his sexuality mediated by his experiences with the prostitute. By the end of his analysis he had married his partner and was no longer using prostitutes. For Mr B, however, the pathway was more complex because he could not be truthful for a very long time about his homosexuality, but he eventually left his marriage and was able to have an open relationship with a man.

These two men shared another important similarity that is germane to this discussion and is relevant in a broader sense to understanding what it means to 'be sexual' and to be able to live out one's sexual self – that is, one's desirous, excited body self – without shame and anxiety. It also touches on the question of why these men could not work through their sexual conflicts exclusively in the transference.

Mr A described a somewhat emotionally impoverished early childhood characterized by the absence of close physical contact with his parents. He was handed over to nannies as a small baby. He recalled his mother being rather 'cold' and never touching him except to stroke his head occasionally when they were out in public as if, he felt, she was using an affectionate gesture to 'good social effect' but that she did not really mean it. As I described earlier, he was physically small and matured late so his body was, from the very beginning it would seem, the site for an experience of rejection and shame. Other people's physical gestures of affection aroused his suspicion: anything ambiguous could not be trusted.

Mr B recalled that both his parents were 'rigid' in everything they did including how they presented themselves physically, which was a 'no frills' look as he described it. He had no memories at all of physical closeness with either parent. His grandmother (who featured in his dream) was the only one who had shown him some physical comfort. His own physical presentation was very conservative and buttoned up. He experienced his body as 'dead' and this was reflected in his appearance, which was smart but 'grey'.

Both Mr A and Mr B therefore reported early histories characterized by what we could formulate as an undercathexis of the body self. Mr A's recurrent dream gives a moving insight into how he represented his body in his mind: a wiry structure that was incomplete. Mr B's 'too fair' skin and his invisible eyebrows conjured up his representation of a body without contours that could so easily disappear into the background and die. In other words both these men approached the development of their sexuality from a weak foundation at the level of their mental representation of the body self. In both cases I gained the impression that their respective struggles to integrate psychosexuality required analysis of this deficit, that is of their undercathected body self in the context of their earliest attachments.

Marked and contingent mirroring of the self's bodily experience is most likely, for us all, a vitally important feature of the development of a coherent sense of self firmly rooted in the body. Without such a foundation the trajectory to the satisfactory elaboration of the sexual self will most likely be compromised to varying degrees. My understanding was that these men's shared deficit at this level undermined their ability to symbolically represent their sexual experience such that they had to first concretely experience the sexual look and touch of the prostitute to enable them to feel safe but excitingly sexual.

Sexuality creates stimulation but also contains otherwise unrepresented, unmentalized experience with significant others. As Laplanche (1995) suggests, after being awakened in the child by the mother, the aspects of sexuality that have not been understood or assimilated become repressed and add to the feeling of strangeness and mystery we all have about sexuality. Sexuality is inherently mysterious and 'excessive' (Stein, 2008) – as exciting as it can be disturbing – because the child cannot translate the adult's message into a conscious representation. In this respect we might say that we all suffer from an unavoidable deficit in our sexual development, but this deficit may be further amplified in some cases depending on the nature of the earliest experiences, especially where there may have been an undercathexis of the body self, hence desire may become linked with excessive anxiety and shame. Where this is the case the anxiety and/or shame associated with sexual desire is such that the sought-after mirroring of sexual desire may be difficult to secure in the context of an emotionally intimate relationship where attachment is also mobilized and thus increases affective arousal thereby rendering the regulation of sexual feelings more complicated.

For both the men in question here the monetary transaction with the prostitute appeared to lead to a degree of de-arousal as it concretely demarcated the prostitute as a non-attachment figure and as someone whose state of mind and intentions towards the self was unambiguous. We might say that Mr A and Mr B were functioning in a teleological mode with respect to their sexuality: they could not make use of anything other than unambiguous explicit visual/sensory evidence – and the clarity of the monetary contract – as a true index of the intentions of the other towards the self. Only action that had a physical impact was felt to be able to alter their experience of their body in a sexually aroused state.

For different reasons both men struggled to feel validated as sexual through their partners' reaction to them. It is of note in this respect that despite being physically attractive they both felt very insecure about whether their bodies were desirable. In the transference I was conscious that they anticipated my critical, non-desiring look: Mr A used the couch to avoid my gaze; Mr B avoided the couch so as to anxiously monitor it. I was conscious too of an absence of any erotic feelings in the transference as if their sexuality had to be kept away from our relationship just as happened with their respective partners. Perhaps the 'advantage' of the prostitute is precisely because she is neither mother nor sexual partner nor analyst and she can thus confirm a phallic sexual self, thereby bypassing Oedipal anxieties that cannot yet be faced.

Anxiety and shame over desires that are felt to be somehow prohibited may of course lead to the splitting off of those desires from an emotionally intimate relationship such that, as Freud (1914) put it, individuals seek others whom they do not need to love in order to keep sexuality away from the people they love. In these cases sexual desire may only be permissible with emotional strangers or denigrated others and may thus result in a perverse[3] use of prostitutes. However neither Mr A nor Mr B used prostitutes in this perverse manner. It could of course still be argued that Mr A and Mr B were splitting off their sexuality from emotionally close relationships and from the transference. Descriptively this is accurate: for different reasons they could not actualize their sexuality in the context of their primary relationship and only did so within the compartmentalized sexual activity with the prostitutes and they could not at first work this through in the transference. However what is so interesting in both these cases is that the men were able to make use of this experience – most likely *because* they were also in analysis and hence were supported in mentalizing their experience – to gradually integrate their sexual self into an attachment relationship.

It is important to question why it proved difficult for Mr A and Mr B to work through their conflicts exclusively at a transferential level. My impression, as I have suggested, is that they both had very specific difficulties in representing their embodied experience of themselves as desirable and desiring and functioned in a teleological mode with respect to their sexuality. The early deficit in the representation of the body could be said to have compromised the development of a phallic sexual self as a necessary step towards the integration of Oedipal sexuality. This phallic self first required the actual mirroring provided by the prostitute allowing the body representation to become consolidated in their minds before these men could work through their Oedipal sexuality in the transference. This raises the possibility that such 'mirrored sexuality' of a narcissistic nature is a precursor of a 'relational sexuality' rooted in two bodies and minds that interact with each other and can then mirror each other reciprocally.[4]

Mr A's and Mr B's individual trajectories suggest that it is important for the analyst to keep an open mind with respect to the use made of prostitutes, which in some instances can be understood as representing a nascent attempt to actualize the sexual self in order to gradually integrate psychosexuality in the context of an attachment relationship. Whilst we are correct, I think, to understand this 'use' as an enactment, in this chapter I have emphasized the importance of considering the possibility that it may also represent a development. To recognize it as such is important therapeutically. It requires the analyst to sensitively steer a difficult path between helping the patient to represent experience and understanding and accepting for a time the teleological imperative that runs counter to that, which may nevertheless be a necessary step towards representing sexuality and living comfortably in the sexual body.

If working with perverse patients sensitizes us to how difficult emotional intimacy is such that anxiety can lead to defensive sexualization (Glasser, 1979) resulting in violent enactments in the most severe cases, work with patients like Mr A and Mr B reminds us more fundamentally of how difficult it is for everyone, to varying degrees, to 'be sexual'.

Notes

1 Most sex worker activists' groups reject the word *prostitute* and since the late 1970s have used the term *sex worker* instead. However, *sex worker* can also mean anyone who works within the sex industry or whose work is of a sexual nature and is not limited solely to prostitutes, hence my decision to retain the word prostitute without wishing to attach any pejorative connotation to the word.
2 And as Berkowitz (2013) details, financial gain was another incentive fuelling the 'acceptance' of brothels, not least by the Church.
3 Here I am using perversion to denote a kind of blueprint for object relations rather than as a set of behaviors, that is what makes a person or a relationship perverse is not the more obvious quest for excitement through sex but the underlying incapacity – or indeed at times refusal – to relate to the other as separate from the self and not as a narcissistic appendage. The pursuit of ecstasy is but a smokescreen for the complex dynamics that transform exhilaration into a mandatory project, no matter the cost to self or others.
4 I am grateful to Heather Wood for her helpful perspective on this matter.

References

Agoston, T. (1945). Some Psychological Aspects of Prostitution: The Pseudo-Personality. *International Journal of Psychoanalysis*, 26, 62–67.

Berkowitz, E. (2013). *Sex and Punishment: 4000 Years of Judging Desire*. London: Westbourne Press.

Corbett, K. (2009). *Boyhoods: Rethinking Masculinities*. New Haven, CT, and London: Yale University Press.

Fonagy, P. (2006). Psychosexuality and Psychoanalysis. In P. Fonagy, R. Krause and M. Leuzinger-Bohleber (Eds.) *Identity, Gender and Sexuality*. London: IPA Books.

Fonagy, P. (2008). A Genuinely Developmental Theory of Sexual Enjoyment and its Implications for Psychoanalytic Technique. *Journal of the American Psychoanalytic Association*, 56, 11–36.

Freud, S. (1914). On Narcissism. *The Standard Edition of the Complete Psychological Works of Sigmund Freud*, Volume XIV (1914–1916): On the History of the Psycho-Analytic Movement, Papers on Metapsychology and Other Works.

Glasser, M. (1979). Some Aspects of the Role of Aggression in the Perversions. In I. Rosen (Ed.) *Sexual Deviations*. Oxford: OUP.

Gordon-Lamoureux, J. (2007). Exploring the Possibility of Sexual Addiction in Men Arrested for Seeking Out Prostitutes: A Preliminary Study. *Journal of Addictions Nursing*, 18(1), 21–29.

Hall, P. (2011). *Understanding and Treating Sex Addiction*. London: Routledge.

Hollender, M.H. (1961). Prostitution, the Body and Human Relatedness. *International Journal of the American Psychoanalytic Association*, 42, 404–413.

Hutto, B. and Faulk, R. (2000). Psychodynamics of a Prostitute. *Bulletin of the Menninger Clinic*, 64(3), 409–423.

Laplanche, J. (1995). Seduction, Persecution, Revelation. *International Journal of Psychoanalysis*, 76, 663–682.

Stein, R.A. (2008). The Otherness of Sexuality: Excess. *Journal of the American Psychoanalytic Association*, 56, 43–71.

Vanwesenbeeck, I. (2013). Prostitution Push and Pull: Male and Female Perspectives. *Journal of Sex Research*, 50(1), 11–16.

Wood, H. (2013). The Nature of the Addiction in Sex Addiction. In M. Bower, R. Hale and H. Wood (Eds.) *Addictive States of Mind*. London: Karnac, 151–174.

Zapf, J.L. and Carroll, J. (2008). Attachment Styles and Male Sex Addiction. *Sexual Addiction and Compulsivity*, 15(2), 158–175.

Chapter 11

On sexual perversions' capacity to act as portal to psychic states that have evaded representation

Avgi Saketopoulou

In this chapter I propose that extraordinarily generative psychic possibilities can sometimes inhere in perverse sexual practices. The set of propositions I will put forward may allow analysts to conceptualize perverse clinical material not from within a state of alarm but with the readiness to identify that sexual transgressions can offer formidable access points to unrepresented psychic bits. These states' inscriptions often arise in the form of sensory traces. Untethered to associatively linked memory, history and meaning, they circulate in psychic space unbound and indecipherable. When brought into the consulting room and are explored in the presence of an analyst who is not too rigidly defended or overly saddled with anxiety these unrepresented mental states can produce a 'generative turbulence' (Civitarese, 2013) in the analyst's psyche. As this turbulence mates with the analyst's own unconscious, spontaneous and unbidden acts may arise (Stern, 2009). These acts are manifestations of the analyst's alpha function (Bion, 1962). Through these acts and how they are taken up in the treatment, an analysand's proto-psychic states can become elaborated into higher levels of psychically represented experience (Levine, 2013).

Cyra

Cyra entered psychoanalysis in her mid-30s with very few memory traces of her early life. For the first two years of her treatment I experienced her as a being that floated in a-historical space and time without legible ties to her past and with an only marginally articulable chronicle of her childhood. Despite the seemingly vibrant tenor of her social and professional life, large parts of Cyra's existence seemed to belong to that domain of psychic life that Winnicott described as incommunicado (1965). There was, of course, 'information' I knew about her: I knew, for instance, that she came from a working class family that had emigrated to the United States – where I treated her – when Cyra was four so that she and her sister would have 'a chance at a better life'; that her mother had had considerable difficulty adjusting to the new country and that she had never learned English well; that her father was a hard-working man who had also struggled with adapting to the new conditions of his life. For the most part, though, this had been conveyed to me as units of data stripped of meaning or implication, information that was unbound by affect and divested of any associative links (Bion's – K). Cyra lived almost exclusively in this universe of associative voids except for her unconventional sexual practices, the only psychic space within which experience seemed to congeal into meaningful relating. The early part of our work revolved around exploring her relationship with her long-term romantic partner, Ann. Cyra felt pleased to find room in our work for these parts of her life and there had been some nominal symptomatic relief.

In the third year of her analysis Cyra recounted a sexual encounter that she described as one of the most consequential experiences of her life. That experience proved to be highly impactful to our work and I will, therefore, relate it here in detail. My hope is to demonstrate how perverse sexuality can, at times, perform meaningful psychic labor in that it can provide unique access to unrepresented psychic states. I will, therefore, sidestep a discussion of Cyra's overall treatment and an in-depth exploration of transference/countertransference dynamics beyond what's immediately relevant to a clinical illustration of my theoretical points. Let us then return to Cyra's experience, which she described as follows: In this particular encounter Cyra positioned Ann naked with her back against the wall. Ann was blindfolded and her hands were tied behind her back. Cyra proceeded to use hypodermic needles to pierce Ann on both sides of her naked body starting below Ann's collarbone, continuing all the way down to her thighs. Cyra then removed her own clothing. Standing naked across her partner, she pierced her own body in a symmetrical way. After she was done, Cyra laced a latex string through the corresponding needles on both of their bodies. The needles on Cyra's right side were intricately threaded through those on Ann's left side and the same on the other side with a different string. When this elaborate ritual was completed Cyra removed Ann's blindfold. Ann looked down to take in the intricate bondage connecting their bodies. When she met Cyra's gaze again, Cyra took a gentle step back causing the strings to become taut. Gently but firmly, the strings pulled on their skins raising them some and resulting in a mildly painful sensation. Cyra understood this as an offering to Ann whose early life had been laced with significant bodily trauma. Cyra felt she was extending to Ann a symbolic, inter-embodied recognition of the somatic and psychic pain that Ann had endured. Further, in this temporary suturing of herself to her partner, Cyra intended to pronounce her commitment to remaining tied to her partner despite the complicated ways in which Ann's torment was bleeding into their relationship. The sexual encounter that followed was saturated: painful skin sensations, their emotional significations and genital stimulation all escalated into a vertiginously intoxicating experience. Cyra felt that she was coming undone, the boundaries of herself dissolving until she eventually felt she was becoming 'dispersed into pieces, as if breaking down into infinitesimal particles.'

This astonishingly potent encounter surprised Cyra and, as analytic time came to reveal, it was more than just sensually enthralling. In her sessions, my patient reported that the moments she had come undone were accompanied by a set of unusual, fleeting sensations. Cyra experienced them as inchoate and resistant to language: any communicable version of them, she insisted, would require that they be contorted into words that would ultimately feel lacking. What she eventually was able to formulate was that they revolved around a vague sensory trace which she could not place well: 'something hovering between a smell and a taste, a kind of burning bitterness, no, just a burning.' She just couldn't tell. While Cyra struggled – and failed – to find the precise wording that would convey her ineffable experience, I wondered if perhaps something else entirely might be at play. In prior work with patients who engage with perverse practices, I have heard accounts of the receding of the boundaries of the self and the outpouring of incommunicable sensation akin to what Cyra had recounted to me. In those instances (e.g. see Saketopoulou, forthcoming) we came to discover a nascent sense of coming into contact with experience that had not yet been psychically organized enough for them to be able to fully discern, experience or communicate it well. Had what flashed before Cyra, I therefore wondered, possibly been an experiential bit that had not yet come into being? A proto-psychic beta-like element of the kind that Bion (1970) described as not yet suitable for thinking?

Before proceeding further, I want to take a step back to reflect on the unusualness of Cyra's experience. How do we maintain a reflective capacity regarding what is happening during this affectively condensed, sexually ionized intersubjective encounter? There are, in my opinion, two sets of obstacles we face as analysts when listening to such challenging clinical material. First, we are often reflexively and unquestioningly inclined to diagnose experiences like Cyra's as evidence of repetition compulsion. While repetition may well be at play in some such instances, repetition compulsion can be a limiting – and, thus, dismissive – framework from which to approach perverse sexualities because it describes attempts at mastery that, despite their intent to repair, are generally doomed to fail. Secondly, sexual material especially when so intense, tends to generate remarkable countertransferential anxiety (Dimen, 2003). When an analyst's mind begins to drown in anxiety, thoughtful reflection becomes instantly thornier. These two sets of difficulties can synergistically interfere with the analytic capacity to maintain an attitude of open and genuine curiosity as to the psychic labor performed by perverse sexualities. As importantly, they tend to incline the analyst to listen for genetic material oftentimes to the exclusion of becoming receptively curious as to the forward reach of these acts. An emphasis on what they may be intending *to move the individual away from* misses that perversity may be unconsciously intending *to help usher the individual towards something.*

Botella and Botella (2005, 2013) were the first to use the term *figurability* to refer to the process by which experience that is not yet organized enough to become representable can build representational traction. The clinical significance of the work of figuration became evident to the Botellas in relation to their encounters with unformulated states in child and adult patients – in other words, when working with the unrepressed unconscious. With such patients analytic work revolves not around the uncovering of disguised unconscious content (as is the case with work that takes place at the level of the repressed unconscious) but around helping them forge links between thought and affect, connecting signifier with signified to birth meaningful connections out of emptiness and void. In those cases, the primary focus of the clinical work is to help proto-psychic material that cannot be thought with or thought about – and which is, thus, not reachable through canonical analytic work – to congeal into better organized, affectively invested associative chains. In these types of treatments, they theorized, the attuned analyst's unconscious spontaneously intercepts the formless elements in the patient's unrepressed unconscious. Salvaging them from a world of formless voids, the analyst's alpha work helps make psychic organization and representation possible.

For the Botellas (2013) the work of figuration occurs through the analyst's spontaneous, unbidden act (on this see also Stern, 2009 who writes elegantly on these matters from a relational perspective). The analyst's own unrepresented states are recruited in the process of rendering the patient's experience figurated. As such, shards of the analyst's own psychic life become folded into the particular way in which the patient's unformulated experience becomes intelligible. The analyst's own unconscious, that is, plays a formative role in the very creation of the patient's mind (Levine, 2013).

At this point, let us return to Cyra's clinical process which I will discuss in light of these formulations. I will subsequently move to fleshing out some of my own reflections around the unique relationship between perversity's capacity to call forth unrepresented states.

In the hour before I was to see Cyra again I found myself having an unexpected and overwhelming craving for Greek coffee. I only fleetingly registered at the time the peculiarity of my craving: ordinarily, I experience these unusually strong cravings in the first couple of months after I return to NY from my visit in the summer, the time when my nostalgia for my country is most acutely with me.

As soon as Cyra walked into the room heading to the couch at the beginning of her hour, I could tell that something had already occurred. Cyra lay down looking shell-shocked. After an unusually long pause she asked me about the smell she could detect in my office. The smell of coffee lingered powerfully in the room yet Cyra could not place it. The particular way in which she reached for language recalled for me her difficulty with describing the ineffable sensory experience that had burst into her sexual encounter with Ann. Instead of inquiring further about her thoughts, I volunteered she could probably smell coffee in the room. Tears started streaming down her face, soon turning into sobs. I was taken aback, surprised by her unexpectedly intense affect which had been quite unusual in the analysis. Feeling uncertain as to what was now rapidly unfolding I quietly commented that something seemed to have made her very upset. Cyra remained quiet and I felt that she required more of an unobtrusive analytic presence (Grossmark, 2012) rather than verbal intervention which could have been experienced as a premature push to formulate meaning. As I remained quietly present for the remainder of the session, Cyra vacillated between tearing and lying in thoughtful albeit stunned reflection.

Cyra started our next session recounting a story. This story drew on some 'facts' that were already superficially known to us: Cyra's mother, we 'knew,' had been incredibly anxious that the family's poverty and immigration status fated her daughters for poor marriage prospects. Her hopes for her daughters' upward class mobility had somehow become encapsulated in the fantasy that learning how to play the piano might secure a favorable pairing for her daughters. To pay for the lessons the mother had accepted a second part-time job involving difficult and painful manual labor that left her body aching and sore. It was such that, when Cyra was five, she and her sister started taking private piano lessons. Upon walking into the teacher's home, they would both be offered a cup of coffee – a common tradition in their culture. Scalding hot, the coffee was more of an expectation than an offering: the lesson would not start till the coffee had been consumed. While Cyra's sister would set the coffee aside until it cooled down, my patient felt persecuted by the thought that every minute of delay wasted time paid for by her mother's painful physical labor. Under her teacher's demanding gaze Cyra would hastily gulp down the bitter and scalding hot coffee. As she recounted this in session, Cyra recalled the burning sensation of the coffee that brought tears to her eyes, the lingering sour taste of the espresso in her mouth, all of which she eagerly endured to prevent wasting precious minutes of her piano lesson.

What emerged over time, nevertheless, as more traumatic than the sadistic ritual itself was Cyra's complicated feelings regarding her mother's suffering which we were only very gradually able to articulate. On a manifest level, Cyra deeply admired her mother's work ethic which was organized around her daughters' well being and which made my patient feel deeply loved and valued. At the same time, however, she felt tremendous anguish and guilt over the mother's suffering. Threaded into her worry about wasted instruction time were also mother's unending verbalizations as to her profound unhappiness living in the US, for the sacrifices she felt were required of her so that her daughters may have a better life and her excruciating longing for her homeland. These sacrifices, of which the piano lessons were but a small symbolic iteration, became an exorbitant debt of mother's pain that could never be repaid, a debt that left a lasting and unrelenting affective balance. The fact that Cyra, as a lesbian, would always fail to produce the kind of 'successful marriage' her mother had been laboring for, added yet another agonizing layer of complexity to my patient's anxiety about having failed to deliver that for which her mother had labored so intently. While some of this material was not entirely new to the analysis it had, prior to this part of our work, only existed as radically unthinkable factoids. As we linked Cyra's drinking of the scalding hot espresso with her mother's suffering, we noted how sacrifice embroiled Cyra's body with her mother's painful physical labor. The depth of her mother's distress and how it lived, hotly and bitterly, in her body were becoming more legible to Cyra, discernible against the backdrop of mother's love and endurance.

Only after all these links became thinkable to us were we able to start considering how sexuality had been productively recruited into living out these unrepresented affects. Cyra and I traced the generational debt in the centrality of sacrifice in Cyra's sexual scene with Ann, the piercing of herself as a way of conveying to Ann her understanding of the traumatic pain which had been inscribed in her partner's body and which we now understood also lived in her mother's. As these traces, now invested with affect, were becoming psychically represented we were also able to begin exploring how other, non-sexual parts of her life were also impacted by these early inscriptions, parts which had been previously inaccessible to analytic inquiry but which, over the next months, came within our reflective reach.

How are we to understand the role of my unusual craving for Greek coffee that day and its role in the cascade of memory, affect and history it set off? For me Greek coffee is bound with my tremendous nostalgia for my country: the culture, the people, the effortless ease of speaking and hearing others speak my native language. For the most part these affects live in repression, rising punctually to the surface of my consciousness in the weeks closely before and immediately after my summer vacation in Greece. Why were they being summoned now? Why with this particular patient? And why in this point in her treatment? I have understood the highly personal and spontaneous impulse of preparing the coffee as an unbidden act (Stern, 2009), indexing how I unconsciously took up my analysand's non-descript yet persistent sensation. My craving and preparing of the coffee can be thought of, then, as the psychic product of how my patient's sexual and sensory experience pollinated my own unconscious. Travelling from my unconscious back to that of my patient to catalyze a range of affects (the tearfulness, the silent self-observation) and actions (a call to her sister), my act appears to have helped bring something about my patient's ineffable experience into the consulting room ultimately making it more intelligible to her and to us. The work of figurability, the Botellas write, 'opens up the analysand's mind to foreclosed affects . . . to an awareness of a reality of suffering of which he was unaware . . . allow[ing] the analysand to . . . form representations of his nameless and shapeless distress' (2013: 107).

Transgressive sexuality's capacity to act as a portal to unrepresented states

In working with perverse sexuality, analysts reflexively and often orient their work towards locating originary traumas that are being reenacted or labor towards identifying perversion's defensive functions. While very useful in many instances, these approaches miss that some such sexualities can be unconscious attempts towards figuration, that is, attempts for individuals to come into contact with experiences that have not yet been fully formed. Put differently, canonical ways of working with perversions are often premised on an unacknowledged – and thus unarticulated – presumption that such sexual practices originate in internal space psychically organized at the level of representation. This, however, cannot be an *a priori* assumption. When we conceptualize erotic transgressions as the sexualized sediment of trauma we fail to identify the organizational level from which these behaviors issue. Their persistence, ordinarily read as the kind of compulsiveness and fixity that Freud described to be the premier features of perversity (1905 – but see also Holtzman and Kulish, 2012 for a more contemporary survey of the literature) can, in some instances, be more fruitfully understood as the placement of an insistent demand on the mind for a particular kind of work: the work of making proto-psychic material psychic. Rather than 'eruptions of impulses . . . manifested through action' (Reed et al., 2013: 22) perversion sometimes has a privileged position vis-à-vis what Levine calls the representational imperative: the 'pressure to form representations and link them into meaningful, affect-laden, coherent narratives' (2013: 45). For reasons I'll shortly explain, sexual perversity is in my opinion an *ideal conductor* for the developmental force that seeks to usher experience that has remained unformulated into psychic representation.

Before further advancing this claim, I want to define my use of the term *perversion*, a term I maintain should be retained in our psychoanalytic lexicon despite its nosological baggage. My commitment to its usage is a luxury I can only afford because others have already powerfully critiqued the term's pejorative misuse (Blechner, 2009; Corbett, 2013; Dimen, 2001; Foucault, 1980; Žižek, 2003). Still, I argue for its continued use because it seems to me that *perversion* captures the phenomenology of sexuality that blends anguish and/or pain with pleasure. *Perversion* maintains vigorous ties with the exuberant physicality with the perplexing, inscrutable dimensions of sexuality in ways that other terms do not – however less colonized by pathological narratives they may be.

I employ *perversion* here, thus, not as the sexual manifest of psychiatric illness,[1] nor am I using it to describe particular sexual practices (e.g. Cyra's sadomasochism). Rather, I rely on it to describe encounters that are *subjectively* experienced as transgressive and which cross the line of prohibition into the too-muchness[2] of experience. The lines of prohibition I have in mind are idiosyncratically sutured, often perched on the divide between the intrapsychic and the social and are always temporally mediated (who does what in what context and at what point in time – see Dimen, 2003). For Cyra it is the transgressiveness of pain and the threading of skin-to-skin that crosses the line. Yet which acts will be experienced as transgressive varies widely across different individuals: for one person it may be the shame of oral sex, for another the pain of anal penetration, for a third the longing to be reduced to begging one's lover.

Transgression and inter-embodiment (Hartman, 2013) synergistically amplify each other. The former lures the self into crashing through its own regulatory walls. The latter inundates the subject with undecipherable messages from the other (what does this person want from me? what did that look/gasp/touch mean?). Together they form the ingredients of what I call perversion: a *sexual process* that is intrapsychic yet activated intersubjectively and which, therefore, materializes on the cusp of one-person and two-person psychologies. The attendant overwhelming experience of excess (Laplanche, 1997; Stein, 2008) pushes the subject into a generative dysregulation. This dysregulation becomes overwhelming to the ego's integrity thrusting the subject through the homeostatic point that guarantees the ego's coherence.[3]

This surge of amplification produces a kind of pleasure that is suffered. At the apex of the interimplication of pleasure and suffering, the literary theorist Leo Bersani has proposed, arises an experience which he calls self-shattering, an experience which leaves the subject momentarily undone (1986). Recall how, in Cyra's experience, suffering and pleasure were described as having shattered her 'into infinitesimal particles,' dissolving her ordinary experience of a bounded self. As the phenomenological correlate of self-shattering, this moment runs counter to our understanding of meaningful experience as revolving around a stable and well-integrated ego. Yet, what's occurring in those moments is neither regressive nor is Cyra in psychotic fragmentation. Whilst parts of her are coming undone, others remain incredibly present, focused on and observing her experience. In this state, which is akin to meditative ones (Epstein, 2004; Ghent, 1990), Cyra may be receding as a bounded subject but she is not in psychotic decompensation.

Why might that be the property of perverse sexuality rather than of all sexuality *per se*? After all, isn't all sexuality by nature excessive and overwhelming (Stein, 2008; González, 2014)? There is a difference, as I see it, between sexuality's undeniable plenitude and perversion's capacity to invite a kind of overflow which does not (ultimately safely) overtake the self but which veritably shatters it. Perversion is ideally suited for this bid for the ego's unraveling because insofar as it is fueled by transgression, it runs on an economic regime of escalating excitations. Transgression's voracious appetite for intensified stimulation can override homeostatic controls, producing the self's undoing. The welling up of pleasure even to the point of exhaustion (Laplanche, 2011: 234) is key to the transient breakdowns I am describing, furnishing perverse sexualities with their anarchic potential. Rather than the homeostatic regulation attained through attachment relations (Benjamin, 2012; Lyons-Ruth, 1999; 2006) and early cycles of non-linguistic and linguistically mediated mother-infant interactions (Fonagy and Target, 1996; Fonagy, 2008), this vigorous pursuit of sensory experience can facilitate generative dysregulations. Being broken open in this particular fashion can allow densely encrypted moments and enigmatic states that have remained encysted into the ego to come forth. In that sense not only is self-shattering not a traumatic experience in the ordinary use of the term but it operates, rather, in some instances in the service of the representational imperative furnishing proto-psychic experience with a chance at becoming intelligible.

A brief metapsychological detour to the work of Jean Laplanche can help better elucidate the intimate links between body, sexuality and the psychic uses of self-shattering. For Laplanche sexuality and subjectivity are intertwined processes and he describes the relationship with the caretaker as flooding the infant with multiple messages (1999). Consciously intended communication directed to the child is accompanied with minor gestures, nuances of a gaze, muscle tone, acoustic elements of speech which are inflected by the adult's unconscious. These transmissions escape the adult's conscious registration and yet are absorbed by the infant in ways that are definitionally outside language. Through this the ineffable in installed inside us all. Consider, for instance, a mother whose speech becomes marginally yet noticeably more tentative when she speaks to her daughter about good genital hygiene. Think of a father who finds himself with a developing erection while roughhousing with his son. In these cases the inter-embodied 'no' of incest oozes into the infant's psyche long before it builds representational traction. Since such messages are installed in us through the medium of our bodies, their plenitudes dwell inside us on a somatic register. To some degree, these inevitably and always exceed representation.

In order to make sense of that which radiates out towards her, the infant is propelled to translate the vast and unremitting array of uncanny transmissions that leak *out of* the caretaker and *into* her. The ego is wrested out of this process of translation, developing as an apparatus that constructs meaning and binds enigma. And yet, several of these messages will remain enduringly impenetrable because these *enigmatic signifiers,* as Laplanche called them (1997), are equally unknown to the adult in whose unconscious they originate. Like Bion's beta elements (1970) these undecipherable enigmas float inside the infant, perplexing and unbound by the ego (Laplanche, 1999) unusable for thinking.

For Laplanche, this developmentally normative failure of de-encryption becomes deposited into the psyche, forming the building blocks of the infant's unconscious and of sexuality. The unconscious/sexuality are, thus, established as fundamentally alien to the self, as persistently and hauntingly other (1999). By definition that which we cannot possess, sexuality is therefore never 'ours,' but rather the way in which we become dispossessed through our relationship with the other (Butler, 2006).

From a Laplancheian perspective all sexuality is fundamentally in some relation to the unthinkable. Sexual contact carries indeed the astonishing potential to re-activate the originary moments of these enigmatic implantations. This is because sexuality draws on inter-embodiment: the bodily materialities *between* subjects place us in a force field of copious untranslatable messages directed at us by our sexual partners. By invoking the body, the site where the tangle of the enigma originated, it showers us anew with the other's enigmatic message.

If the subject comes into being through early implantations and the excess of meaning which eludes the infant's understanding, the ego's breakdown has the capacity to release forth these enigmatic implants, unrepresented bits that had originally escaped translation. As the self shatters, condensed meanings which had never become organized, akin to beta elements, spring forth. Able to breathe and as they rise more to conscious awareness, these enigmatic states may become available to analytic engagement. To the extent that such enigmatic states carry intergenerational meanings, the experience of unraveling may make it possible to find a way to take possession of the intergenerational errands (Apprey, 2013) and excesses (Stein, 2006) that have been installed into us, entering us through our bodies in the early somatic relationship with our caretakers (Laplanche, 2011). Such sexual scripts open up portals that may offer up these parental infusions for reinterpretation: early mysterious communications that have always circulated in this torrent announce themselves, making their presence known. When these implants become intersubjectively apprehended by the analyst's unconscious and reconfigured through the work of the psychoanalytic dyad, the self may be stitched together in novel and personally meaningful ways.

Perverse sexualities are especially potent agents in the enlisting of the body, for working to turn intergenerational errands and debts (Apprey, 2013) handed down to us through primary object relationships into a relationship to oneself, to appropriate that which may not have been originally ours yet has become ours to carry. Through the unconscious activity of the analyst's psychic apparatus sediments of the parental other can be thus brought more into our own possession. That which has been generationally injected can become assembled anew as it becomes threaded through with subsequent experience and shreds of the analyst's own unrepresented experience. This reconfiguration applies equally to enigmatic signifiers that arise from the *normative* trauma of implantation (Laplanche, 2011), as it does to trans-generationally transmitted elements of unmourned personal or historical trauma that saddle an infant of a tormented parent. In that sense pleasure that is suffered can, through the work of figurability, become a site of increased freedom.

It's important to clarify here that the portal opened up by self-shattering is not to be confused with structural regression. The self's unraveling is not a regressive variant which imbricates the subject in an *earlier* developmental stage of psychic operations. Neither is it a nostalgic return to a primal undifferentiated fusional state with the mother (Loewald, 1980; Milner, 1969). Cyra's experience is best understood as a process where the self is catapulted back in time to a developmental moment similar *but not structurally identical* to that earlier time, an instant in which one comes undone yet is not collapsing into a prior level of psychic organization. The Botellas use the term regredience to describe this process which they understand not as a return backwards but as a point en route to evolution, a reach towards transformation (2013). Put differently, the ego is pulled, almost tempted towards a productive kind of breakdown, always already with forward momentum towards achieving representation.

Analysts often conceptualize these enigmatic sediments and beta elements as the unproductive and unusable debris of human experience. Without the alpha function's psychically organizing operations, beta elements occlude thought and preclude associative links. Perverse sexuality however, as I have tried to illustrate in this chapter, has the potential to release forth beta elements in ways that can be thought of as generative, as creating a productive pulsion towards the reinscription of unformulated states. Some sexual perversions, in other words, may be best understood as proto-attempts towards figuration. When met by the responsive conscious as well as unconscious presence of an analyst, perversions can constitute a conduit towards the transformation of beta elements into alpha, of the enigmatic into the representable.

It is critical to emphasize, however, that the objective when these enigmatic states leap forward is not to exhume original meanings. What remained originally unbound can never be brought into experience or articulated into language fully. Even as they were implanted during infancy, these messages were already bathed in parental excess. To begin with unconscious, they were at the time of their formation unknown to the parent herself: as such, there are no *essential* meanings to be recovered (Plant, 2007). The adult who unravels, that is, does not become necessarily more able to revisit – to return to my earlier examples – the moment of hygiene lesson to decode mother's anxiety or the father's arousal in playing with his son. Those embodied affects, laced with parents' own history, defensive operations and unconscious fantasy, can never be recovered in their original version. They can, therefore, never become accessible to the patient, let alone to the analyst in their pure and unadulterated form. As they become figurated, the patient's proto-psychic material runs through the mesh of the analyst's own unrepresented states midwifing the particular representational form with which this material will appear in consciousness. There is no way to know, for example, what of Cyra's unformulated experience is intercepted by the work of figuration that has been produced through my nostalgic preparation of Greek coffee, my own alpha function that leads to my patient's surge of memory and affect. 'This mode of being' writes Matte-Blanco in his discussion of the unrepressed unconscious,

> cannot enter consciousness. Consciousness does not have enough dimensions to contain it: in a similar way one cannot pour water into a jug in a painting because this jug has only two dimensions and to receive the water it would need three.
>
> (1980: 45)

As unformulated experience becomes figurated, some of its dimensions, we should always be aware, are eternally inaccessible to us, impossible to bring into knowable experience.

Notes

1 There is, of course, a vast body of analytic literature that offers a plethora of understanding perversion in very textured and rich ways: as sexuality conscripted into repetitions of the traumatic past (Bach, 1994; Kernberg, 2012; Novick and Novick, 2012); a characterological problem that issues from constitutional destructiveness (Joseph, 1972, 1982; Steiner, 1982); the psychotic obliteration of generational and gender differences (Chasseguet-Smirgel, 1996); Oedipal dynamics gone awry (Holtzman and Kulish, 2012; Ornstein, 2012). While certainly useful for particular patients, reflexively approaching perversion in any of the above ways obscures the unconscious, forward reach of some – though not all – perversions. Understanding perversity as a potential topos of productive, rather than defensively driven, possibility is not taken up in the analytic literature even by analysts like McDougall (1995) and Stoller (1986) who have worked more expansively on the multivalent nature and psychic function of sexual perversion.

2 I use 'too-muchness,' a term also used by Atlas and Benjamin (2015), to refer to the overflow of affect and sensation that can be uniquely potentiated by transgressive sexuality. I, thus, differ from Benjamin and Atlas in the use of the term in that I am not discussing

here too-muchness as symptomatic of a failure of regulation (see also note 3). I am committed, rather, to exploring its emergent potential. I also differ from Ruth Stein's use of the term *excess* with which she referred to the expectable and inevitable ways in which all sexuality can be overwhelming to the subject, insofar as I am interested in the kind of too-muchness that vertiginously seizes individuals who cross *regulatory* lines.

3 To think of perverse sexuality as aspiring to the unraveling of the ego through the pushing of limits is a methodologically different approach to sexuality's excitatory potential than that adopted by theories of infantile sexuality which emphasize maternal attunement and mutual regulation of excited states (Atlas and Benjamin, 2015; Benjamin, 2012). Instead of focusing on identifying and maintaining optimal levels of stimulation, this way of thinking follows pleasure to the land of overstimulation, tracking what occurs in the too-muchness of experience that presses into the unbearable.

References

Apprey, M. (2013). *Representing, Theorizing and Reconfiguring the Concept of Intergenerational Haunting in order to Facilitate Healing.* Unpublished paper, presented at the Wounds of History conference, NYU Postdoctoral Program for Psychotherapy and Psychoanalysis, March 2nd.

Bach, S. (1994). *Narcissistic States and the Therapeutic Process.* New York: Jason Aronson, Inc.

Benjamin, J. (2012). Containing excess: sexuality, attachment and intersubjectivity in theory and transference. *American Journal of Psychoanalysis*, 72, 187–189.

Benjamin, J. and Atlas, G. (2015). The 'too muchness' of excitement: sexuality in light of excess, attachment and affect regulation. *International Journal of Psychoanalysis*, online 2/20/2015. DOI: 10.1111/1745-8315.12285.

Bersani, L. (1986). *The Freudian Body.* New York: Columbia University Press.

Bion, W.R. (1962). *Second Thoughts.* London: Karnac.

Bion, W.R. (1970). *Attention and Interpretation.* London: Karnac.

Botella, C. and Botella, S. (2005). *The Work of Psychic Figurability: Mental States without Representation.* London: Routledge.

Blechner, M.J. (2009). *Sex Changes: Transformations in Society and Psychoanalysis.* New York: Routledge.

Botella, C. and Botella, S. (2013). Psychic figurability and unrepresented states. In Levine, H.B., Reed, G.S.,and Scarfone, D. (Eds.). *Unrepresented States and the Construction of Meaning: Clinical and Theoretical Contributions* (pp. 95–121). London: Karnac.

Butler, J. (2006). *Precarious Life.* London: Verso.

Chasseguet-Smirgel, J. (1996). *Creativity and Perversion.* New York: Free Association Books.

Civitarese, G. (2013). The inaccessible unconscious and reverie as a path of figurability. In Levine, H.B., Reed, G.S., and Scarfone, D. (Eds.). *Unrepresented States and the Construction of Meaning: Clinical and Theoretical Contributions* (pp. 220–239). London: Karnac.

Corbett, K. (2013). Shifting sexual cultures: the potential space for online relations, and the promise of psychoanalytic listening. *Journal of the American Psychoanalytic Association*, 61, 25–44.

Dimen, M. (2001). Perversion is us? eight notes. *Psychoanalytic Dialogues*, 11, 825–860.

Dimen, M. (2003). *Sexuality, Intimacy, Power.* New York: Relational Perspectives Book Series.

Epstein, M. (2004). *Thoughts Without a Thinker*. New York: Basic Books.

Fonagy, P. (2008). A genuinely developmental theory of sexual enjoyment and its implications for psychoanalytic technique. *Journal of the American Psychoanalytic Association*, 56, 11–36.

Fonagy, P. and Target, M. (1996). Playing with reality I: theory of mind and the normal development of psychic reality. *International Journal of Psychoanalysis*, 77, 217–233.

Foucault, M. (1980). *The History of Sexuality: Volume I: An Introduction* (R. Hurley, Trans.). New York: Vintage Books. (Original work published 1976.)

Freud, S. (1905). Three Essays on the Theory of Sexuality (1905). *The Standard Edition of the Complete Psychological Works of Sigmund Freud, Volume VII* (1901–1905): A case of hysteria, three essays on sexuality and other works (pp. 123–246).

Ghent, E. (1990). Masochism, submission, surrender-masochism as a perversion of surrender. *Contemporary Psychoanalysis*, 26, 108–136.

González, F. (2014). Pleasure principles: reflections on Saketopoulou's 'To suffer pleasure'. *Studies in Gender and Sexuality*, 15, 278–284.

Grossmark, R. (2012). The unobtrusive relational analyst. *Psychoanalytic Dialogues*, 22, 629–646.

Hartman, S. (2013). Bondless love. *Studies in Gender and Sexuality*, 14, 35–50.

Holtzman, D. and Kulish, N. (2012). Introduction. In Holtzman, D. and Kulish, N. (Eds.). *The Clinical Problem of Masochism* (pp. 1–14). London: Jason Aronson.

Joseph, B. (1972). A clinical contribution to the analysis of perversion. *International Journal of Psychoanalysis*, 52, 441–449.

Joseph, B. (1982). Addiction to near-death. *International Journal of Psychoanalysis*, 63, 449–456.

Kernberg, O. (2012). Clinical constellations of masochistic psychopathology. In Holtzman, D. and Kulish, N. (Eds.). *The Clinical Problem of Masochism* (pp. 15–28). London: Jason Aronson.

Laplanche, J. (1997). The theory of seduction and the problem of the Other. *International Journal of Psychoanalysis*, 78, 653–666.

Laplanche, J. (1999). *Essays on Otherness*. (J. Fletcher, Trans.). New York: Routledge.

Laplanche, J. (2011). *Freud and the Sexual*. (J. Fletcher, J. House, N. Ray, Trans.). New York: Unconscious in Translation.

Levine, H.B. (2013). The colourless canvas: representation, therapeutic action, and the creation of a mind. In Levine, H.B., Reed, G.S., and Scarfone, D. (Eds.). *Unrepresented States and the Construction of Meaning: Clinical and Theoretical Contributions* (pp. 42–71). London: Karnac.

Loewald, H. (1980). Ego and reality. In *Collected Papers in Psychoanalysis* (1989) (pp. 3–19). New Haven, CT: Yale University Press.

Lyons-Ruth, K. (1999). The two-person unconscious: intersubjective dialogue, enactive relational representation, and the emergence of new forms of relational organization. *Psychoanalytic Inquiry*, 19, 576–617.

Lyons-Ruth, K. (2006). Play, precariousness and the negotiation of shared meaning. *Journal of Infant, Child and Adolescent Psychotherapy*, 5, 142–159.

Matte-Blanco, I. (1980). *The Unconscious as Infinite Sets: An Essay in Bi-logic*. London: Karnac.

McDougall, J. (1995). *The Many Faces of Eros: A Psychoanalytic Exploration of Human Sexuality*. New York: W. and W. Norton.

Milner, M. (1969). *The Hands of the Living God*. London: Karnac.

Novick, K.K. and Novick, J. (2012). Some suggestions for engaging with the clinical problem of masochism. In Holtzman, D. and Kulish, N. (Eds.). *The Clinical Problem of Masochism* (pp. 51–76). London: Jason Aronson.

Ornstein, A. (2012). Self-abuse and suicidality. In Holtzman, D. and Kulish, N. (Eds.). *The Clinical Problem of Masochism* (pp. 113–128). London: Jason Aronson.

Plant, B. (2007). Playing games/playing us: Foucault on sadomasochism. *Philosophy and Social Criticism*, 33(5), 531–561.

Reed, G.S. (2013). An empty mirror: reflections on non-representation. In Levine, H.B., Reed, G.S., and Scarfone, D. (Eds.). *Unrepresented States and the Construction of Meaning: Clinical and Theoretical Contributions* (pp. 18–41). London: Karnac.

Reed, G.S., Levine, H.B. and Scarfone, D. (2013). Introduction: from a universe of presences to a universe of absences. In Levine, H.B., Reed, G.S., and Scarfone, D. (Eds.). *Unrepresented States and the Construction of Meaning: Clinical and Theoretical Contributions* (pp. 3–17). London: Karnac.

Saketopoulou, A. (2014). To suffer pleasure: the shattering of the ego as the psychic labor of perverse sexuality. *Studies in Gender and Sexuality*, 15(4), 254–268.

Stein, R.A. (2006). Unforgetting and excess, the re-creation and re-finding of suppressed sexuality. *Psychoanalytic Dialogues*, 16, 763–778.

Stein, R.A. (2008). The otherness of sexuality: excess. *Journal of the American Psychoanalytic Association*, 56, 43–71.

Steiner, J. (1982). Perverse relationships between parts of the self; a clinical illustration. *International Journal of Psychoanalysis,* 63, 241–251.

Stern, D. (2009). *Partners in Thought: Working with Unformulated Experience, Dissociation and Enactment.* London: Routledge.

Stoller, R. (1986). *Perversion: The Erotic Form of Hatred.* London: Karnac.

Winnicott, D.W. (1965). *Maturational Processes and the Facilitating Environment: Studies in the Theory of Emotional Development.* London: Hogarth Press.

Žižek, S. (2003). *Perversion and the Social Relation.* Durham, NC: Duke University Press.

Chapter 12

Working with problems of perversion

Heather Wood

Psychoanalytic psychotherapists increasingly find themselves treating patients who present with problems of compulsive sexual behaviour or sexual perversions. Drawing from clinical examples and theoretical perspectives, the author delineates six key themes which encapsulate her own learning when commencing work with perverse patients. The first is the heterogeneity of this group of patients, both in terms of symptoms and presentation, but also in terms of the depth and developmental implications of the pathology. Further themes are the patient's fear of the object and the inability to bear separation. The author explores the significance of negative countertransference which may be experienced in relation to perverse patients, as well as the risks of being drawn into exhibitionistic or voyeuristic dynamics. Finally, the nature of the superego in perverse patients and the impact of this on the transference are discussed drawing on O'Shaughnessy's notion of the abnormal superego.

Addressing compulsive sexual behaviours is no longer a specialism within psychoanalytic psychotherapy, but has become an integral part of everyday practice. Internet pornography, the use of the internet to facilitate casual sexual liaisons, and online sexual encounters have became widespread, and feature in the material of patients seeking therapy for a wide range of problems (Wood, 2011). Whether the easy availability of internet-facilitated sexual behaviours is leading to increasing preoccupation with sexual issues in the consulting room, or whether internet content reflects an existing social trend, is difficult to disentangle. But after decades in which sexuality was eclipsed in psychoanalytic preoccupations by concerns with attachment and early infancy (see Fonagy, 2008), issues about sexual behaviours are returning to the foreground. In some cases, the troubling behaviours reported by patients are compulsive and repetitive; in others they become associated with extreme or perverse sexual fantasies or wishes. In both groups, the search for sexual stimulation and gratification appears to function defensively, being primarily concerned with avoiding mental pain, evacuating unbearable mental contents, and managing the anxieties aroused by intimacy.

This chapter attempts to articulate the key lessons that I learned in my first five years working at the Portman Clinic, an NHS (state-funded) outpatient psychotherapy clinic for people with problems of compulsive sexual behavior, violence and criminality, and part of the Tavistock and Portman NHS Foundation Trust. Patients presenting with compulsive sexual behaviours may or may not have criminal convictions, but all attend voluntarily, rather than as a requirement of the courts. Through linking clinical observations to some classic theoretical perspectives on perversion, my aim is to assist others who find themselves working with people who present with compulsive sexual behaviours. I have structured these reflections according to six themes.

A heterogeneous group

The clinical problems that are regarded as perversions are a diverse group of problems. Limentani (1989) makes the useful point that a perversion is 'not an illness but only a symptom. As a symptom it can appear at any time in the life of an individual for an infinite variety of reasons' (p. 237). A sexual perversion is not in itself the underlying pathological process, but is indicative of such a process in the same way we might think of depression as a symptom with a very wide range of potential underlying causes.

Both of the major classificatory systems – the International Classification of Diseases (ICD 10 – WHO, 1992) and the Diagnostic and Statistical Manual (DSM IV – American Psychiatric Association, 1994) make a distinction between 'disorders of sexual preference' (ICD 10) or 'paraphilias' (DSM IV), and gender identity disorders. The paraphilias or disorders of sexual preference involve fixed, repetitive sexual behaviours involving unusual sexual stimuli, or may involve potential harm to the self or the other, and to qualify as paraphilias, must be enduring and persistent, often felt to be essential for full sexual satisfaction, rather than being an expression of casual sexual experimentation. 'Disorders of sexual preference' include fetishism, exhibitionism, voyeurism and paedophilia. The second group, the gender identity disorders, includes transsexualism or confusion about gender identity; ICD 10 also includes 'dual role transvestism', where there is cross-dressing but this is not associated with sexual excitement.

The aetiology of transsexualism is hotly debated at present, with neuropsychological and hormonal explanations competing with psychological and psychoanalytic explanations (Lemma, 2012). Whatever the pathway to these conditions, the experience that some people have that their brain, psyche or identity belongs to a different gender from their anatomical body contrasts with the situation in which the personality becomes organised around an obsessive sexual fixation on a particular type of person, physical object or activity that we would regard as abnormal or potentially harmful. It is this latter group of problems, the paraphilias, which most obviously correspond to the psychoanalytic notion of perversions, and I will limit the discussion here to paraphilias.

Paraphilias/perversions/disorders of sexual preference appear in a wide range of guises and it is important to have a good clinical description of the problem in each case. This would include the extent to which the behaviour deemed paraphilic or perverse is the exclusive means of achieving sexual gratification, or whether it exists alongside a capacity for fulfiling sexual engagement with another adult who is valued and desired as themselves, and not simply as an instrument in the achievement of sexual pleasure. In assessing readiness for psychoanalytic treatment, the extent to which the paraphilia is ego-syntonic or ego-dystonic may be crucial; if the gratification from the behaviour continues to outweigh any distress or concern about the impacts of the behaviour on the self or others, there may be little motivation for treatment at that point in time.

It is beyond the scope of the present paper to provide a comprehensive theory of perversions, yet it is important to outline a theoretical position, since this will structure the clinical approach. With respect to theories of sexuality, Fonagy (2008) criticises an exclusively drive theory model which neglects the inherent relatedness of sexuality, but also finds an object-relations position wanting, because of its lack of emphasis on the visceral quality of physical sexual experience. In a similar vein, any contemporary theory of perversions needs to encompass the interpersonal or relational (the evident difficulties which many people with perversions have in maintaining sexual and emotional intimacy with another adult, and the often traumatic histories of such patients), the intrapsychic (the function served by these compulsive behaviours), the issue of meaning (the significance of the chosen 'object of desire' or ritualised behaviour), as well as the bodily experience of sexual urges and acts and the psychological significance of sexual arousal, pleasure and orgasm. I have suggested elsewhere (Wood, 2013) that perverse behaviours may be thought of as the enactment of scenarios in the person's mind, comprising actors and dramas, which function as: a means of evacuating intolerable feelings; enacting punishments on the self and others either in fantasy or reality (Stoller, 1975); avoiding the perils of genuine intimacy with another who is separate and different (Glasser, 1979; Joseph, 1997); and filling unbearable empty spaces in the person's emotional world with excitement.

When working with patients who present with problems of perversion, there are important differences in terms of the depth and nature of the underlying pathology. The classical psychoanalytic notion that one can trace a problem in adulthood back to a point of fixation in childhood has been irrevocably blurred by insights deriving from the Kleinian school and others concerning the primitive aspects of much psychopathology; problems that might once have been thought to reflect, say, Oedipal conflicts originating at age 4 or 5, are now often seen to be underpinned by difficulties in the first months of life which will have shaped, in turn, the experience of every subsequent developmental stage. Nevertheless, it is still the case that we tend to think of problems in adulthood reflecting degrees of non-resolution of developmental challenges. This highlights the importance of both obtaining a clinical description that may indicate more primitive or psychotic phantasies and taking a clinical history that may identify points of developmental trauma or challenge.

The extent of splitting and denial may be one indicator of the depth of disturbance and the accessibility of the patient for treatment. It was in relation to the subject of fetishism that Freud (1927) first posited the idea of a vertical split in the ego, in which something known in one part of the mind can simultaneously be disavowed and not known. Such splitting and disavowal is often evident in those with perversions, who, may, for example, 'know' (intellectually) that child abuse harms children emotionally and is punishable by law, while simultaneously convincing themselves that they are bestowing love, or that they are exempt from such laws. The capacity to reflect on such splits will be significant in an assessment.

Within psychoanalytic writing, there is widespread agreement that perversions are characterised by a fusion of sexuality and aggression, or specifically the sexualisation of aggression (see for example Glover, 1933, 1964; Stoller, 1975; Glasser, 1979). If the defence is successful the aggression may be obscured; but the extent of evident or inferred aggression, in masochistic as well as overtly sadistic acts, may be one indicator of the severity of disturbance.

Perversions are often viewed as inherently narcissistic, involving the use of the object in the enactment of the individual's own sexual 'script'. While it would be expected that the transference with a patient presenting with these problems will involve sadomasochistic and narcissistic elements, the extent to which there is also a capacity for engagement and internalisation will be pivotal in the therapeutic work.

A clinical example[1] illustrates some of these issues: the patient, a man in his fifties, sexually abused a boy for the first time in his life when already a grandfather. In the eyes of the law his was a serious crime and he served a significant prison sentence prior to seeking therapy. His history involved a narcissistic mother with whom he had a gratifying, but hollow, relationship of mutual admiration. This appears to have primed him to be vulnerable, pre-puberty, to sexual abuse by a tutor who both offered similar admiration and took his education and development seriously, for which he has never ceased to be grateful. The unfortunate consequence was that the abuse was experienced by him as ego-syntonic, as a precious and secret experience. He made two marriages and was successful in his working life, though reliant on manic defences, believing that he could triumph over any adversity. He remained fascinated by the image of the body of a young boy that seemed pure and beautiful. This fascination was only enacted sexually at a time in his life when he was particularly disturbed, in the months after his mother's death, having witnessed his mother, the 'beautiful peacock', reduced to a poor 'featherless fledgling' in his eyes. The manic collusion collapsed and he, her 'Adonis', unconsciously diminished and enfeebled, found himself with a child into whom he could project both the idealised boy and the unwanted vulnerability, and transformed his experience of loss and depression into one of admiration and sexual excitement. There is a sense when working with him of a man determined to pursue the truth about himself. In terms of the framework outlined above, while his early experience may have set in place a narcissistic pattern of relating, the major trauma of the abuse occurred later, when he could mobilise existing manic defences to deal with it. For most of his adult life his sexuality was not overtly paedophilic. While his action was cruel and destructive, constituting an assault on the boy's psychosexual development, overt sadism was not a salient feature. On entering therapy he was troubled about his lack of empathy for the boy he had abused, thus expressing concern about a degree of splitting that he recognised in himself. Thus there were many positive indicators in his presentation, which have been borne out by the subsequent experience of working with him.

The patient's fear of the object

Working at the Portman Clinic with people who present with compulsive sexual behaviours, it is striking how commonly patients are preoccupied with the dangers posed by the therapist. There may be a phantasy[2] that, if they allow the therapist to become close to them, they are bound to be abused or become abusive themselves, that they will seduce or be seduced, they will be taken over and annihilated, or that abandonment will surely follow. More commonly the underlying fear is hidden beneath strenuous efforts to regulate the distance between themselves and the therapist, by missed appointments and lateness, and by subtle manoeuvres in the sequence of the session to lead the therapist away from areas where the patient might be exposed to feelings of anxiety, vulnerability or shame. In this context, working in the transference is a necessity if there is to be any chance of patients being held and contained.

Glasser's (1979) description of the core complex is invaluable in directing our attention to the primitive anxieties regarding object relations that may underpin perversions. What Glasser calls the core complex is an unconscious conflict which arises as a response to the frustrations of separation from the object, and we may think of the prototype of this situation occurring in the first months of life. Clinically however, we can recognise the core complex from patients' descriptions of acute conflicts and terrors about intimacy. Glasser proposes that, in response to separation, there is an urge to get back inside the object, to have an experience of blissful fusion or merger. However, to get right inside or to fuse with the object arouses a terror of annihilation – to be taken over completely by the other would be to lose oneself. This evokes aggression towards the other, in self-protection. But to express this aggression, which seeks to annihilate the object which poses such a threat, leaves the individual at risk of total abandonment. The core complex is a conflict which thus has elements of a claustro-agoraphobic dilemma. Glasser suggests that, for people who develop perversions, the solution that is found to this dilemma is to sexualise the aggression, and to convert aggression into sadism. In sadism we do not want to destroy the object, but to control it, to see it suffer and to derive pleasure from its suffering. Thus the object is preserved, the relationship to the object is preserved – though now distorted by sadism – and the individual is protected from total abandonment and isolation.

Glasser's formulation has a number of important implications. The first is that sexual perversions have very little to do with sex (in the sense of a bodily intimacy between two adults), but are about the use of sexualisation as a defence to deal with primitive terrors in relationships. When working clinically with people with problems of compulsive sexual behaviour it is very easy to get preoccupied with the sexual behaviour and the way in which this impacts on the transference. It is more useful to keep reflecting back on the anxiety in the relationship which triggered the flight into perverse fantasy or relating at that moment. This anxiety is often about being taken over, about falling into a state of helpless dependency, and about the therapist knowing about how dependent the patient feels and apparently thereby gaining power over the patient.

The idea of the core complex illuminates the fact that, for some patients, intimacy is not only a longed-for state which promises comfort and gratification: it is a terrifying minefield of primitive terrors and destructive impulses. The cost of obtaining some comfort or gratification may be to entirely lose the self, agency or potency. Freud (1927) noted the centrality of castration anxiety in perversions, and this indeed may be a feature of them, but Glasser draws attention to the way that castration anxiety may actually be founded upon much earlier anxieties about being helpless and overwhelmed in a relationship.

Beyond the need to think and work in the transference, I have also come to see the imperative of taking up the anxieties which underpin the negative transference which often prevails. Glover's (1933, 1964) and Glasser's (1979) assertions that perversions are about the libidinalisation of aggression are central here. Patients with sexual perversions are struggling with their own cruelty, destructiveness and aggression. They are also likely to have histories in which they have experienced marked cruelty, destructiveness or aggression in others. In my experience this is a group of patients who are principally preoccupied with anxieties about the destructiveness that will be unleashed by intimacy – in one party or the other. A therapist who only focuses on the positive transference may be experienced as, at best, naïve and uncontaining, or at worst, as seductive and dangerous.

One man verbally attacked me on and off for the best part of nearly three years, seeing me as a devouring spider, a witch, or as completely helpless and useless in the face of his omnipotent destructiveness. When this omnipotent destructiveness was in control he described it as 'the fucker in the driving seat'. He would set me challenges: how would I deal with his religious beliefs, how would I cope with his badgering questions? And then, if I refused to answer and gratify him, he would berate me for being withholding and cruel when all he wanted was this one bit of reassurance that would relieve his intolerable distress. He surprised me when, having landed a particularly good job, he told me that this would not have been possible two years previously, and that he felt he had been 'wrapped in love' during that time by me and his partner. This did not seem as though it was said entirely sarcastically, but it was soon brushed aside, and in a subsequent session, he said he felt he and I had been snarling at each other like dogs from opposite corners of the room for the last two years. And then he added, 'Well, I've been snarling at you'. For this patient, withstanding his attacks without retaliating may have been a kind of 'love', but to have talked about a loving or positive transference would have evoked his scathing contempt when he was primarily concerned with his own snarling aggression and the fear, based on projection, that I was snarling back at him.

This does not mean that it is not appropriate at times to take up the way the patient may attack the therapy on which he depends, or which may be, for him, a lifeline; to that extent one can acknowledge that the therapy might represent a valued object. But it does mean holding in mind that, for patients with intense core complex anxieties, intimacy does not herald comfort, fulfilment and pleasurable connectedness. They imagine that their sense of themselves, their whole being, may be at risk if they allow anyone to get close to them, or that they may do some terrible harm to the other.

Glasser's framework also draws attention (and interpretation) away from the aggression and destructiveness *per se*, to focus on the underlying anxieties which it defends against. In Glasser's view, sadism and masochism are two sides of the same coin and express profound core-complex anxieties about intimacy. A therapist who focuses unduly on the aggression and destructiveness risks being experienced as sadistic and retaliatory, and the sadomasochistic dynamic may be perpetuated. Glasser's focus on the underlying anxiety underpins an analytic stance that is less likely to be experienced as persecutory or punitive.

Patients who are constantly preoccupied with what is in the therapist's mind are often trying to second-guess what the therapist may do next, lest it pose a danger to them. In such cases the patient's agenda may be to get through to the end of the session unscathed. The therapy can then become a kind of pseudo-therapy in which the patient has just enough material to fill the time; they may appear to become anxious on realising there are 10 or 15 minutes of the session left, as if the prepared script has run out and they are now going to have to improvise for the remainder of the session. This may be when the fear of the therapist as an object really becomes apparent. Steiner's (1993) notion of patient-centred and analyst-centred interpretations is often useful: someone who is not yet ready to understand himself might first be able to tolerate interpretations which communicate under-standing of how he experiences the analyst or therapist.

Inability to cope with separation

We are all used to recognising the impact of breaks on patients, who may experi-ence separation in a range of ways. It is probably true for most patients in therapy that it is only in the later stages of the work that they are able to experience the absence of the therapist as the loss of a whole person who can be missed, reproached and with whom the relationship can be repaired on reunion. We are probably all used to the patient missing the odd session before or after the break. What I have been surprised to experience at the Portman Clinic is patients disap-pearing over a break and never making contact again. The level of enactment on either side of the break is striking.

In Glasser's two seminal accounts of the core complex (1979, 1992) he starts to describe this phenomenon by describing the longing for fusion, 'the fantasy of *fusion* [his italics] with the idealised mother as a means of meeting the person's (originally the infant's) deep-seated longing for satiety and security' (1992: 496). In his 1979 account, he describes 'a deep-seated ànd pervasive longing for an intense and most intimate closeness to another person, amounting to a "merging", a state of "oneness", a "blissful union"'(1979: 278). What this presupposes is that there has first been a separation from the object, which is experienced as intolerable; thus the core complex becomes a response to the experience of disturbing separation (Don Campbell, personal communication).

Whatever the therapist may represent for the perverse patient in the transference at a particular time, the impact of a break is to enforce the therapist's separateness and to confront the patient with their dependence. When perverse dynamics prevail, the therapist's absence may be experienced as a deliberate act of cruelty, a retreat from a patient experienced as disgusting or repellent, or a sadistic flaunting of the therapist's other relationships. But the person who resorts to sexualisation to manage the unconscious terrors of separation from the object is unlikely to be able to manage separation from the therapist without some enactment. The enactment may take the form of a retreat into the perverse act – an increase in the use of sadistic pornography or exhibitionism, for example – or retaliation.

The negative countertransference

We may think that, as therapists, we are above the perception of sex offenders or people with perversions as 'creepy', 'disgusting', 'vile', and even 'monstrous', that we are immune to reactions of contempt and disgust. But there is no doubt that this is a reviled group, and sometimes they confront us with shocking or disturbing histories or behaviours, and with both personal reactions and countertransference reactions that are hard to bear.

In this situation there are three main issues that are pertinent. The first is that we live by powerful social rules about when and where sex belongs. It belongs in the bedroom, in private, in intimate relationships, between consenting adults, in mutually consensual engagement. Cross these boundaries and the behaviour might be regarded as distasteful or disgusting. At the more innocuous end of the scale, the man who is inappropriately sexually preoccupied and flirtatious with a work colleague, or who is seen to be harbouring unwelcome sexual thoughts, may be seen as 'creepy'.

The second factor that may evoke a reaction of distaste is the patient's distaste or contempt for himself. This may be disguised and defended against, but evident through the countertransference. Sexualisation may serve as a manic defence against depressive anxieties to do with guilt, ambivalence or imperfection. It may serve as a narcissistic defence, when the underlying anxieties are of inadequacy, of being pathetic or contemptible. Sexualisation may also conjure feelings of desirability and serve as a defence against feelings of being disgusting, soiled or tainted.

A feeling of disgust or contempt can be evoked in others, and in the therapeutic context, in the therapist, when the defence is thin or precarious and the self-doubt or self-loathing beneath the defence leaks through or is communicated via the countertransference. For example, a man who feels unattractive and lacking in confidence may foster a sense of himself – through perverse sexual activity – as daring and potent. The discrepancy between the bravado of his inflated, sexualised self-image and the underlying contempt or disgust for himself may evoke scorn or distaste in others.

One man needed at all times to be in control and triumphant, and he achieved this by baiting others, including me, in a sadistic way, or demolishing himself in a cruel way, attacking his physical appearance, longing for cosmetic surgery and feeling himself to be deformed and grotesque. He was able at times to recognise that his feeling of being despicable and repellent could be self-induced. After some time in therapy, he started to talk about how he covered himself in 'shit' – in self-loathing and self-hatred – and acknowledged his dependence on his therapy, which was the only way, at that stage, that he felt he could experience this shit being washed away. The power of Freud's insight about the bodily nature of experience is that at some level this man felt himself to be literally covered in excrement, and talking in these terms seemed to address both the symbolic concerns of the adult and the much more concrete bodily experience that he had had of himself as a child as disgusting and repellent.

This links to a third factor that may engender a sense of disgust. Every culture is founded on rules about what Douglas (1966) has called 'Purity and Danger', about separating the clean from the dirty, separating food preparation, for example, from toilets. Some cultures dictate that certain animals or methods of food preparation are unclean. And what is unclean, if it strays out of its allocated place, is seen to be dangerous. The classic Freudian notion of developmental stages echoes these demarcations: we deal with the oral function, and then we progress to the anal function, and when that is resolved we have the possibility of approaching genital sexuality. People with perversions often blur these safe distinctions. We encounter patients who derive sexual excitement from eating faeces or who are aroused by being urinated on. Chasseguet-Smirgel (1985) has emphasised the anality of perversions. Feelings of nausea or disgust in the therapist may reflect a personal reaction of distaste to the patient's material. Such feelings may also be a countertransference response to the patient's communication of their own disgust about aspects of themselves, involving, for example, their confusion of oral and anal functions, or their experience of being invaded, over-filled or overstimulated by an intrusive object (Rob Hale, personal communication). All of these can be challenging to manage.

Similarly, our culture assumes that we can make a distinction between what is life-giving and what is destructive, between Eros and Thanatos. In common parlance, 'perverse' has come to mean that good and bad cannot be distinguished, that someone appears to value or idealise something that is corrupt, dangerous or destructive; or conversely that they corrupt, attack and spoil that which is good.

Returning to Glover's insight, a crucial aspect of sexual perversions is that they appear to represent a fusion of sexuality and sadism or destructiveness. Thus perversions are inherently confusing and this confusion can be used to obscure the real function of the behaviour. The paedophile may believe himself to be expressing love for a child, while it is evident to others that what is being enacted is envy or sadism. In the countertransference we may feel disgusted by such a confusion of functions, tricked by sudden shifts from constructive to destructive, or cheated as if something we thought was constructive has suddenly been hijacked and distorted.

Some of the anxiety about working with people who present with compulsive sexual behaviours may be that the transference will become sexualised. Freud (1905) applied the term 'polymorphously perverse' to the child's early normal sexual development rather than to a specific group of patients. Yet in clinical practice with patients with compulsive sexual behaviours we often make an informal distinction between those whose sexual behaviours seem rigidly scripted and others whose sexual practices and objects are so varied that it appears that variety and novelty are a prerequisite of their achieving sexual excitement. It is this latter group whose problems seem to warrant the description of 'polymorphously perverse'. Patients of this type seem to be constantly preoccupied with sexuality, almost every engagement is viewed for its sexual potential, and they often seem to sexualise the transference almost immediately, in a very indiscriminate way. With patients who have more narrowly focused, tightly scripted perversions or paraphilias, I have been struck by how infrequently the transference seems to be sexualised. It is as though the perversion functions to encapsulate and contain sexual feelings, so that there is no risk of them becoming focused on another with whom there is an affective bond. In this situation, sexual feelings in relation to the therapist would compound the patient's anxieties about intimacy, and so are largely kept at bay.

Where there is sexualisation of the transference, if one keeps in mind the function of sexualisation as a defence – as well as the anxieties about engagement which it defends against – then the use of sexualisation becomes less disconcerting. As with any transference reaction, there are always questions about what kind of object the patient needs the therapist to be at that moment: whether the apparent sexualisation is about control, sadism, intrusion, seduction, and so on. There are also questions about what the sexualisation defends against: does it defend against a fear/longing for merger; is it an attempt to tame a frightening object; does it defend against destructive wishes or urges, or a fear of abandonment? Where there is an apparent sexualisation of the transference, there is always something to be 'unpacked' and understood.

Occasionally, after considerable work, there may be the emergence of tentative sexual feelings towards the therapist, which seem to grow out of the intimacy of the therapeutic relationship rather than to defend against it. It may be important that these feelings are tolerated rather than viewed as defensive if true integration of sexuality and dependency are to occur.

Exhibitionism/voyeurism

A specific and important dimension of the transference and countertransference is the dimension of exhibitionism and voyeurism. As therapists, we may feel that we have had a more satisfying session when we have seen something in the patient that has previously been hidden. We welcome 'new material' as if the more we see, the more we will understand. We talk all the time about 'seeing' patients. What happens to this therapeutic 'watching' and 'seeing' with a patient for whom looking and seeing has become highly sexualised?

In all of the patients that I have seen who present with exhibitionism there has been a failure of intimacy in childhood, a lack of contact, engagement and experienced affection. All have described an experience as a child of an adult glimpsing their genitals or seeing them urinate, and the child-self imagining that this has stimulated or excited the adult in some way. Suddenly they have the capacity to evoke interest and curiosity in an adult, and it is through exposing their body and being seen from a distance. The eyes and looking become charged with excitement. They also become the means for expressing aggression towards the object for the deprivations and frustrations that have been endured. As the boy matures, he turns from passive to active: by choosing when and how to expose himself he imagines he can now control the interest of another in him; rather than helplessly waiting to be seen or appreciated, he has the power to draw attention to himself, and to evoke strong feelings in the other. He can arrange to expose himself to the particular type of object that meets his unconscious need: a group of boys, a lone woman, a group of animated women out for the evening, or whatever. The conscious intent is often not to frighten but to arouse or amuse the other. But on exploration, the aggression implicit in the act becomes apparent: it is an assault on the person's innocence, tranquillity or indifference.

When a patient such as this is faced with a therapist who is offering them attention, this may be experienced as something highly desirable but also terrifying. The more vulnerable the patient feels, the more likely they are to assume control of the situation in the way they know how: by taking control of what they expose and reveal, deriving excitement from disturbing or unsettling the therapist, or by trying to arouse an excited voyeur in the therapist through sexual clinical material.

For the man obsessed with viewing pornography there may be a similar flight away from contact and engagement towards viewing. One patient who had served a prison sentence for downloading child pornography had moments of being extremely insightful and honest about himself. I felt as though I was being given a privileged glimpse into some of the processes underlying paedophilia. And yet when I tracked the material through an entire session, often such reflections were followed by him taking off into a perverse world where he justified his paedophilia or mused about internet pornography and its rewards. Through him I came to understand more about the use of sexualisation as a defence against anxiety, as well as a defence against aggression. It was difficult for him to stay in contact with the anxiety of knowing about his emptiness, his sense of powerlessness, or his sense of becoming completely subsumed by his mother's (or my) needs and concerns.

In the therapeutic relationship it often happens that a moment of apparent engagement is followed by a flight into exhibitionistic display, in which the therapist is made the excited voyeur watching the images created by the patient. Whether we are being allowed to see something deeply personal and significant about the patient or being treated to a perverse display is often not clear-cut. I have had the experience of presenting material in a clinical meeting that I had experienced in the session as searching and illuminating, about how a man had sexually abused a 13-year-old girl, but some seminar participants heard the material as an exhibitionistic display by the patient and a sadistic attack on me in the transference. They might have been right, but it also sometimes happens that something that was authentic and revealing leaves the patient feeling anxious and so they retrospectively sexualise the situation; in this way what was genuine therapeutic work may be hijacked and turned into a seemingly perverse interaction. In a clinical seminar, different members may pick up these different aspects of the session.

For the therapist there is always unease about being seduced into the role of excited voyeur, rather than maintaining the stance of a neutral therapist with an enquiring mind. To some extent this can be limited in the course of the therapy by avoiding questions and sticking strenuously to the analytic task of interpreting anxiety and the transference. However, there are occasions, particularly when trying to gauge risk and when conducting an assessment, when we might feel we need more factual information about what the patient has done; here the tension between professional rigour and seeming to be voyeuristic may be most acute. An assessment that I had conducted with an exhibitionist was discussed in a clinical meeting. A colleague wanted to know whether the man's penis was erect or flaccid when he exposed himself, as this is typically associated with different patterns of pathology. I had not asked, and would not have asked, as I think this would have conveyed exactly the same curiosity about his genitals that he was trying to evoke in his victims. However, to not ask leaves one waiting to construct a clinical picture in a slow and piecemeal way, or taking up the dilemma created in the consulting room. In that situation the patient had effectively tantalised me with glimpses of what he did. I knew that he had exposed himself approximately every two weeks in a specific, crowded public place for the last 20 years. I said that he must be very adept at deception to have done this every two weeks for 20 years without getting caught. At this point he let some of the deception slip, and told me, as much as he wanted to, about what it was that he did.

Superego functioning

The last feature of this work that I want to address is the nature of the superego. When working with people whose sexual behaviour is often deemed by society to be transgressive or illegal, it is difficult to disentangle the patient's reaction to social disapproval they have experienced from their own internal judgement of themselves. The patient's superego is initially evident as a projection onto the therapist: either the therapist is experienced as disapproving and punitive; or as potentially collusive and indulgent; or as corrupt. These dynamics can also become projected into the institutions in which we work, when rules about cancellations and non-attendance, for example, are enforced in an autocratic and unthinking way; or are ignored while we protect and indulge our patient; or the rules are deliberately ridiculed and flouted in a delinquent or defiant manner.

At the Portman Clinic we have a policy that states that any patient missing more than five weeks of therapy in one term should have their treatment reviewed by the Clinic. This is considerably more generous and accommodating than the original policy that was proposed, in which therapy was to be terminated after a patient had missed three consecutive sessions. One patient did not return for seven weeks after my summer break. In his first session back my response could be seen as collusive and indulgent: I waited to hear his account of what he had been doing, and learned that some of what he had gained by going away during this time had undoubtedly been positive. I was also somewhat identified with the delinquent flouting of rules, viewing the missed appointment policy as something that could be overridden by clinical considerations. But when, in the second session, I tried to raise with the patient his failure to keep me informed during his absence, he tried to create a sadomasochistic fight, insisting that I was angry with him, I was trying to punish him, I was going to leave him feeling awful by spoiling everything he had gained from the time away, and so on. Amongst his attacks was a reproach: I was a bad, cruel therapist who was unprofessional and enacting my own anger towards him. Thus, he became a persecutory superego wagging his finger at me. As he attacked me in this way, he succeeded in arousing my anger towards him. The temptation was for me to enact the punitive superego back: to let him know the repercussions of his actions for the Clinic, that he came close to jeopardising his therapy, and that it was at my and my colleagues' discretion whether the therapy continued or not. I managed not to voice these thoughts, but I imagine my irritation was evident.

Freud's account of the formation of the superego will be familiar: that the superego is formed through the resolution of the Oedipus complex as the boy internalises the authority of the father – conveyed through the prohibition on incest – and forms an identification with the father that enables him to sublimate his incestuous longings. In many of our patients with perversions it is possible to see how this process has been distorted because the father fails to embody the Oedipal authority but represents an abusive or corrupt object with which the superego then becomes identified.

While there is often powerful evidence for the impact of external experience on the developing superego, I think one has to look beyond a Freudian model to a Kleinian and post-Kleinian view of superego formation to really understand the ferocity that the superego may have in some patients. For Klein, the superego originates in the splitting of the paranoid-schizoid position. The bad object and good object may be projected into both external objects and internal objects

(Rosenfeld, 1952/1965). The superego may thus contain elements of early idealisation and primitive persecution. Under benign conditions, this superego may develop so that the persecutory elements are modified by the introjection of a good object, so that a 'normal' superego may develop which includes aspirations and ideals, and watches over the ego (O'Shaughnessy, 1999). Bion (1962) proposed that if there is a failure of containment or communication between mother and infant, a 'super' ego is internalised which destroys links. Bion (1962) describes this superego:

> It is a superego that has hardly any of the characteristics of the superego as understood in psychoanalysis: it is a 'super' ego. It is an envious assertion of moral superiority without any morals. . . .
>
> (p. 97)

I think this account is particularly pertinent to the superego one encounters when working with patients with problems of perverse or compulsive sexual behaviours. The superego may seem to become fused with a sadistic attempt not to know or understand, not to take an overview or to experience guilt, but to condemn, destroy and invalidate, as in my description of the patient who returned late from the break above. O'Shaughnessy describes how patient and analyst become locked in a battle of 'abnormal superego' to 'abnormal superego', as I think I undoubtedly did with that patient.

In other situations, the superego may seem to be hijacked in a more subtle way, so that the patient apparently claims the moral high ground and pronounces on others' immorality, although the high ground on which he purports to stand may be built from a bogus, perverse morality. One patient, as he was awaiting trial on a second charge of downloading child pornography, responded to feeling persecuted – by the external superego of the legal system and his persecutory internal superego – by setting himself above the legal system and pronouncing on its failings. He sacked his solicitor, insisting he would represent himself, alerted the court to the fact that he would be bringing complaints against the solicitor for his initial handling of the evidence, and railed against police incompetence in their dealings with him. He dedicated himself to studying the law and legal procedure, and was gratified when, appearing in the magistrates court for a pre-trial hearing, a security guard mistook him for a solicitor. When in this pseudo-legal, pseudo-moral superior state he was completely unavailable for therapeutic work. One day when he came there was a break in this armour. In a subdued way he was able to talk about how the part of him that railed against everyone had now put him in a position where he risked a further prison sentence; he was able to talk with me about how a prison sentence risked a break in or the ending of his therapy; he was able to talk about how he was terrified of messing up in relationships with women, but how a part of him still hoped he would one day be able to have such a relationship. In this more depressed state, there was more sense of a 'normal' superego, that recognised the authority of the law, the destructiveness of something in him, but that could still have aspirations and hope. This was quite different to the superior 'super' ego of the previous sessions, which was out to triumph and to destroy links and hope.

Concluding remarks

Compulsive or paraphilic sexual behaviours are underpinned by widely differing dynamics and levels of disturbance, but have in common the use of sexualisation as a defence to manage anxiety, often the anxieties evoked by physical and emotional intimacy with another person. The therapeutic relationship therefore confronts the patient with many aspects of the situation which they find most difficult: an experience of a deeply personal relationship in which they risk feeling taken over, intruded upon, emotionally exposed and vulnerable, and one in which, they imagine, they will have to face their own and the other's aggression and destructiveness. These are also patients who may provoke or evoke an abnormal superego in others: a persecutory, judgemental revulsion or rejection. If enacted in the consulting room, this can provide the patient with a 'gratifyingly' sadomasochistic exchange, but it does not further the therapeutic task of enabling the patient to find and tolerate a different mode of engagement.

As in all analytic work, when working with patients who present with perverse sexual behaviours, we are trying to be as accurate as we can be in naming the underlying anxieties or phantasies that drive pathological behaviours. With these patients the things that need to be properly named are frequently about a terror of the object, fears of the person's own destructiveness, the desolation of failed early relationships and underlying depression. These are often heavily disguised by sexual excitement. They come in and out of focus in the consulting room. But when they are recognised there can be a sense of real contact and productive work.

Notes

1 I am grateful to this patient for giving permission for the inclusion of this case material.
2 In accordance with psychoanalytic convention, I will use 'fantasy' to denote a conscious fantasy in the popular sense of the word, and 'phantasy' to denote an unconscious fantasy.

References

American Psychiatric Association (1994) *Diagnostic and Statistical Manual of Mental Disorders, 4th Edition*. Washington DC: APA.
Bion, W.R. (1962) *Learning from Experience*. London: Karnac. Reprinted in *Seven Servants: Four Works by Wilfred R. Bion* (1977). New York: Jason Aronson.
Chasseguet-Smirgel, J. (1985) *Creativity and Perversion*. London: Free Association Books.
Douglas, M. (1966) *Purity and Danger*. London: Routledge and Keegan Paul.
Fonagy, P. (2008) A genuinely developmental theory of sexual enjoyment and its implications for psychoanalytic technique. *Journal of the American Psychoanalytic Association*, 56, 11–36.

Freud, S. (1905) Three essays on the theory of sexuality. *Standard Edition*, 7. London: Hogarth Press.

Freud, S. (1927) Fetishism. *Standard Edition*, 21. London: Hogarth Press.

Glasser, M. (1979) Some aspects of the role of aggression in the perversions. Ch. 12, pp. 278–305 in I. Rosen (Ed.) *Sexual Deviations*. Oxford: Oxford University Press.

Glasser, M. (1992) Problems in the psychoanalysis of certain narcissistic disorders. *International Journal of Psychoanalysis*, 73, 493–503.

Glover, E. (1933) The relation of perversion-formation to the development or reality-sense. *International Journal of Psycho-Analysis*, 14, 486–504.

Glover, E. (1964) Aggression and sado-masochism. In I. Rosen (Ed.) *The Pathology and Treatment of Sexual Deviation*. London: Oxford University Press.

Joseph, B. (1997) 'Where there is no vision': from sexualisation to sexuality. Ch. 9, pp. 161–174 in D. Bell (Ed.) *Reason and Passion: A Celebration of the Work of Hanna Segal*. London: Karnac.

Lemma, A. (2012) Research off the couch: re-visiting the transsexual conundrum. *Psychoanalytic Psychotherapy*, 26 (4), 263–281.

Limentani, A. (1989) Perversions: treatable and untreatable. Ch. 15, pp. 230–249 in *Between Freud and Klein*. London: Free Association Books.

O'Shaughnessy, E. (1999) Relating to the superego. *International Journal of Psychoanalysis*, 80, 861–870.

Rosenfeld, H.A. (1952) Notes on the psycho-analysis of the superego conflict in an acute schizophrenic patient. *International Journal of Psycho-Analysis*, 33. Reprinted in H.A. Rosenfeld (1965) *Psychotic States*. London: Karnac and Hogarth Press.

Steiner, J. (1993) Problems of psychoanalytic technique: patient-centred and analyst-centred interpretations. Ch. 11, pp. 131–146 in *Psychic Retreats*. New Library of Psychoanalysis. London: Routledge.

Stoller, R. (1975) *Perversion: The Erotic Form of Hatred*. London: Quartet.

Wood, H. (2011) The internet and its role in the escalation of sexually compulsive behaviour. *Psychoanalytic Psychotherapy*, 25, 127–142.

Wood, H. (2013) The nature of the addiction in 'sex addiction' and paraphilias. In M. Bower, R. Hale and H. Wood (Eds) *Addictive States of Mind*. London: Karnac.

World Health Organization (1992) *The International Classification of Mental and Behavioural Disorders*, ICD 10. Geneva: World Health Organization.

Index

abnormality 5, 9
abuse 222–223, 230
acting out 66–67, 70
addiction 63, 67, 70, 189–190
adolescence 48, 105, 141–143, 150, 193
Adorno, Theodor 186
affairs 53
affect regulation 44, 46, 192, 201
affection 142
aggression 46, 48, 50, 152; attachment
  theory 44; core complex 223, 225;
  maternal 51; perversions 222, 224, 225,
  233
Aisenstein, Marilia 7, 63–70, 76–79
Alexander, Franz 22
'alien self' 47, 53, 54, 163
alienation 45, 52, 61
Allison, Elizabeth 2, 125–137
alpha function 205, 208, 214, 215
American Psychiatric Association (APA)
  26, 27, 29, 89, 129–130, 220
American Psychoanalytic Association 28,
  33, 63, 89, 90, 184
anal function 227
anal sexuality 12, 143, 144–146, 153, 170,
  211
analysability 77
analysts: being desired 74–76; fear of 225;
  figuration 208, 210; gay and lesbian
  33, 34, 90, 181; 'generative turbulence'
  205; homosexuality 129, 130;
  intersubjectivity 214; mirroring by 154;
  patient's phantasies about 223; perverse
  sexualities 207; separation from 225–226;

sexual aberrations 181–182; voyeur
  role 230; *see also* countertransference;
  therapeutic relationship; transference
androcentrism 87
anger 55, 59, 60, 106
anima 86–87
animals 3, 14n1, 86, 116n5
animus 86–87
anonymity 151
anti-Semitism 23
anxiety 67, 77, 93, 141, 185, 192;
  about therapists 223; core complex
  224, 225; countertransferential 207;
  defensive sexualization 203, 229, 233;
  homosexuality 128–129, 143, 153;
  impotence 193; intimacy 219; prostitute
  users 199–200, 202
Aquinas, Thomas 189
archetypes 86–87
arousal 49, 50, 58, 70, 201, 221; clinical
  example 52; Laplanche's theory of
  psychosexuality 50–51; mirroring 159;
  same-gender desire 160
Atlas, G. 215n2
attachment 4, 43, 44, 53, 192; to analyst
  58; developmental model 152;
  embodiment 5; failures of attunement
  and mirroring 47; gender identification
  106; Lewes on 34, 35; prostitute users
  202–203; relational approach 152
attunement 47
Auchincloss, Elizabeth 10
Austen, Jane 101
autoerotic excitement 50